Also by Judith Milner

Assessment in Social Work, with Patrick O'Byrne (1997), Palgrave

Women and Social Work (2001), Palgrave

Brief Counselling: Narratives and Solutions (2002), Palgrave

Assessment in Social Work, with Patrick O'Byrne, 2nd edition (2002), Palgrave

Assessment in Counselling, with Patrick O'Byrne (2003), Palgrave

Working with Violence

Policies and Practices in Risk Assessment and Management

Judith Milner and Steve Myers

palgrave
macmillan

First published 2007 by
PALGRAVE MACMILLAN
Houndmills, Basingstoke, Hampshire RG21 6XS and
175 Fifth Avenue, New York, N.Y. 10010
Companies and representatives throughout the world

PALGRAVE MACMILLAN is the global academic imprint of the Palgrave Macmillan division of St. Martin's Press, LLC and of Palgrave Macmillan Ltd. Macmillan® is a registered trademark in the United States, United Kingdom and other countries. Palgrave is a registered trademark in the European Union and other countries.

ISBN-13: 978-1-4039-4307-1
ISBN-10: 1-4039-4307-9

This book is printed on paper suitable for recycling and made from fully managed and sustained forest sources. Logging, pulping and manufacturing processes are expected to conform to the environmental regulations of the country of origin.

A catalogue record for this book is available from the British Library.

10 9 8 7 6 5 4 3 2 1
16 15 14 13 12 11 10 09 08 07

Printed in China

To Dave and CCW

Contents

List of Figures

Acknowledgements

We owe much to the many clients and colleagues who have helped and encouraged us in writing this book, in particular Jo Campling for inviting us to consider the project and Penny Simmons, our copy editor, who has been outstandingly efficient. Lorell Webster, Manager of Barnardo's The Junction Children's Service also deserves a special mention (as well as the dedicated staff group); she has the rare ability to combine level-headed criticism and inspiration. We are also deeply appreciative of Dr Alasdair Macdonald's helpful comments on specific chapters, as well as his general advice and support.

We also are deeply indebted to the many service users who have provided us with challenges, questions and solutions. Their stories of the different sorts of therapies they have received have been invaluable in supplying the detail to the research findings about what works, how it works, and what doesn't work and when. Their information influenced the structure of the book. We also extend our thanks to the Duluth Domestic Abuse Intervention Project for permission to reproduce the Wheel of Equality and the Wheel of Power and Control in Figures 5.1 and 5.2.

Particular thanks go to 13-year-old Thomas for his impressive computer skills; to Jayne Langlands for formatting when our own limitations became apparent; and His Honour Judge Robertshaw for his critical comments.

CHAPTER 1

Introduction

Our starting point in writing this book is that *everyone* who works with people in whatever capacity will at some time have to respond to violence; whether this is a young child telling a nurse of an abusive experience, an adult with learning disabilities telling their carer about experiencing harassment, a young woman explaining to her social worker that she has aggressive feelings towards her baby, a boy who has sexually abused his sister talking to their youth offending team worker, or a frail older man in hospital who tells the community care manager he does not want to go home because his wife physically assaults him. You will come across these situations as a student on placement or as a qualified practitioner working with people, and responding to violence is an increasingly common element within social and health education and training programmes. When you turn to a book for guidance on how to deal effectively with these complex manifestations of violence, you will quickly discover that the literature divides unhelpfully into two distinct types. First, there are a number of books telling you how to work with people who are violent (mainly men and mainly groupwork). Second, there is a vast literature on how to respond to the victims of violence (mainly female and individual counselling). You will probably find that the situation you are dealing with is far more complicated; for example the young woman who has aggressive feelings towards her baby may well tell you that she has been a victim of abuse too. Similarly the older man who is physically abused by his wife may turn out to have been financially and emotionally abusive to her for most of their lives. Also with older people their expression of violence and/or their acceptance of violence towards them will have been mediated through culturally informed attitudes. Older people have not necessarily been informed by feminist thinking on the courses of male violence.

Professional practice is also informed by agency policies and practices, which in turn may change regularly in response to the large number of government consultation papers, guidance and legislation. Not only does government policy change frequently, but it varies from government department to department. For example, in the United Kingdom the Home Office has much to say on male violence, favouring a cognitive behavioural explanation and treatment. At the same time whilst cognitive behavioural programmes are recommended for male offenders within the community and prison, it largely ignores organized violent crime although it is increasingly expecting people who work with people to be able to rescue and rehabilitate those who are the victims of sex trafficking. On the other hand the Department for Education and Science has very much more to say about victims, especially children, favouring psychotherapeutic explanation and treatment. What dominates in this approach to violence is a commitment to reducing the domestic violence inflicted by men on women and reducing the emotional and physical harm to children. Despite a common interest in domestic violence across government departments, government guidance reflects different ways of intervening with victims and offenders.

These sources of guidance can often prove inadequate for dealing even with what are quite common situations. For example, a family where the man is violent to his wife but no-one wishes him to be removed from the home, a family where both the man and the woman fight each other physically and emotionally, or a less traditional family where one woman regularly beats up her female partner. In this book we acknowledge that violence in relationships is almost always complex and that there is no single way of dealing with it. We are aware, however, how tangled it becomes when a worker attempts to combine two totally different approaches to one situation. For example, what is the rationale for deciding that an adult who is violent requires a brief cognitive behavioural programme to correct their distorted thinking, whilst the victim requires psychodynamic intervention over a long period of time to repair the emotional damage?

Using one single (probably familiar) domestic violence scenario throughout the book we explore a range of interventions, detailing the theoretical basis on which they have been developed and critically analyse their effectiveness in different situations. At the end of each chapter are brief examples of government and agency guidance that have been developed from the theory and intervention outlined. Our intention in this is to make clear where an intervention originates (the theories and research findings), how selective use has been made of this material in the development of people's working hypotheses about violence, and the actual interventions themselves and where they can most effectively be used. We illustrate them with a single case example but the reader will be able to examine examples from their own practice. The examples of government guidance, agency policy and examples of practice at the end of each chapter allow the reader to reflect on how they have been influenced by the theories outlined. We aspire to making the links between social policy and practice more transparent.

We hope that this book will be useful both to students trying to make sense of different ways of working with violence in different placements and to experienced practitioners who find that their multi-disciplinary colleagues hold different allegiances to different interventions (and whose agency policies are informed and regulated by their respective government departments which in themselves take often contradictory theoretical treatment positions). We also provide ideas for informing your practice in reducing risk and promoting the safety of the people you work with.

In Chapter 1 we emphasize the complexities of violence, outlining the social, cultural and political context in which it is constructed and identifying the key drivers of current explanations of, and responses to, violence. We look at the role of the media in influencing perceptions of the prevalence and severity of violence, contrasting this with official statistics and political statements. We then outline government policies and strategies, highlighting the very real contradictions, complexities and confusions that exist despite the confidence with which government guidance promulgates specific ways of working, promoting them as effective, evidence-based and straightforward. We then address some of the consequences for workers attempting to reduce risk and promote safety within these narrow frameworks.

In Chapter 2 we explore some of the key issues in the assessment of violence, including the notion of 'risk' and the different ways in which assessment can be constructed. The models and protocols commonly used to assess violence are critically analysed in terms of their limitations and strengths. Clinical and actuarial approaches are explored, questioning the usefulness of dynamic and static risk factors. The consequences of increasingly sophisticated ways of identifying people who may be 'risky' at the expense of developing effective risk-reduction approaches is also explored, particularly the dangers of pathologizing those subjected to them and how this undermines the traditional values of social care.

Chapter 3 introduces the earliest and most enduring approach to working with violence in social and health care. There are three main components: how interpersonal violence is understood in terms of a response to grief and loss (attachment theory); how the theory informs risk assessment; and the implications for prevention and intervention. As attachment theory evolved from psychoanalytic theory and practice this is briefly described. The research evidence supporting attachment theory as an explanation for interpersonal violence is presented. The clinical implications of attachments for the prediction of violence and the assessment of risk are explored using the examples of child, sibling, peer, spouse and elder abuse and the practice implications are critically explored.

Chapter 4 explores a currently favoured approach to working with violence (particularly offenders), that is cognitive behavioural therapy. We outline how the theory explains violent behaviour; how it is used in the prediction and assessment of violence and the various forms it takes in managing violent behaviour. This theory has become an increasingly influential one in the development of policies, protocols and practices to tackle violence and has made claims to be the most effective intervention. We explore the evidence base for this.

Chapter 5 focuses on Feminist explanations of violence, particularly how men's violence to known women and their children is understood in terms of patriarchy; how this theory influences risk assessments; and the implications for prevention and intervention. The various forms of feminism are briefly introduced and the huge impact of 'second-wave' feminism on professional practice and government policy and guidance is explored. The limitations of this theory as an explanation for all family violence is also discussed, with reference to elder abuse, same-sex violence, female sexual abuse, and female-on-male violence.

Chapter 6 looks at the changing expectations of mental health services in responding to and managing violence and the potential for violence with people, especially those who also use drugs. How this has been influenced by political and media representations of violence associated with those who have mental health problems is outlined, and legislative initiatives are critically analysed. The effectiveness of traditional classification and treatment paradigms are considered within the demands made on mental health services to deal with both offenders and victims within both hospital and community-based programmes.

Chapter 7 introduces Solution Focused approaches which are emerging ways of working with violence. Unlike the more established approaches, it does not attempt to explain and categorize violent behaviour, on the grounds that it is not necessary to understand a problem to arrive at its solution. The basic principles and techniques of solution focused practice are described, followed by a detailed discussion of assessment and intervention using a signs of safety approach. Outcome research is detailed, plus examples of how solution focused practice 'works' in a variety of service provider settings.

Chapter 8 introduces another emerging approach to working with violence, Narrative Therapy. Although it shares certain commonalities with solution focused approaches, it is more explicitly influenced by postmodern theorizing and deconstructs the problem in order to understand, assess and reduce risk. It takes a more explicitly 'political' stance through the recognition of power relations within society and how these impact on people's behaviour and potential for change. The theoretical principles and practices are described and its usefulness in working with violence is critically evaluated.

Using the case example, Chapter 9 brings together the various approaches outlined previously, assessing their potential effectiveness within a criminal justice policy which emphasizes the safety of victims and the control and management of offenders. The limitations and pitfalls of government policy, including the What Works agenda, are also summarized.

Case example: Mark, Kelly, Billy and Luke

This example has been constructed from our experiences of working across a range of violences and (of course) is neither clear-cut nor discretely drawn, as most lives are complicated, messy and cross professional boundaries.

Mark (28 years) and Kelly (24 years) have been referred to a Domestic Violence Programme by their health visitor following an incident when Mark took a hammer to the front door which Kelly had locked behind him when he stormed out of the house during an argument. Kelly was very frightened and rang her father. He arrived and had a noisy altercation with Mark which led to her father telling Mark that he was not good enough for her and to get out of her life. Mark and Kelly were reunited the next day. She has accompanied him for the first assessment session.

They describe how arguments develop: first they 'pick' at each other, this escalates to raised voices, then they begin shouting, swearing, and saying really hurtful things. Mark usually threatens Kelly at this point of the argument and she tells him to leave. They describe feeling out of control during these arguments. Even when Mark goes out of the way, they both brood and come back together as wound up as they were before. The arguments can last for days. They are both fed up with this way of conducting their relationship as they have a lot of love for each other. Equally, they do not wish their young son to see them like this.

Kelly says that she 'picks', first, as frustrations about money (Mark does not stick at any job long enough for her to feel financially secure) then turn to resentments. She attends college two days a week to continue her business course, which was disrupted by the birth of Luke. Her mother childminds for her although Kelly's relationship with her parents is not good. The rest of the time she is stuck in the house with 14-month-old Luke whilst Mark goes out with his mates. She has lost touch with her mates. She describes this as whirling thoughts in her head and tends to say the hurtful things first (about his failure as a provider in comparison with the rest of her family, who disapprove of the relationship). Mark finds his heart beating faster when Kelly 'picks' at him, gets a sick feeling and paces about with his hands clenched. He 'picks' back a little about her failure to make his 4-year old son, Billy, from a previous relationship, welcome at weekends, or help him when Billy is 'difficult'. He then explodes; shouting, swearing and making threats of violence. Kelly feels embarrassed when he does this in case their neighbours can hear. Luke and Billy get upset when these incidents occur.

On a few occasions, such as when Mark tried to break the front door down with a hammer, Kelly has feared for her safety and rung her father for assistance. This causes Mark to feel humiliated and fearful: 'I know she must have been frightened but she didn't need to send for her dad. I was right shown up. I said to him, "don't you realize, I'm losing my wife, my son, my family, my home ... everything". I had to do something.'

The referral form describes Mark as having had a difficult upbringing, with strict discipline including physical chastisement; a series of petty offences when he was a teenager; long unauthorized absences from school; poor behaviour when he was attending school and suspected use of cannabis. Mark was admitted briefly to residential care at the age of 10, where he was assessed as suffering from an Attachment Disorder. He had a second short period in care at the age of 14 where he was assessed as suffering from Conduct Disorder. Mark's first foster placement broke down after he alleged that he was sexually abused by an already established older foster child. He received a Caution for Unlawful Sexual Intercourse with Billy's mother when she was 15 and he was 16.

Public reactions to violence

Periodically, the newspapers fill with another terrible story of an innocent bystander killed by a mentally disordered man who has recently been released from hospital. There are many possible reactions to reporting of this kind. Some professionals will feel relief that they were not part of the decision-making team that came to the conclusion that this man no longer posed a risk to the public. Some may be reminded of a long-standing concern about the lack of effective treatment programmes for people who are violent. Some may feel like most members of the public, that 'something must be done about this!'. Some may be susceptible to feelings of personal insecurity in an increasingly dangerous world, where they feel random acts of violence severely compromise their quality of life. Some may remain confident about their own ability to assess risk and provide treatment for the people they work with who are violent.

We are interested in what informs risk assessment and management decisions: the knowledge base that informs practitioners' understanding of violence and those who commit it; the values that inspired people to enter this work; and how helpful professional and government guidance is in performing this hugely responsible task. As we consider the plethora of policies and practices published almost weekly on government websites, we wonder how far the guidance reflects practitioners' accumulated wisdom, how much it reflects a knee-jerk reaction to media and public fears of violent crime, and how much it reflects what seems to be an increasing trend to establish ways of undertaking risk assessments and devising interventions which treat violent people differently according to age, sex, gender, mental health status and type of violence.

In this book we want to explore the commonalities and complexities of violence, for example how people can be both victim and perpetrator depending on the position they hold in society at any particular time; how dominant explanatory and treatment approaches tend to totalize the experience of violence, based on global accounts that subsume individuals into categories such as 'male', 'youth' 'sex offender' and 'psychopath'; and how responses to violence are based on these constructed 'types' rather than exploring the meaning of the behaviour for those people in that specific time and place. We want to argue that this has led to the development of formulaic assumptions and techniques that restrict the capacity for meaningful change by imposing pathologized problem identities on people who are, or have been, violent.

We will examine current explanatory theories of violence, how these theoretical positions influence risk assessment and risk management, and identify the strengths and weaknesses of each approach in order to assist the reader in clarifying what they do, why they do it and how effective it is. Our hope is that this will assist you to reflect critically on your practice.

This book stems from our engagement with violence through our professional lives, and probably through our personal lives as well. We both have backgrounds in social work and counselling where violence and risk assessment have been the focus of work with service users. Judith is in her tenth year of working with adults and young people who are violent or who have experienced violence, whereas Steve is now more involved in education and training. Our struggle to make sense of the violences involved; what we are told the explanations for these are; what may be effective interventions; and how we can maintain some sense of values when working within a highly charged field have influenced the structure and content of this book. We have used a variety of theoretical understandings and methods depending on the 'flavour of the month' and on the more directive guidance promoted by government and agencies. All of the approaches described have something to offer in responding to violence; however, we have come to the conclusion that practices based within a broad social constructionist approach produce the best results for the widest group of service users, as well as providing constructive and respectful ways of working, and this is reflected in the tone and content of this book.

The social and political context of violence

Victimization studies show that criminal violence in the United Kingdom is actually in decline; for example, the incidence of common assault and domestic violence went down by 25 per cent between 1997 and 2001/2, with the latter reduction accelerating to 29 per cent between 1999 and 2001/2 (Simmons et al., 2002). However, the punishment of violent offenders has become substantially harsher over that same period. The probability that an offender convicted of an indictable offence will be sentenced to imprisonment has doubled, and lengths of sentences have steadily increased. As is discussed in the chapter examining mental health and criminality, the government is planning to build more high security psychiatric hospitals to accommodate lengthy waiting lists. This is despite research showing that a number of people with personality disorder who are already in these hospitals could be accommodated elsewhere; Harty and colleagues (2004) estimate that 40 per cent of the population of the three high-security hospitals (some 500 people) could be safely transferred to less secure hospitals.

Historically high imprisonment rates have been confined to the United States, China, Russia and South Africa, with European rates remaining low. However, the imprisonment rate in the United Kingdom and the Netherlands has quintupled over the last 20 years (Downes, 2001). There is an over-representation of African-Caribbean male prisoners in the United Kingdom and the proportion of non-Dutch prisoners rose by 26 per cent in Holland in 1992. The rates of female imprisonment in the United Kingdom have risen more slowly, but the introduction of short sentences for repeat minor offences (mainly drug offences) has disproportionately affected women, of whom 26 per cent are from ethnic minorities, with 10 per cent of these women being foreign nationals (Carlen and Worrall, 2004). Carlen (2002) estimates the increase in women's over men's imprisonment at 87 per cent to 37 per cent. The emphasis on 'persistence' as a factor in dangerousness has meant that disproportionately more women than men are imprisoned for violent offences; women convicted of violent offences make up the second largest group of prisoners after drug offenders (Malloch, 2004). The introduction of Detention and Training Orders in the Crime and Disorder Act 1998 has resulted in the trebling of the number of juvenile girls in prison, all of them being in closed prisons on the grounds that if they were considered suitable for open imprisonment they would have received community sentences. Adult women are therefore more likely than men to be in closed prisons. Because of the relatively small numbers of women prisoners, there are only two categories of women's prisons compared with four for men. The number of open places for women has declined to fewer than 250 (Carlen and Worrall, 2004), thus less than 10 per cent of women are in open conditions, subjecting the majority of women to over restrictions.

Garland (2001a) refers to this mass imprisonment – the systematic imprisonment of whole groups of the population. He suggests that this is a result of a converging series of policies and decisions: determinate sentence structures; the war against drugs; mandatory sentencing; the emergence of private corrections; and political events that have made everyone tough on crime. Tonry (2004) asks why a nation as historically tolerant as the United Kingdom has adopted so many US measures uncritically – three strikes and you're out, minimum sentencing, boot camps, zero tolerance, and so on – when these measures have significantly failed to reduce prison populations in the United States. He argues that the 'get tough' approach ignores careful research into violence, being influenced more by a heightened awareness of risk and populist punitiveness. Nowhere in the Labour party policy statements or government papers is violence generally addressed as a serious social problem in its own right, even the Halliday report being ambiguous and unsatisfactory on the subject. Rather, he says, criminal justice policy making has been theatrical rather than substantive; for example, *Justice for All* talks about violence in polemic terms:

> The public are sick and tired of a sentencing system that does not make sense. They read about dangerous, violent, sexual and other serious offenders who get off lightly, or are not in prison long enough.
>
> (Home Office, 2002: 86)

Several reasons have been put forward to explain this heightened perception of risk and willingness for greater control. Consumerist practices encouraged by government to avoid the possibility of a recession may seem like the permissiveness to enjoy oneself without restraints; for example, the relaxation of prosecution for cannabis use, but says Loizidou (2004), behind this permissiveness comes a baggage of conditions and restraints. People do not feel in control of even their family lives; they must send their children to school – which may be plagued with bullying and drug pushing – or face fines and possible imprisonment, but are not allowed to smack them or take them out of school on holiday. This perceived lack of control is reflected in local crime audits; people express concern about crime, are very worried about robbery, burglary and violence, but their main concern is young people on the streets. This concern is echoed in government strategy where children and young people are specifically targeted in terms of the preventing a supply of new prolific and/or dangerous offenders. *The Prolific and Other Priority Offender Strategy* identifies three groups of children and young people in need of intensive interventions:

■ young offenders within the youth justice system who are not yet prolific offenders

■ older children and young people who are involved in less serious offending but not yet within youth justice interventions

■ children from an early age in need of support now and at risk of a range of poor outcomes, including criminality.

(Home Office, 2004)

This latter group is also targeted in the government initiative *Every Child Matters* (www.everychildmatters.gov.uk), where avoiding crime is one of the desired five outcomes, and also in the Children Act 2004. Use of the word 'yet' in this guidance assumes that all these children are likely to become prolific offenders, thus adults who offend have a dual responsibility for their own behaviour and in creating the next generation of offenders.

The development of Anti-Social Behaviour Orders reflects some of the ways in which crime is (re)conceptualized and (re)defined, as it is clear these orders, first introduced in the Crime and Disorder Act 1998 and developed in the Anti-Social Behaviour Act 2003, have passed into common parlance. The acronym (ASBO) has become an accepted term ('asbo') to describe certain people as undesirable. We have even come across professionals describing families as 'asbotic'. Of course, defining ASB is problematic, as inviting people to do this generates identification of behaviour from spitting to gun crime, thus drawing a wide (and confused) boundary around the unpleasant to the downright dangerous. Victims are central to the construction of ASB as it can be any behaviour that causes 'harassment, alarm and distress' (Anti-Social Behaviour Act, 2003), terms that could be used to turn all of us into victims for what can be everyday events. We may be 'alarmed and distressed' by aggressive and foul-mouthed individuals who abuse their positions to bully others, yet would we wish to name ourselves as victims? If a loud group of children make someone feel alarmed, should that be enough to trigger an ASBO? If the children are black and the 'victim' white, to what extent does racism play a part in constructing these children as anti-social?

Another reason commonly cited in changing perceptions of violence is the role of the media, the portrayal of violent crime as an overwhelmingly visual narrative (Loizidou, 2004). Whilst it cannot be argued that there is a direct link between the media and individual behaviour, there is little doubt that public fears are heightened by daily images of violent crime. These range from the public execution of hostages abroad, terrorist activity at home, the linking of crime with migration, the deaths of James Bulger and Sarah Payne (accentuating the fear of 'others' or strangers), to the gruesome reporting of deaths of small children such as the Soham children and Victoria Climbié (increasing the suspicion and fear of known people). Added to these regular headline stories are numerous documentaries on violence in all areas of life – nurses who kill elderly patients, cruel and insensitive nursery workers, and sexually predatory priests and teachers (nowhere is safe). And these stories fuel perceptions that government is dishonest in its presentation of crime statistics; for example, the Home Office reports that most violent crime recorded by the police is low-level thuggery that involves little or no physical violence to the victim and that the United Kingdom has one of the lowest homicide rates among EU member states, but newspapers report a huge increase in violent crime (see, e.g., 'Violent crime soars during police crackdown', *The Sunday Times*, 03.10.04; 'A gun crime every five hours as the crisis grows', *The Times*, 16.10.04; 'Violent Crime soars but Labour puts gloss on it', *Telegraph*, 22.10.04; 'Kicking to death: the new brutality of savage streets', *The Times*, 22.10.04)

Cavender (2004) argues that politicians are merely articulating the public's insecurities, invoking a fearful, angry public to justify neo-liberal and conservative social policies and to revitalize a punitive approach to sanctions. But a daily diet of violence on television and in the newspapers cannot be held solely responsible for heightened fears. Other than visually, it differs little from the media coverage of the Hummel and Kuschera child-death cases in Freud's Vienna, when people faced similar worries about immigration (largely from rural Czechoslovakia) and the vilification of Jews as blood-drinking child murderers mirrored today's anti-Islamic expression (for a detailed account, see Wolff, 1984). People have always been fascinated by violent crime simply because it has all the ingredients of good narrative structure: social equilibrium is disrupted by a villain, the victim is seen to suffer tremendously, and after a successful denouement punishment is meted out and equilibrium is restored.

What is qualitatively different in media representation nowadays is how the victim is portrayed, whether this is an individual or a community. Not since Euripides have victims, largely identified as women and children, been so sympathetically and *comprehensively* delineated; see, for example, *Safety and Justice: The Government's Proposals on Domestic Violence* (2003b, Cm 5847), which outlines strategies for prevention (particularly changing young people's attitudes), protection and justice, and support for victims (mostly assumed to be women who wish to leave their relationships), but is silent on how adult violence may be prevented or how violent adults whose partners leave them may be helped. Government, influenced by pro-feminist theory and research, has actively sought to influence the media in this regard: 'The prevalence of media images and publicity about violence is a big factor in our attitudes to violence', giving as an example of good practice in *Living without Fear*:

> Television soaps can be an effective way of raising awareness of social issues. Channel 4's *Brookside* has had a number of stories of violence against women in recent times. In 1998 domestic violence was covered and in 1999 a character involved in a date rape involving the use of Rohypnol. Both *Coronation Street* and *East Enders* have covered domestic violence.
>
> (Home Office, 2003a)

Indeed, it may be that portraying the effects of violence on victims has had an effect on the reduction in violent crime; we have experience of service users telling us how ashamed it made them feel about their behaviour. However, this is merely anecdotal evidence and one that has not been researched, offenders being less likely to be represented in current media or official discourses as socially deprived citizens in need of support. They are depicted instead as culpable, undeserving and somewhat dangerous individuals to be managed:

> The critical measure is the probability of harm to the public. Accordingly, the offender is to be confronted about offending behaviour, challenged to accept responsibility for the crime and its consequences, made aware of the impact of the crime committed and motivated towards a greater sense of personal responsibility and discipline.
>
> (Caddick and Lewis, 1999: 63)

Thus a victim's experience of violence would be the salient factor when represented as a local newspaper item or a documentary, not the offender's experiences or mitigating circumstances. The victim is individualized and the offender is objectified; their interests being assumed to be diametrically opposed. Where there is what was previously regarded as a victimless crime, it is the future victim who is the focus of attention – the safety of the community (Garland, 2001b).

The official discourse of the criminal justice system is not interested in understanding why someone has offended; it merely assumes that his criminal act was voluntary, the result of a misguided choice (or cognitive distortion). This means that an offender's violent behaviour would not be seen as a possible presenting problem of deeper troubles, it is **the** central problem to be addressed. Indeed, in the current guidance on prolific offenders (*Prolific and Other Priority Offenders Strategy*, Home Office, July 2004), the offender is not individualized at all. The concern is to 'catch and convict' those 10 per cent of active offenders who commit at least 50 per cent of all serious crime but who are not a static group: 'In the group of 100,000 most *active* offenders, we estimate that approximately 20,000 offenders drop out and are replaced by similar numbers each year', and especially the 'super prolific' group of 5000 who commit 9 per cent of all crimes. The offender's self-esteem, levels of insight, social and economic problems become irrelevant as the welfare mode becomes more conditional (can the offender benefit from treatment?), more offence-centred (has he developed victim empathy, is he likely to re-offend?) and more risk conscious (how can the victim(s) be kept safe?). The prominence of the penal mode means that the offender is more likely to be punished and have restrictions placed upon him: 'It is future victims who are now "rescued" by rehabilitative work, rather than the offenders themselves' (Garland, 2001b: 176).

This loss of the individual, subsumed into categories, controlled in a physical sense and dehumanized through policies and practices, is the element we wish to make claims upon. We believe that these are 'people worth doing business with' and we seek to retain the sense of the person in front of us in all their (sometimes unattractive) complexity despite pressures to place them in a small box labelled 'violent offender'. This is not to say that we ignore or marginalize victims. On the contrary we are committed to developing safety for all through a rigorous engagement with those who have been violent to hear how they can take responsibility for their actions, and in doing so create the conditions for a more just and lasting change in behaviour.

Summary

- Although serious violence is reducing in frequency, the punishment of violent offenders has become harsher.

- Imprisonment rates have increased most rapidly for men of ethnic minorities and all women.

■ Government plans to reduce prolific and violent crime by targeting children and young people assessed as being at risk of becoming offenders.

■ The media plays a large part in fuelling public concerns about violent crime.

To aid critical reflection we invite you to consider the framework and questions below.

Prolific and Priority Offender Strategy
(www.crimereduction.gov.uk/ppominisite01.htm)

Purpose and Scope of the Strategy

The **Prolific** and other **Priority Offender** (PPO) **Strategy** is a single, coherent initiative in three complementary strands to reduce crime by targeting those who offend most or otherwise cause most harm to their communities. ... It will replace the existing national Persistent **Offender** Scheme. ...

...

The **strategy** should be operated on a case by case basis, with interventions being both proportionate and lawful.

...

The problem

1. Home Office modelling work (Annex B, Criminal Justice White Paper 2001) suggests there are about one million active offenders in the general population at any one time. Of these, around [10%] will accumulate more than three convictions during their criminal careers and ... commit at least 50% of all serious crime. In addition, it can be reasonably assumed that this group is responsible for a disproportionately high amount of unsolved crime.

2. The active **offender** population is not static. As offenders give up offending and leave the population, a steady stream of new offenders replace them. ...

3. ... [A]nalysis suggests that ever smaller numbers of offenders are responsible for disproportionately greater amounts of crime. We

estimate that the most **prolific** 5,000 offenders ... are responsible for around 9% of all crimes. This **strategy** is aimed at tackling this 'super **prolific**' group.

The strategy

4. The **strategy** builds on expertise learned over two years of the Street Crime Initiative and from numerous, successful local initiatives.

5. The **strategy** is in three complementary parts designed to tackle both **Prolific** offending and its roots, comprising:

   ■ Prevent and Deter;

   ■ Catch and Convict; and

   ■ Rehabilitate and Resettle

6. The **Prevent and Deter** strand will help to stop the supply of new **prolific** offenders by:

   ■ reducing re-offending, so that those who are already criminally active do not graduate into becoming **prolific** offenders;

   ■ reducing the numbers of young people who become involved in crime.

7. It will do so by focusing in particular on three specific target groups:

   ■ young offenders within the youth justice system, but who are not yet **prolific** offenders, ... through youth justice interventions;

   ■ older children and young people at high risk of criminality. Some of this target group may already be involved in less serious offending, but not yet within the youth justice system. There are intensive targeting programmes that focus on this group;

   ■ children (from early age) in need of support now and at risk of a wide range of poor outcomes including criminality, who are targeted by early intervention programmes.

8. This work will be taken forward within the broader context of the reforms set out in the Green Paper Every Child Matters and the Children Bill, which is now before Parliament. ...

9. The basic proposition for the **Catch and Convict** and **Rehabilitate and Resettle** strands is to develop a joined up approach, with all partners focused on the same group of offenders through the setting up of a **Prolific** and other **Priority** Offenders (PPO) Scheme in every Crime and Disorder Reduction Partnership (CDRP) area. Each local scheme will, based on intelligence, select the individuals who are causing the most harm to their communities and will ensure all agencies prioritize their resources on these offenders, with the explicit aim of putting an end to the harm which they are causing.

10. For smaller CDRP areas, we expect a minimum of 15–20 **Prolific** and Other **Priority** offenders. There is a requirement for very much more substantial targeting – and therefore larger numbers – in those CDRP areas which cover two or more Police Basic Command Unit areas. In these much larger (city) areas, ... we expect between 60–100 PPOs to form the basis of the ... programme. ... There should be a single group of PPOs identified as the focus for Catch & Convict and Rehabilitate & Resettle strands. Where juveniles are identified as PPOs, Youth Offending Teams need to be closely involved at all stages.

11. **Catch and Convict** reflects the need for robust and proactive criminal justice processes, to ensure effective investigation, charging and prosecution of PPOs. ... We expect all areas to adopt a Criminal Justice System (CJS) Premium Service, building on that agreed for the Persistent **Offender** Scheme (POS) and Street Crime Initiative (SCI), to ensure that these offenders are consistently prioritized throughout the Criminal Justice System.

12. The **Rehabilitate and Resettle** strand aims to present PPOs with a simple choice: reform or face a very swift return to the courts. This will be undertaken through management of offenders, whether in the community or in custody, through provision of support and **priority** access to services, including multi-agency, pre-release support for those serving custodial sentences, and monitoring these individuals on release (using surveillance and

other intelligence methods). Interventions with these offenders should ensure that they are prioritized at Area and Regional level in work taken forward as part of the National Reducing Re-Offending Action Plan.

13. ... Our work to target PPOs aims to encourage partners to build on existing important initiatives (e.g. Street Crime Initiative, Criminal Justice Intervention Programme) within a single **strategy** to focus on the same group of offenders.

14. Although leaving very wide **scope** for local discretion, the scheme is not an optional one. ...

Questions

- The above strategy is mandatory for all local areas. How would you implement the Prevent and Deter element of the strategy?

- How would you identify those children at risk of 'criminality'?

- What criteria would you apply to decide who is a Prolific and other Priority Offender?

- Which types of criminal behaviour are unlikely to be targeted in this strategy?

CHAPTER 2

Assessing Violence

The core of many professional interactions with violence is assessment, underpinned and reinforced by a plethora of governmental and departmental policy initiatives in crime, health and social care. This focus on assessment, or in it's guise of 'risk' assessment, leads to approaches that can be rather mechanistic in nature, providing the busy professional with a series of protocols and instruments that all make claims to 'truth' in the prediction of future violent acts. This in itself may be of use to those under pressure and clearly if the assessment can be done quickly and effectively, based on evidence, then future victims have been protected through the identification of those who have the propensity for committing further damage. However, there are difficulties with this approach both in concept and in practice which we will explore. We will look at some key issues in the assessment of violence in this chapter, exploring how assessment is, and can be, constructed, with a view to illuminating some of the benefits and pitfalls of varying approaches to assessment.

Trouble with assessment

Prediction of events is something that seems to be prevalent in all human societies throughout history, with a variety of methodologies used to anticipate what may happen in the future. These have been, and still are, based on notions of signs and symbols, through rituals designed to facilitate the illumination of the not yet known. We can see how many of these pre-industrial approaches still have currency in our society, with the popularity of astrology, palmistry, card-reading, religious interpretations and so on, but the advent of a scientific, Western, industrial-technological society has generated its own ways of thinking about prediction, specifically a statistical approach that uses an empirical method to calculate risks. This can be seen most clearly in weather forecasting, in which data is collected on variables that are known to influence dangers; these are analysed using regression-based actuarial risk-assessment models that predict the likelihood of those dangers occurring. Our current ways of thinking have their own signs and symbols (clouds; barometric pressure; wind patterns) and the rituals to make sense of these (statistical analysis).

Assessment is a concept that is subjected to ways of making sense of the world to the same extent as any other professional task in people-working. It is constructed by and through knowledge, and the type of knowledge used will influence the design, implementation and interpretation of the assessment. Postmodern and poststructuralist approaches have assisted in illuminating what are often taken for granted ways of working (Fook, 2002) and these perspectives will be used to explore the dominant methods of assessment. In particular, notions of power, subjectivity and identity will be central in considering the different ways that workers can make sense of the same event (violence), depending on the epistemological (knowledge-base) construction of the assessment. The following chapters will add to this knowledge base by their exploration of specific theoretical areas, hopefully assisting the reader in understanding the very practical ways in which a preferred knowledge may have consequences for the outcome of interventions.

Locating assessments

Smale and Tuson (1993) provided a helpful structure for understanding assessments and the different ways in which they may be categorized. They focus on the processes involved as much as the technologies or tools that may be utilized in making an assessment:

1. **Procedural Model.** The information is gathered using a model or tool that is prescriptive about what constitutes a relevant fact. This list of facts is then placed within a matrix that provides a ready-made analysis of the situation and this leads to a specific outcome. The worker is an information-gathering machine who has to make sure that they provide the correct input to this system.

2. **Questioning Model.** In this approach the worker undertaking the assessment takes an 'investigatory' role; asking questions that are relevant to the situation in an attempt to find out more about the circumstances and nature of the problem. This gathering of facts

may be led by protocols that assist in deciding which questions to ask and how the answers/information may then be analysed. The analysis leads to the making of a professional judgement based on theory, research and/or organizational requirements. The worker in this process is central; they decide which questions to ask, which facts are relevant or have more weight than others, make deductions and interpretations from the information and create an assessment that reflects their understanding of the situation.

3. **Exchange Model.**   In this approach the subject of the assessment is seen as the expert in their situation, and the worker is there to assist the person to identify strengths and strategies to overcome the problems. The process is much more collaborative in nature than the previous models and may go some way to addressing the clear power imbalance of other models.

The above structure will be helpful to readers in identifying their current practice(s) and in reflecting on the dominant ways of assessing people who have been violent. We suspect from our experience and understanding of the subject area that most assessments undertaken **on** people follow either the Questioning or Procedural models, or mixtures of the two. Of course, the models are never completely discrete, with elements that may be recognizable in many assessment processes. Indeed, in working with violence there are clear ethical considerations about effecting change and preventing recidivism which may lead workers to take a more anxiety-led, directive model. This is understandable when 'getting it wrong' could lead to someone being harmed, although the responsibility for future harm remains with the person who commits this. Certainty in this matter is probably unachievable whichever model is used and acceptance of uncertainty is perhaps important to bear in mind (Parton and O'Byrne, 2000). Decisions are always temporary and contingent, awaiting further developments, despite pressures to make them definitive. Organizational demands can severely proscribe what approach workers are allowed to take, yet we consider that creative professionals have the capacity to work in ways that acknowledge limitations, introducing or combining ways of working that enhance the quality of service.

We have a preference for the Exchange model, an acceptance of informed Questioning models, and some major reservations about the Procedural model that we will discuss further in this chapter. The following chapters will include ways of working that are more likely to be located within Exchange and Questioning models.

Art and science

The influence of a scientific approach to assessment is clear from the general construction of most of the processes involved. The 'scientific' method of rational enquiry has a privileged position within our society and ways of thinking, but in many ways can be seen as a further human development in seeking certainty about the world. Collecting data, analysing it and making a judgement on the problem(s) to decide on effective intervention to ameliorate the problematic aspects is fairly accepted practice. However, this is often achieved through the identifying of causes that can then be assessed for appropriate intervention, a linear model that makes assumptions about the nature of cause and effect. These assumptions include the premise that causes can be objectively determined through rigorous investigation and that once this 'truth' is determined, then there is an indicated intervention that can deal with the problem and its causes. This will be familiar to most of us from our experiences of visiting the doctor. Symptoms are diagnosed (aches, a temperature and sore throat) and categorized (as a cold) and the established treatment is given (bed rest, lots of fluids, Paracetamol). This may even be subject to review (come back next week if the symptoms persist). This approach has its basis in a medical model which is relatively effective in identifying and managing diseases, although many medical staff may raise questions about the purity of this model in practice (trial and error is common in medicine).

Parton and O'Byrne (2000: 136) use the example of the Home Office *National Standards for the Supervision of Offenders in the Community* (1995) to demonstrate this process in practice guidance. As this guidance is relevant to violence (our case example Mark could easily have found himself subject to criminal justice intervention), it is worth exploring this to illuminate some of the points above. The expressed purpose of this assessment is to '*set out factual data concerning the service user in an accurate and truthful way, stating how the information was obtained, what were the sources, and "identifying steps taken to verify the information"'* (Home Office, 1995: 8). This data is intended to be objective or at least free of subjective reframes or of the '*terminology of aggravation or mitigation*' (ibid.: 9). The guidance then proceeds to analysis of the person and their behaviour, offering an explanation of why this may have occurred, leading to a summary of the person's needs, resources and risks. This in turn is followed by a recommendation of the most appropriate form of intervention to remedy the situation, including some prognosis of likely success.

In our case study, Mark would be asked questions about the violence, a judgement would be made based on the facts elicited, and he would then be categorized as in need of a certain strategy to deal with this behaviour. He may be asked about the circumstances of the incidents; how he felt in the lead-up to the violence; what were the 'triggers' to the violent feelings and actions; what his own experiences of violence have been as a child; whether he uses drugs or alcohol; what his attitudes to violence (and women) are. All these questions are designed to find out 'who' he is and to place him within a category that indicates his 'riskiness' and how to prevent him from future acts.

Yet this process is much more complex and less straightforward than it first appears. An assumption is that the worker asking the questions is an objective and passive actor in this; that all that has to be done is to establish the presence of known facts about people who are violent and then analyse these facts to produce a rational judgement. Protocols are there to assist in this process, providing 'facts' to look for and indicate outcomes based on these. This assumes some notion of objectivity on the part of workers, much like a computer when fed particular information would 'crunch' these numbers and come out with the answer, but the interaction between worker and client is ignored and the sense that the worker makes of the world is not acknowledged. The worker is in the powerful position of directing the conversation towards what they need to know, rather than listening to what the service user wants to say. There may well be scepticism on the part of the worker if Mark is not admitting any of the factors that are 'known' to be significant in their understanding of violence. Questions may be aimed at reinforcing the search for underlying meaning or events that he is unwilling or unable to discuss, for example pursuing information about the style of parenting he was subjected to or any childhood abuse he had experienced. Of course, such facts may be of significance to the interviewer which when found may lead to the end of this line of questioning, thus marginalizing any view Mark may have had about the significance *for him*.

This is illustrated by the experience of a colleague undertaking an assessment on a boy who had committed a sexual offence. Protocols indicated that it was important to identify the sexual fantasies of the offender to see how they might support abusive behaviour. When asked by the (self-categorized) white, middle-class, middle-aged, professional woman what the black, teenaged, working-class boy fantasized about, he looked aghast and then said '*Oh, stockings, suspenders and that sort of stuff*'. It was clear to the colleague that the boy was saying what he felt was acceptable and appropriate in the circumstances, striving to perform a 'normal' role. This was mediated by who they were but also raises questions about the ethics of such questions (are sexual fantasies always acted upon?), particularly as there is currently no way of knowing absolutely whether someone is telling the truth when they tell you about their inner thoughts. The paradox in this situation is that if someone is truthful and admits to having some 'illegal' fantasies then they may well be propelled into a more 'risky' category. If they choose not to discuss (or lie about) it, then this factor will not be recognized and the outcome will be different.

Mark may offer answers that can be interpreted in different ways, depending on who is making sense of them. If Mark talks about early behavioural problems at his school, then this could be seen as indicating a pattern of difficult behaviour that demonstrates he has a history that may be of concern, perhaps entrenched behaviours that make his likelihood of continuing violence more probable. This could be viewed as biological in nature or due to his upbringing, giving him 'traits' that lend themselves to violence. Another interviewer may see the troubles as the product of an education system that is loaded against certain children from particularly disadvantaged backgrounds, looking at the social context rather than locating the problem purely with Mark. The sense making of the events depends on what someone brings to them.

How the questions are asked can also affect the outcome. For example if Mark is asked directly if he has been subjected to parental violence, he may well believe this not to be the case, yet if he is asked to describe his disciplining by his parents this may identify behaviour that would constitute abuse from a professional perspective. This problem of agreeing what constitutes some of the concepts used recurs in assessments, with little agreement on what is, for example, 'abuse', 'violence' or 'frequency'. We can all recognize extremes, but it would be difficult to gain complete agreement about the range of events in between. What may at first appear to be a definitive category is often dependent upon personal interpretation.

The importance of communication skills is often underplayed in processes, viewed as simply a vehicle for eliciting information. Yet we know from research into any therapeutic relationship (and any intervention into people's lives to deal with problems can be construed as such) that the impact of the therapist/worker is of central importance in the experience, to the point that how a person is communicated with can impact on their responses (Wampold, 2001). We know this from our own experiences, yet there are examples of practice guidance within violence that encourage aggressive approaches to interviewing (see Vizard, 2002, for examples of this with children who sexually offend). Challenging violence at every opportunity is also commonly held in some practice (see, for example, Dobash, Dobash, Cavanagh and Lewis, 2000), yet this may well precipitate a certain response from those assessed that confirms preconceptions of their violent nature.

This drive to locate people within categories may have an organizational function, as limited resources are often only available for those who are deemed really in need of them and this is demonstrated through the process of assessment. Making arguments for services are supported when significant need and risk factors can be collected and used to argue for a particular service to address the circumstances of that individual. Workers who are concerned about the person not reaching the threshold for services may well be tempted to subvert the process by over-emphasizing certain factors in order to gain some assistance for the individual in need.

Although it may seem paradoxical, this assessment process has been criticized for actually losing the individual within the factors and categories used. Despite the best intentions of workers to really understand the individual and their behaviour, the outcome is to place the individual within categories that make them *like others* who have committed similar behaviour or who are in similar circumstances.

The role of identity

The notion of identity has become increasingly important in thinking about how we conceptualize people and their behaviour and has a particular significance in assessment. It has been recognized that we have a tendency to construct the social world into binary opposites (Healy, 2000), where people are placed into an either/or category; for example, we are black or white, rich or poor, powerful or powerless, or in our case victim or perpetrator of violence. This dichotomous thinking (Berlin, 1990) has the consequence of creating, accentuating and 'fixing' difference, in effect generating an identity for the person subjected to the categorization. Once this identity is given, the focus of investigation and sense making of the person is framed within this construct, leaving little room for the uniqueness of the individual. Mark has been violent but he may well become a 'violent person', with certain attributes and characteristics that are expected of such people. There is an implicit working assumption that Mark is 'different'; that his behaviour indicates a type of person who is not-normal; that his violent identity is the core of his being rather than contextual. He may well have accepted this identity and consider his actions to be an integral part of who he is, his 'violent streak' or 'short fuse'. Within this framework change is difficult to achieve or to imagine (both for Mark and his worker) and questions may be asked of him that serve to reinforce this identity, rather than to seek individual differences away from the label.

This is often reflected in the language we use about people who behave in ways that we disapprove of. There is a tendency to 'other' these people, to distance them from 'us' who are 'normal'. Using the term 'perpetrator' is a useful example of this, as it can be argued that this is a word that has been linked specifically with the commission of violence and in particular sexual abuse. Although the word itself merely indicates the commission of a criminal act, it would be unusual for it to be used in the context of 'the perpetrator of car theft', or 'the perpetrator of financial fraud'. The use of 'paedophile' is a further categorization that creates an identity of difference. Dominelli and Cowburn (2001) have discussed the inherent problems in uncritically using the concept, as it tends to psychologize, pathologize and deny social power relations, generating an image of child abuse as a personal abnormality rather than the reality of adult abuse of power situated in (usually) gendered relations. A person who sexually abuses children is not statistically the 'dirty old mackintosh-wearing man in the park', but a father, mother, sibling or trusted friend. Identities are linked with personality characteristics that tend to be seen as 'essential', that is of a fixed nature, which limits any notion of personal agency on the part of the person subjected to the label.

Thinking about identity has developed within a postmodern framework to raise questions about the above assumptions. Rather than seeing identity as static, fixed, psychologically constructed, unable to change and unrelated to social context, this approach views identities as changeable, often consisting of contradictions and constructed by and through the social environment. Newton (1988: 99) helpfully describes the 'postmodern' identity (or 'subjectivity' as it is sometimes referred to) as 'multiple, contradictory and in-process', giving a sense of complexity that is often absent from more scientific, modernist notions. Time and space are also key mediators of this, with Mark for example being violent at certain times in particular places, rather than having a 'violent personality'. Mark may also have contradictory behaviours where he can be not-violent, or behave in ways that are much more ambiguous or complicated than his violent identity may indicate. He is also subjected to forces that have shaped his understanding and expression of feelings and behaviour, where he has been 'invited' to behave in ways that are socially sanctioned, in particular the destructive elements of masculinity. Traditional modernist approaches to identity have tended to reduce the person to a rather mechanistic 'vessel', driven by internal or external forces that are beyond their control and of which they are only vaguely aware, if at all. The postmodern approaches allow for consideration of the person as actively engaging with these forces; continually making sense of the rich social environment in which we find ourselves. Of course, many of the cultural stories and discourses around are very powerful and may limit the choices people feel able to make, or encourage the choice of certain ways of being. Sands (1996) discusses the term 'narrative identity', where people construct their many and varied experiences as a 'story' about themselves in order to make sense of their place(s) in the world. This story often fits with culturally acceptable ways of being, but also changes when subjected to interactions with others in different situations that may contradict or not-quite-fit the self-story.

Risk or 'risk'

The term 'risk' appears in many assessment protocols of violence as an indicator of the purpose of the exercise. Predicting the risks involved usually relates to the likelihood of something negative recurring, in this case the chances of the violent behaviour exploding in the future. In the laudable drive to try to decide how probable it is that a particular individual will hurt someone again, many professionals will be party to agency or disciplinary imperatives to make some judgement on this recurring. Yet the concept of risk is not entirely without its problems and it is worthwhile exploring the meaning(s) attached to this before we move into assessing risk.

There is little doubt that most people-workers (and lay people) when using the word 'risk' associate this with danger, as evidenced by our experiences within child protection, criminal justice and in teaching social work students. When people are asked about the risks involved in situations, they have a tendency to dwell on the negatives of a situation or the potential for negative events to happen. Research on professional attitudes exists to confirm this (see, for example, Alaszewski and Manthorpe, 1998). This has become so entrenched within our professional and cultural discourses that we often forget that 'risk' originated as a neutral term to describe the probability of an event happening, linked with the scale of the outcome in terms of losses *or gains*. This latter part of the concept has become eroded to the point where Douglas

(1992: 24) states that '… the word *risk* now means danger; *high risk* means a lot of danger.' The probability of gains and losses is now reduced to negative outcomes, what Parton, Thorpe and Wattam (1997: 235) describe as '… hazard, danger, exposure, harm and loss'. Douglas pursues the argument further by raising questions about the consequences of this change, locating this use of language within a drive to make events more calculable. She considers that although danger is a more fitting description of what people are trying to explore, 'danger does not have the aura of science or afford the pretension of a possible precise calculation.' (Douglas, 1992: 25). By re-creating danger as risk, this allows for its incorporation into a scientific, objective way of thinking, therefore improving its status in our rationalist world-view. It also lends itself to scientific prediction of future events.

The use of risk in this context has significant consequences in terms of the function of assessment; Beck (1998), for example, proposes that we are living within a 'risk society' that has a focus on future dangers/risks, demanding and expecting prediction and prevention through the application of rational science. If events should be calculable, then people or systems can be held to account for failure to predict, generating a blame culture. Douglas identified that all societies have had blaming structures, be they natural or supernatural, and that currently risk has this function in our society. The anxiety to reduce perceived risk is fraught with contradictions given the basic uncertainty and unpredictability of modern life (Ungar, 2004), and the belief that danger/risk can be identified, calculated and prevented in an absolute manner is clearly a goal which will never be achieved. Reliance on experts to predict and manage danger/risk has been seen as crucial in illuminating the way in which society conceives of and makes use of science, knowledge and professionals (Luhman, 1993). As trust in science and professionals has decreased, perhaps partly due to truth-claims that could not be substantiated; claims which changed as scientific investigation developed and the growing awareness of scientific debate and difference, the pressure to proceduralize risk assessment into a testable framework is enormous. The resulting 'scientific' opinion can also be questioned and challenged at a later date as new 'evidence' is discovered, as happened in the case of Professor Roy Meadow, who diagnosed Munchausen's Syndrome By Proxy. Thus risk-assessment protocols can be seen as organizational tools to make defensible decisions in order to minimize the 'blame' when dangers inevitably occur. If the tool has not been followed, then the person responsible for its completion is at fault; if the tool predicts violence and this occurs, then the organization is defended; if the tool has been followed and an unexpected outcome occurs, then it is at fault and requires further development. Frequently the inquiries following the violent deaths of children at the hands of their carers have concluded that procedures need to be changed and modified in the light of failings, in the belief that such events can eventually be predicted and prevented through the increasing refinement of structures.

Castel (1991) also considers the consequences of distinguishing between risk and danger, observing that danger is a potentiality embodied in an individual, whereas risk is potentiality embodied in a population aggregate (Silver and Miller, 2002: 152). Risk factors are distilled from studied populations through the scientific method and are applied to the individual, thus creating an aura of calculation and certainty. To use the term danger about an individual is to locate this from and within the person, but this does not have the statistical sweep of risk and therefore has less currency in our privileging of the numerical. There are difficulties with this use of risk, particularly in conceptualizing problems, that we will consider further.

Approaches to risk assessment

There are two broad approaches to risk assessment; *actuarial prediction*, which uses statistical information and processes, and *clinical prediction*, which is based on expert judgement. Clinical prediction utilizes the knowledge base, experience and expertise of professionals to make sense of someone who has been violent, and may include the use of actuarial or otherwise structured assessment protocols to inform the overall decision making. Guidance exists for both approaches and we will consider some of these within this book. However, it is important to note that neither actuarial nor clinical methods of risk prediction are supported by evidence that demonstrates more than modest accuracy (Grubin, 1998). The following chapters in this book will explore the knowledge that underpins most clinical judgements. They are what Smale and Tuson would locate as 'Questioning' models, whereas the actuarial approach is more 'Procedural'.

Actuarial risk assessments

In the field of violence assessment there is a preponderance of actuarial risk assessments that make claims for the accuracy of their predictive validity. We saw at the beginning of this chapter that the use of actuarial approaches in weather prediction has been seen to be helpful, and these successes have been used to support the transfer of these techniques into the field of social control systems. Interpersonal violence has been an issue that has attracted this approach, with the development of a plethora of protocols to be used in the prediction of future recidivism. These include the *Violence Risk Assessment Guide* (VRAG) (Quinsey et al., 1998; Webster et al., 1994) for serious violence prediction and the *Static-99* (Hanson and Thornton, 1999) for sexual offenders.

Silver and Miller (2002) identify three key elements of an actuarial assessment:

1. **Decisions are grounded in statistical relationships.** Statistical algorithms are used to categorize individuals into population subgroups with shared characteristics and similar levels of risk. Individuals can be given a numerical score based on high and low risk attributes, where certain risk factors can be weighted to gain the numerical score. As a consequence of this process, individuals can be grouped into homogenous risk classes based on shared high or low risk attributes.

2. **Actuarial prediction moves decision making from professional knowledge and expertise to the actuarial model.** Relevant information is input into a risk-assessment algorithm, similar in principle to the introduction of data into a computer. This information may be gathered from a variety of sources by a variety of techniques. In this process the professional–client relationship becomes a one-way exchange of information, as all that is required is the accurate gathering of relevant information in a format that can be processed by the algorithm.

3. **Actuarial prediction uses aggregate data in prediction.** As in motor insurance, risk is determined by individuals who share characteristics. Aggregate data allows for estimating the likelihood that a certain group will commit violence. It is claimed that actuarial algorithms tend to be more accurate and consistent than human decision makers therefore there is an ethical imperative to use them, particularly when predicting harm against people.

The history of actuarial risk assessments has been subject to various developments and reflects the social and political context of the time (Auerhahn, 1999). There have been two recurring criticisms of this approach: that of false positive predictions (predicting cases to re-offend that do not do so) and false negative predictions (predicting cases not to re-offend but do so). These false prediction rates could be extremely high, in particular the false positives where an error rate of up to 48 per cent was recorded (Greenwood and Abrahamse, 1982). The ethical consequences of this are obvious, with large numbers of people being dragged into a net of stringent social control based on a mis-labelling. In view of this fundamental problem with the models, actuarial approaches have changed to a less definitive and certain way of predicting behaviour with a 'probabilistic' model. This model again explores characteristics that place people within a category, but this category is deemed to have a certain percentage of them who will go on to re-offend. Thus the model can claim that a particular person is within a group that has say a 50 per cent chance of re-offending over a specified time period. This person can then be said to have a 50 per cent chance of re-offending during the time period, therefore avoiding definitive statements about recidivism that cannot be absolutely supported. What sense systems make of this information is dependent on thresholds that may be set based on a perception of un/acceptable likelihoods. A person within a 90 per cent likelihood of recidivism will presumably warrant a more controlling response than someone with a 10 per cent likelihood, but these are decisions that will be made in a socio-political context. Beaumont (1999) provides a useful discussion of some of the key difficulties with the prediction of offending, and Craig (2004) outlines the complexities of the methodologies of actuarial risk assessment, including details of the various statistical processes involved.

Despite developments in actuarial risk assessments, there are still major questions about the purpose to which they are applied. Feeley and Simon (1992) identify these approaches as responding to a social and political context that demands increasing predictive accuracy to allocate limited resources more effectively. Not only do they assist in providing for effective management of offenders, they also have the potential to marginalize those professionals who have skills in working with people, as the required data can be collected and codified through computer programs, claiming to reduce the variable of individual interpretation to produce a 'purer' outcome. Actuarial risk assessments are not designed to explain, judge nor question the causes of violence and recidivism, but are there to predict the likelihood of violent events, thus ignoring the moral decisions about social and political change and focusing the problem back on to the individual. Risk markers may include poverty, poor education and unemployment; however, the actuarial risk assessment provides no imperative to deal with these issues; it simply treats people who are victims of these circumstances as 'a high-risk group that must be managed for the protection of the larger society' (Feeley and Simon, 1992: 192). In this sense actuarial risk assessment is an inherently political process, focusing as it does on the shortcomings of the individual and marginalizing the social context.

The drive to find those factors associated with violence in order to predict and manage people has produced a wealth of research and we will now look at an example of how studies inform the assessment of risk within this construct. Powis (2002) undertook a review of the literature of the risk of serious harm by offenders for the Home Office in order to inform the OASys, a joint prison/probation Offender Assessment System to be used within the UK criminal justice system. This review categorizes various types of offender (violent, domestic, stalking, sexual, arson, self-harmers and suicide risks) and seeks to explore the relevant literature. Under the category of Violent Offender, a list of risk factors have been identified including: previous offences; being a man; being young; being from a lower socio-economic group; being unemployed; having a low IQ; having a difficult or abusive upbringing; use of drugs and alcohol; poor housing; everyday problems such as finance; brain abnormalities; some mental illnesses; personality disorder; psychopathy; hostility and anger; difficulty in delaying gratification; impulsive behaviour; lack of insight or remorse; lack of victim empathy; callousness and lying; difficulty in recognizing emotions; being under- or over-controlled; and having sado-masochistic tendencies. These factors are supported by extensive research evidence and inform violence prediction tools. Yet there are some difficulties with the construction, interpretation and application of this approach which it is worth highlighting as they raise questions about the way in which we conceptualize problematic behaviour.

Clearly there are some factors that are static (unchangeable), such as biological gender, that are unlikely to change and are beyond the capacity of the individual to reasonably do anything about, modern surgical procedures notwithstanding. This is based on studies about the prevalence of violence by men as opposed to women, which have shown that men are more likely to commit violence. This fixed biological category can be read as due to some inherent male traits or due to socialization within masculinity. However, the explanation becomes irrelevant as the key is the sex of the person and not how we (or they) make sense of that, thus creating a label of inherent danger, that of 'male'. The same process can be seen in the identification of 'youth' as problematic, where the over-representation of younger people ('youth' being defined as aged below 29) within the violence statistics leads to assumptions that they are more likely to be violent, therefore any assessment needs to take into account that the younger the person, the more likely they are to be violent. However, both these factors require reflection on how they are constructed, as they are creating a homogenized identity from a large number of individual experiences.

Static factors such as age, gender and previous offences are key determinants in many actuarial assessments, yet they are actually self-evident and ultimately unhelpful in assisting how to change the behaviour and to reduce risk. As Horsefield says:

> the application of risk assessment within criminal justice is a bit like betting on a race where the outcome is known in advance. A probation officer sitting across a desk from a male person under the age of 25 who is there because he has to be, can say with considerable confidence that he will commit another offence, and with equal confidence that it will be similar to the last one.
>
> (2003: 374)

The static factors do not provide the worker with any strategies for reducing the danger someone may pose, nor can they be used to measure the effectiveness of interventions. Dynamic (interactive and changeable) factors may have some benefit in stimulating thinking about how to respond to them since these factors are potentially more amenable to change, be they social problems or specific behaviours that can be modified. If someone has problems with anger and this has been identified as a risk factor, then it makes some sense to change this through interventions, currently Anger Management programmes. Yet actuarial risk assessments have tendency to make definitive statements about people and their propensity for future violence ('This person has a 90 per cent likelihood of re-offending within 5 years'), which raises questions about the impact of interventions. If people are so firmly categorized as having a certain 'riskiness', then what is the point of intervention and how do you go about it? In constructing a risky *identity* for people, actuarial assessments can reduce the hope or potential for change.

Studies into violence have demonstrated that many factors do have significance, while most of these studies are not focused on *re-offending* but rather on the *incidence* of violence. Actuarial approaches have been criticized for utilizing research that is retrospective rather than prospective, where studies show that certain factors occur more frequently when there is violence, but there are few studies which have identified factors as predictive of *future* violence, which is the key issue in assessment.

Indeed, there are major methodological problems in the prediction of violence due to the relatively low re-offending rate within the majority of studies. The identification of factors within a small number of recidivists does not provide a robust statistical basis for prediction and indeed can lead to a high false-positive error rate (Szmukler, 2001).

Powis (2002) identifies those from the lowest social classes as being more likely to be violent. This stark statement raises several questions about the nature of policing and the identification of those who are violent. The inherent bias of agencies of social control and the ability of those with socio-economic power to avoid the gaze of surveillance systems may well be factors that have influenced the construction of the dangerousness of a specific class, yet how the research has been developed is deemed irrelevant to the exercise. If those subjected to deprivation (poverty, unemployment, poor housing, etc.) are more likely to experience difficulties with their behaviour then this could reasonably be viewed as a call to arms to alleviate their poverty, yet within this way of constructing assessments their socio-economic status is viewed as yet another problem with which to burden them; in effect they are made responsible for the situation they find themselves in. The complications of being damned by such categorizations can be highlighted through the debates around the significance of ethnicity and crime, where if a particular ethnic group is over-represented in the crime figures, then does this mean that any individual from that group should be viewed as a higher risk? The ethical considerations are obvious and can lead to the demonization of minority ethnic groups, denying the significance of how these 'facts' were constructed.

Investigation of those who are categorized as violent has uncovered other factors which are said to be indicative of this type of person, such as low IQ and a problematic family background. One can question the relevance of IQ testing as culturally and class bound, related more often to educational and social opportunity rather than any inherent biological trait, but the notion that families generate criminality is a strong one supported by a substantial body of evidence. Indeed, the idea of criminogenic families has become a firm factor to explore, with the assumption that something must have 'gone wrong' for someone to turn out violent. Family environment may well create the conditions for someone to behave badly, but there are problems in that this is a normative judgement, which requires information not just about those people identified as violent but also from those who have experienced a difficult background but not subsequently offended. The 'normal' family experience remains very elusive and studies interested in those who have been violent rarely investigate the family backgrounds of those who have *not* been identified as violent, thus reducing the chances of a balanced understanding of the impact of their upbringing. Simply because a factor appears within a limited population does not necessarily mean that this factor does not appear with those outside the study group. This process accentuates a notion of difference between an imagined 'normality' and the 'deviant'.

Many of the factors identified within research about violence appear at first to be scientific and authoritative in their claims, with an air of certainty that the words and concepts used have specific and agreed meanings. However, the difficulties in reaching agreement about what constitute factors is not just about 'finding them', but in defining what they are. This can lead us into contested territory about definitions of what is, for example, 'substance misuse' or 'alcohol problems', as these are laden with cultural, social, moral and familial expectations that may lead to the same person's drinking pattern being assessed as either 'having a problem' or 'typical of people today', depending on who is bringing what values to the understanding of the behaviour. The use of illicit drugs is often viewed as a risk factor, yet there is little effort to differentiate between the plethora of drugs available with their multitude of effects, nor to view violence by those who use drugs as instrumental in the search for further supply. Illegal drug use may well lead to a higher propensity for becoming involved in violence as this is a marginal and criminal behaviour, which by definition involves risky situations and actions, as well as meeting often unpleasant people, but the prevalence of cannabis use in the United Kingdom would indicate that 'drug use' in itself is a very poor predictor of violence. The subjective interpretation of what constitutes a 'fact' is downplayed in this approach, with an assumed acceptance that there is agreement about what constitutes, for example, 'poor housing', 'over or under controlled' and 'personality disorder', all of which are dependent upon normative judgements.

These approaches are helpful in providing labels for people rather than in understanding or resolving their problem behaviour. An actuarial risk assessment does not assist in clarifying why a particular individual behaves badly; it is not interested in changing behaviour but in placing the individual within a distilled category of population aggregates. Issues such as how the person came to commit the offence; their responsibility in this and the individual circumstances are lost in the drive to classify dangerousness. The emphasis is on the management of offending, rather than eradicating/treating the social/individual factors that may lead to it. Reichman provides a useful critique of this by stating that:

> One of the most significant effects of utilizing risk management systems for controlling crime is a shift in the locus of criminal responsibility from identifiable (guilty) offenders to categories of behaviour. Conditions, characters, and modes of life supplant traditional moral choice as a sufficient justification for the imposition of criminal penalties.
>
> (1986: 165)

In other words, it is not what you have done, but who the system has decided you are that leads to the nature of intervention. This is further developed by Silver and Miller:

> Membership in a particular population subgroup is as important as or more so than individual acts of deviance. To be placed in a particular risk category, it is enough to display the appropriate combination of characteristics identified as risk markers. The individual is transformed from an autonomous subject who may or may not choose to engage in a particular behaviour to a nexus of factors made meaningful by the levels of risk they represent in the aggregate.
>
> (2002: 152)

Returning to our example of Mark, practitioners are faced with the need to make as accurate a judgement as possible in order to respond to the expectations of society for protection. Is Mark suitable for treatment? Where can this treatment most safely be undertaken – in prison or the community and what is his risk of re-offending? The development of 'scientific' methods of risk assessment is a logical result of the adoption of new management practices in the probation service – influenced originally by the ethos of private business involvement in prisons (Ryan, 2002). A preoccupation with accurate risk assessment has led to an increase in the numbers of psychologists working in prisons and the joint recruitment of psychologists for prison and probation (Towl, 2003). Psychologists frequently express high levels of confidence in their ability to identify appropriate and accurately defined predictor and criterion variables through their knowledge of both dynamic and static risk factors involved in violent behaviour:

> The question of 'How well can dangerousness be predicted?' dissolves into another question, 'How well is the VRAG [Violence Risk Assessment

Guide] able to predict violence in this or that context?' Such questions can be answered with relative ease given the existence of the requisite detailed coding manual.

(Webster and Bailes, 2004: 23)

Assuming psychopathy to be the 'flagship' variable in violence risk prediction, Webster and colleagues have adapted the VRAG and Hare's Psychopathy Checklist to identify ten historical (static), five clinical and five future-oriented (dynamic) risk variables – the HCR-20 (see exercise below). They consider the variables most powerful to be the childhood ones – early childhood maladjustment and separation from parents before the age of 16, although the main strength of the assessment schedule is considered to be the integration of careful research into prediction with clinical practice of assessment: 'the general view from experienced and thoughtful psychologists is that it is well within our grasp to assess and manage violence risk at standards appreciably higher than those presently in routine' (Webster and Bailes, 2004: 27). Thus Mark would be somewhat curiously assessed on this sort of schedule, part of which would be actuarial and part traditionally psychodynamic in its exploration of his (possible) childhood trauma. Unfortunately such optimism is not born out by the research:

Despite the fact that considerable research has been carried out into the prediction of anti-social behaviour generally, this has merely tended to suggest that although actuarial techniques can discriminate between high-risk and low-risk groups, there will always be a residual majority in the middle-risk groups, whose re-offending rates are too near 50-50 to be of much use prognostically.

(Prins, 1995: 231)

Mosson (2003) argues that the identified static and dynamic factors all relate to male prisoners and have little relevance to women prisoners and, more seriously, Grevatt and colleagues (2004) found that relationship instability, the number of young offender convictions and violence throughout the lifespan appeared to be protective factors for prisoners. This finding has confirmation in the research carried out by Rutter and colleagues (2004), who found that the most violent inmates in high security psychiatric hospitals were actually young women with special learning needs. And Monahan whose work is cited in support of Webster and Bailes's claims, cautions that risk prediction is plagued with false positives, and that clinical predictions of dangerousness are often less accurate than actuarial predictions (Monahan, 2004).

The assessment of risk in sexual offenders is even more difficult, the main preoccupation being with a behaviour that is extremely difficult to measure – recidivism. Hanson (2004) has carried out a meta-analysis of adult sex offender recidivism studies (where the same factors come up in many independent studies). He finds that the strongest factors relate to sexual deviance: deviant (however this is defined) sexual interests, a variety of sexual crime being committed, offending at an early age, and targeting boys or unrelated victims. Of these, deviant sexual interest in children was the strongest predictor but, again, this is extremely difficult to assess as it depends on the offender being open and honest about it. Younger, less sophisticated offenders are most likely to be open about their sexual deviance and this could explain why offending at an early age figures as a predictor.

And, despite commonly held working hypotheses that sex offenders are likely to re-offend (see, for example, Scourfield's, 2003, analysis of social work attitudes towards sex offenders), the reconviction rate is lower than commonly believed. This is around 12 per cent to14 per cent during a five-year follow-up, but this increases to 35 per cent to 45 per cent over 15 to 20-year follow-up. The long-term rate for child molesters is similar to that of rapists although the latter re-offend somewhat earlier on release. However, this may reflect no more than an increased likelihood of rape victims reporting the offence.

Overall, the research shows there to be no single factor that is sufficient to determine whether or not a person will re-offend. There are no dynamic factors identified and the predictive accuracy of actuarial scales is low (see, for example, Bates et al., 2004), therefore there are likely to be many false positives. This means that such factors as may indicate a likelihood of re-offending are static or highly stable, thus offenders with such a profile may well be labelled as high risk, and incarcerated for long periods:

> In assessing risk, and talking about 'serious risk', we should distinguish between what we call the mathematics and the morals. Talk of 'serious risk' can refer to questions of probability, with no comment on whether what is very probable is also very harmful. On the other hand, it can also reflect judgements as to what is very harmful, with no comment on whether what is held to be very harmful is also very probable.
>
> (Caddick and Lewis, 1999: 56)

The capacity of risk assessments in predicting dangerousness is not only low, but there is no way they can be used to determine how to intervene, or assess whether interventions have been successful: 'They [predictive factors] are useful for assessing enduring propensities to re-offend but they cannot be used to assess treatment outcomes or monitor risk on community supervision' (Hanson, 2004: 40).

To sum up, actuarial risk assessments are increasingly common and popular within violence, yet they are often limited in scope and have a narrow and unacknowledged focus that will lead to particular outcomes. Their usefulness for understanding and responding to individuals is proscribed, and they can reduce people to a collection of factors that minimize their choices, actions, agency and ultimately their personal responsibility for violent behaviour. However, they may have some validity in assisting in what Quinsey and colleagues (1995) describe as providing an 'anchor' for clinical judgement, helping to bring some structure to what can be a daunting and responsible task, the prevention of future harm. However, (to pursue the analogy further) when anchored, a boat does not remain static; it moves to position itself in the direction of the prevailing (and changeable) wind and tide. How people are positioned by assessment 'anchors' will depend on the winds and tides of different worker perspectives, organizational needs and general social conditions. The following chapters will explore some of the influences on how violence is made sense of, with a view to providing readers with a range of theoretical and practical approaches to working in this area.

Summary

- There are so many variables in any one violent incident that absolute risk prediction of it being repeated is always uncertain.

- Actuarial and clinical risk assessments have only modest predictive accuracy.

- Static risk factors tend to identify only the most obvious enduring characteristics of a person who is violent and are of little use in helping professionals determine effective treatment modes or measure change.

- Dynamic risk factors have some slight predictive value in determining effective treatment, especially where this relates to improving people's life chances.

■ Claims are made that 'objective' risk factors can be identified for specific forms of violence, yet the research on which this is based is mediated through selected theoretical and/or worker perspectives.

■ Risk assessments often pathologize individuals for their socio-economic location within society.

■ Risk assessments tend to be once and for all static events which fix individuals within a narrow group identity.

To aid critical reflection we invite you to consider the framework and questions outlined below.

Assessment factors in the HCR-20 (Webster et al., 1997)

Historical Factors

■ Previous violence

■ Young age at first violent incident

■ Relationship instability

■ Employment problems

■ Substance use problems

■ Major mental illness

■ Psychopathy

■ Early maladjustment

■ Personality disorder

■ Prior supervision failure

Clinical Factors

■ Lack of insight

■ Negative attitudes

■ Active symptoms of mental illness

■ Impulsivity

■ Unresponsiveness to treatment

Risk Management Factors

- Plans lack feasibility
- Exposure to destabilizers
- Lack of personal support
- Non-compliance with remediation attempts
- Stress

Questions

- Which of the above are static and which are dynamic factors (or both)?
- How would you quantify each of the factors?
- Which of the factors require professional judgment?
- How would undertaking this assessment inform your intervention plan with a service user?

CHAPTER 3

Grief and Loss: Psychodynamic Approaches

This chapter has three main components: how interpersonal violence is understood in terms of a response to grief and loss (attachment theory); how the theory informs risk assessment; and the implications for prevention and intervention. As attachment theory evolved from psychoanalytic theory and practice, Freudian personality development will be briefly explained. Klein's development of Freudian ideas on aggression is also explored, and the differences between object relations and attachment theories are outlined. The research evidence supporting attachment theory as an explanation for interpersonal violence is presented, particularly the work of Ainsworth and colleagues and of Main. The clinical implications of attachments for the prediction of violence and the assessment of risk are explored using the examples of child, sibling, peer, spouse and elder abuse. The practice implications of a theoretical explanation which does not have a distinct therapy are critically analysed.

Psychoanalytic explanations of violence

Understandings of violence that are based on broadly Freudian theory view violent behaviour, and possibilities of changing that behaviour, as intertwined with personality development, particularly the oedipal stage. In his early writing Freud elaborated his concepts of id, ego and super-ego (Freud, 1962), with the concomitant oral, anal and genital stages of personality development, as the means by which we control, or fail to control, our emotions. As Jacobs reminds us, Freud's structural division of the psyche serves 'more as crude pictures of the relationship between conscious and unconscious functions within the psyche' and can be 'more fully understood and appreciated if they can be seen as much as metaphors as literal statements' (1988: 9).

Freud's earliest distinction was that between the conscious and unconscious mind, considering the latter as the greater part, consciousness being only the tip of the iceberg above the surface. While a large part of the ego, although by no means all of it, can be conscious, the vast majority of the superego and probably all of the id are unconscious. Freud also identified the 'pre-conscious' as that part of the unconscious that we can readily recall, that is just under the surface.

The *superego* develops through a process of *internalization*. The child internalizes the values, rules, prohibitions and wishes of the parent and of authority figures, but the process is one that magnifies these rules and records them in the raw, without editing, and laden with amplified feelings. Admonitions and rules go straight into memory, carrying the weight of total truth, never to be erased from the tape (Penfield, 1952). The superego may be restrictive or permissive (Caplan, 1961). People riddled with guilt can be said to have an over-restrictive superego and people with too little guilt an over-permissive or weak superego. Those with no internal rules, no conscience about hurting others, are labelled sociopaths (commonly called psychopaths). The *id* is that aspect of the person which is primitive, the animal drive, full of feelings, capable of rage, operating on instinctual drives and urges, hungry to fill any voids that are felt. There are two main id drives: *libido*, which is sexual impulse, desire and attraction; and *mortido*, which is the killing instinct, hating, attacking and hitting out violently. Berne (1978) suggests some people are more prone to one rather than the other, although these are close relatives born of the need to propagate and survive. They explain something of what some people are looking for, so the id is described as being governed by the 'pleasure principle' (which is seen as our motivating force); the lack of sufficient pleasure leaves the id hurting, demanding and wanting irrationally, sometimes leading to a chaotic life of acting out, living for 'kicks' or sending out cries for help, such as the abused person who shoplifts or 'flashes' to attract attention to his/her plight, behaving in a way that could be interpreted as asking to be caught. Campbell (1997) explains an adolescent sex offender in terms of being overwhelmed by guilt arising from the revival of Oedipal fantasies, thus attaching the guilt to something conscious and finding some temporary relief when caught. As the id is in the service of both the pleasure principle and the death drive, it can be seen that how the ego and superego mediate the demands of the id is central to a Freudian understanding of violence.

The *ego*, the I and Me, thinks, decides, plans and relates to the world of *reality*. It is governed by the 'reality principle', exploring and testing, born

of curiosity. The ego acts as a referee between the id and superego, struggling to keep a balance between the gratification of needs and impulses
and the sacrifice of this gratification to the demands of reality. Freud
saw the ego as a man on horseback, striving to control a superior force
(the id), whereas later ego psychologists saw the ego as masterful, at least
potentially. This giving of primacy to the ego goes hand in hand with
Western individualism (Fromm, 1985). There are, therefore, always ten-
sions between the ego, id and superego, and this is what the term psychodynamic means; the psyche is seen as active not static. Jacobs (1988)
reminds us that this activity is not confined to relating to people, or to
objects outside of the self; it also takes place within the psyche, in relation to itself. This dynamic is referred to as internal relations which are
formed over the long years of a child's development. They are counter-
parts of external relationships which predominated in early childhood,
principally those with the child's mother and father. Campbell (1997),
for example, says that an act of child abuse bisects the line of normal
development and disrupts the natural timing of the biological clock,
thereby turning the Oedipus complex upside-down.

In his later writing, Freud placed more emphasis on aggression and
the death instinct, an aspect of his work that was taken up by Klein (1988),
whose *objects relations* theory was to influence a major strand of British
psychotherapy, whereas ego psychology was more influential in the
development of psychotherapy in the United States. There are, therefore,
different emphases on the roots and treatment of violence. The latter
will focus on the strength of the ego as adaptable, flexible, resilient,
reality based and stable in the face of anxiety and loss so that anger can
be handled. The former focuses more on the pre-Oedipal period.

Kleinian objects relations theory

Klein was interested in how emotions are triggered by early experiences
and how they shape or affect identity. Where Freud concentrated on the
three-person relationships of the Oedipal period, her clinical work with
young children led her to stress the importance of the two-person relationships of the pre-Oedipal period. These relationships were not just
with the mother; the infant's 'object' is eventually the mother but, initially, is the part-object of the mother's breast, her smell, her touch. Early
experiences lead to fantasies concerning other people, parts of people,
even animals or symbolic objects of various sorts. Where Freud saw
individuals as driven by biological needs, Klein saw people as essentially

social; she stressed that individuals need relationships with others, object-seekers rather than pleasure-seekers. Problems stem from early relationships with care-givers and from early emotional deprivations that result in '*splitting*' in the unconscious. Klein emphasized fantasy by which we shuttle our inner and outer worlds, while we are caught up in a mass of 'part objects'. In adulthood, our object relations are similar to personal relationships, but more – there are one's own internal objects (the internalized aspects of personality), part-objects (for example, parts of the body), and non-human objects (such as a security blanket).

Our tendency to destruction is directed at the earliest part object (the breast) but as anxieties become too terrifying, the infant 'splits' the mother into good and bad objects and fantasizes about attacking the mother – this is called the *paranoid-schizoid* position. To move past this position, split objects need to be integrated and the mother accepted as a separate integrated person with some good and some bad aspects. However, the child fears that its violent fantasies have injured that separate person and so it has to make 'reparation', entering a *depressive position*, with feelings of guilt and ambivalence. In the depressive position, tolerating ambivalence, pain and concern for the other person is striven for. If the feelings become unbearable, there is a return to the paranoid-schizoid position with intolerance of the experience of separation, stirring up of violent and manic defences against pain, or an overemphasis on guilt. Briggs sees adolescence as a developmental stage where this return is likely, resulting in anti-social behaviour, delinquency, drug taking, and racism in which gang membership turns passive suffering into active cruelty (2002: 115).

Like Freud, Klein was interested in interpretations of unconscious processes, in understanding the past so as to understand the present, and in understanding resistance and the defences used to cope with the discomfort of inner conflict, but she was more willing to leave defences intact if it is assessed that the person is too fragile to let go of them. A key element in her work is the understanding of identity; like Erikson in the United States (1948), there is concern over identity confusion and the lack of clear boundaries of the self; like Bowlby (1979, 1988), attachments are also seen as important. Self-formation is enhanced by the emotional provisions of others. As the child comes to trust responsive and consistent parents, a secure self can go on to develop meaningful relationships later. Thus the early mother relationship sets the pattern for later relationships – self evolves out of these interactions and motivation is based on the need to establish and maintain relationships and human contact.

Attachment theory

Bowlby (1963, 1979) agrees with one of Klein's main hypotheses: that childhood experiences of mourning link to ways of responding to loss in later life, but he does not regard her theory of the depressive position as a way of accounting for the diverse ways in which some people respond to loss with healthy mourning and others with pathological mourning. He differs from her over the age at which particular events are thought to occur, considering the vulnerable period to extend over a number of years of childhood and for the significant object to be the mother (and sometimes the father) rather than the breast. He also disagrees with Klein about the nature and origins of anxiety and aggression. Bowlby considers that the loss of a parent not only gives rise to primary separation anxiety and grief but also to processes of mourning in which aggression plays a major part:

> A little paradoxically, behaviour of an aggressive sort plays a key role in maintaining affectional bonds. It takes two distinct forms: first, attacks on and frightening away of intruders and, second, the punishment of an errant partner, be it wife, husband, or child. There is evidence that much aggressive behaviour of a puzzling and pathological kind originates in one or other of these ways.
>
> (Bowlby, 1979: 69)

Thus attachment theory provides a means of understanding aggression across a whole spectrum of behaviours from the temper tantrum of a toddler to the murder of a parent (see, for example, Bowlby, 1988: 30–1). It also claims predictive power, making it a useful theory for those who have to assess risk. Whereas psychoanalytic theory and practice (particularly the work of Goldstein, Freud and Solnit, 1973, 1979, 1985) influenced the emphasis on the welfare of the child in the Children Act, 1989 and, at the same time, court decision making (Mr Justice Thorpe, 1997), attachment theory has been particularly influential in shaping subsequent child protection policy and practice. It has long been the dominant theory in assessment guidance: of a list of 23 texts that social workers undertaking a comprehensive assessment of children at risk were recommended to read (Department of Health, 1988), ten were by attachment theorists (BAAF, 1996; Bowlby, 1953, 1979; Fahlberg, 1981a and b, 1982, 1984, 1988; Fraiberg, 1980; and Winnicott, 1986). Although later guidance on assessment (Department of Health, 2000) considers a broader range of factors in the assessment of risk, attachment theory predominates as both explanation and prediction. Attachment theory has, therefore, become the official discourse of child protection work, **the** way of talking about it. It has also been invoked as an explanation for dysfunctional behaviour in all forms of interpersonal violence: marital disharmony (Weiss, 1982, 1991); poor relationships between elderly parents and their children (Cicirelli, 1991, 1991; Yan and Tang, 2003); dysfunctional family systems (Byng-Hall, 1985; Marvin and Stewart, 1990); and adult bullying (Randall, 1997). We make no apology, therefore, for spending some time examining both the theory and research evidence before going on to talk about practice implications.

Attachment theory is an ethological theory of interpersonal relationships that emphasizes the evolutionary significance of intimate relationships, also referred to by Bowlby as *affectional bonds*, particularly those in early childhood. Bowlby believed that people possess an inborn need for close attachments to significant others that serve a survival function. Throughout childhood and adolescence, people develop expectations regarding the availability, or otherwise, of attachments through specific attachments in the first instance (usually the mother, but sometimes the father), and then through multiple attachment relationships. Each relationship builds on the previous one and contributes to the construction of what Bowlby called the *internal working model*, a characteristic way of thinking about and responding to others in relationships. As the person matures, these models become more stable and part of the personality, serving as an interpreter for new information regarding attachment relationships, and thus influencing behaviour. Attachment patterns not only persist but they also self-perpetuate; for example, a securely attached child is happier and more rewarding to care for than an anxious ambivalent child, who is apt to be clingy and whiny, or an anxious avoidant child, who will be distant and prone to bully other children (Bowlby, 1988).

The terms 'secure', 'anxious' or 'anxious attachment style', derive from the research findings of Ainsworth and colleagues (Ainsworth et al., 1978; Bretherton and Waters, 1985), who researched mother–toddler relationship styles by means of a 20-minute miniature drama known as a *strange situation*. They observed toddlers' behaviour in a sequence of three situations. First, the toddler was left with the mother in a small room with toys. The mother was then joined by an unfamiliar woman who played with the toddler while the mother briefly left the room. A second separation ensued, during which the toddler was left alone before the mother finally returned. The researchers were interested in the reunion behaviour between the mother and toddler.

They found that the toddlers exhibited three basic relationship patterns. These were those with non-expressive, indifferent or hostile relationships, in which the toddlers devised a strategy whereby maximum
closeness to the mother was obtained without fear of rebuff; those with
strong, positive feelings towards the mother, where the toddler looked
for the mother, but played freely; and those with markedly ambivalent
relationships, characterized by the toddler being clingy and angry. The
researchers labelled these reactions as types A, B and C; type C was later
subdivided into two related types (for an overview, see Bretherton, 1992).
Type B was the normative response among the white, middle-class sample. Although the researchers reported that they did not impute that any
one type of response was better than another, these attachments styles
soon developed labels which imply healthy or unhealthy psychological
development. Type A became known as insecure-avoidant; type B secure;
type C anxious-ambivalent; and Type D anxious-disorganized. Although
similar research in Germany found that type A relationship styles were
the dominant pattern (Grossman, Grossman and Spangler, 1985), and
Type C more frequent than anticipated in Israeli kibbutzim (Sagi, Lamb
and Lewkowicz, 1985) and Japan (Myake, Chen, Compos and Waters,
1985), a secure attachment style has been translated into the desirable
style in child protection work:

> All children need secure attachments if they are to flourish and develop
> their potential. In any assessment of children, therefore, it is important
> to get to know the details of the current and past attachment figures in
> a child's life.
>
> (Department of Health, 1998: 38)

Ainsworth and colleagues (1987) found that the toddlers' behaviour in
the *strange situation* could be explained by the behaviour of their mothers.
For example, secure children had mothers who were sensitive to their
emotional signals, while insecure children had mothers who could be
observed to be insensitive, rejecting or unpredictable. This does not mean,
says Bowlby, that mothers should be blamed for treating their children
in a way that is a major cause of mental ill health: 'the misguided behaviour of parents is no more than the product of their own difficult and
unhappy childhood' (Bowlby, 1988: 145), pointing to an intergenera-
tional effect. Main and colleagues (Main and Weston, 1981; Main, Kaplan
and Cassidy, 1985) found a strong correlation between how a mother
describes her relationships with her parents during her childhood and
the pattern of attachment her child now has with her. Her interviews

have been developed into an *Adult Attachment Interview*, in which a person is invited to talk openly and at length about childhood experiences and memories that may be quite painful, and then analysed for style and manner in which the story is told rather than content (see also Hesse, 1999). Whereas the mother of a secure child is able to talk freely and with feeling about her childhood, the mother of an insecure child is not. Four types of attachment style were identified; these are similar to the categories used in the strange situation research:

- **Secure-autonomous.**   The mother's story is coherent, consistent and objective. She is able to collaborate with the interviewer.

- **Dismissing.**   The story is not coherent. Although she claims in a generalized, matter of fact way that she had a happy childhood, she has no supporting detail and may say that she can remember nothing of her childhood.

- **Preoccupied.**   The story is incoherent and will describe an unhappy relationship with her mother about which she is still clearly disturbed.

- **Unresolved disorganized.**   This is similar to dismissing or preoccupied styles but may include long silences or overtly erroneous statements.

Main also identified an exceptional category of mothers, those who could describe an unhappy childhood in which positive experiences are integrated with negative ones also had securely attached children. She hypothesized that these women seemed to have come to terms with their experiences and her theorizing on how they could reflect on their internal working models has influenced the practice of counselling (Fonagy, 1999). We return to this shortly but, first, how does the theory outlined so far help us to understand Mark's violence? The emphasis so far has been on the anxiety produced by unsatisfying relationships between parents and children; we hinted earlier that aggression plays a role in the maintenance of affectional bonds, but how does it link to anxiety?

Bowlby (1979) makes the important point that because affectional bonds, such as those between mother and child or husband and wife, are subjective states of strong emotion, thus the threat of loss arouses (separation) anxiety, which in turn arouses anger in various degrees. It is the situation that signals an *increase* of risk that creates a fear response, he says, therefore threats of abandonment are terrifying. These threats create intense anxiety, and they also arouse anger, often also of intense degree. For Bowlby, anxiety and anger as responses to the risk of loss go hand in hand, thus attachment theory explains **all** interpersonal violence:

> in the right place, at the right time, and in the right degree, anger is not only appropriate but may be indispensable. It serves to deter from dangerous behaviour, to drive off a rival, or to coerce a partner. In each case the aim of the angry behaviour is the same – to protect a relationship which is of very special value to the angry person … a great deal of the maladaptive violence met with in families can be understood as the distorted and exaggerated version of behaviour that is potentially functional, especially attachment behaviour on the one hand and care giving on the other.
>
> (Bowlby, 1988: 79–81)

We can reasonably infer from this that Mark's anger is both a response to his intense fear of abandonment, a fear he makes plain to his father-in-law, and an attempt to deter Kelly from ejecting him from the house. But how much of his anger is functional, and how much is distorted? Could his response to her hurtful words with shouting and threatening her be classified as a sensible survival strategy? Is taking a hammer to a door locked against him an exaggerated version of functional behaviour? Although attachment theory provides a compelling explanation of Mark's behaviour, it leaves any distinction between what is functional and what is exaggeratedly dysfunctional to a subjective interpretation. Kelly's subjective response was fear for her life. Unfortunately Bowlby has little to say about the specifics of male violence, other than that men who are violent to their wives are likely to have been battered as children, as are their partners. He would probably suggest that Mark and Kelly were anxiously attached to each other and have developed a co-dependency relationship in which they each control the other and try to keep each other from departing from the relationship:

> In most marriages, it was found, each party was apt to stress how much the other needed them, whilst disclaiming their own need for the partner. By need, of course, they meant what I am calling their desire for a care-giving figure. What they dreaded most was loneliness.
>
> (Bowlby, 1988: 95)

He also ducks the question of what to do about Mark. In answering his own question: 'What actions are then called for?', he replies with: 'Since every study has shown how very difficult and time-consuming

all such work is, we ask about prospects for prevention. Here lies hope'
(Bowlby, 1988: 96). He would probably have much more to say about
Luke and Billy; if their parents both have anxious attachment styles, then
the theory would predict that they would develop similar patterns.

How attachment theory informs risk assessment

The links between the attachment patterns of children and adults who
are violent and their parents is the subject of research aimed at predicting which specific attachment patterns are the most likely to precipitate people to behave violently to their children, partners and peers.
Parents who abuse their children have been demonstrated to have
experienced poor childhood experiences themselves (for an overview,
see Howe, 1995), although there is some disagreement over which
parental attachment pattern is the more damaging for children.
Crittenden (1988) and Finkelhor (1983) suggest that anxious-ambivalent and anxious-disturbed attachment patterns, which lead to emotional abuse and neglect, have more serious consequences for children
than an avoidant attachment style, which leads to physical abuse.
Browne and Hamilton (1998), however, found that a smaller percentage of their respondents who reported emotional maltreatment was
violent compared to those who reported either physical or sexual maltreatment. Bowlby also highlights the damaging effect of physical
abuse, citing research that shows physically abused children were not
only more likely to assault other children but were also notable for a
'particularly disagreeable type of aggression, termed "harassment"...
malicious behaviour that appears to have the sole intent of making the
victim show distress' (1988: 91). This links with findings on adult bullying (Randall, 1997). Inter-sibling aggression is rather more complex,
with children being both victim and perpetrator: 'Bullying occurs
when there is a reciprocal fit between the projection of murderousness
into someone identified as vulnerable and the victim of bullying pro-
jecting aggression with the aggressor' (Briggs, 2002: 116). Hardy (2001)
found that whilst financial stresses predisposed towards physical
aggression, marital strains and losses predisposed towards sexual contact between siblings.

Links between poor childhood experiences and men assaulting their
partners has also been a recurring finding in the research into violence

and attachment style; a particularly large study (8629 participants) found correlations between adult violence and childhood physical or sexual abuse or witnessing domestic violence (Whitfield et al., 2003). Hazan and Shaver (1987) add to Bowlby's analysis of male violence; they found that men with avoidant attachment styles had relationships that were characterized by fear and extreme jealousy, and anxious-ambivalent individuals' relationships were characterized by emotional highs and lows, accompanied by obsessive thoughts concerning the other and a strong desire for union with others. Later research (Bartholomew and Horowitz, 1991) reconceptualized avoidant attachment styles in adulthood as dismissing and fearful, the latter category being significantly related to measures of anger, jealousy and verbal abuse, which Dutton, Saunders, Starzomski and Bartholomew (1994) describe as an *angry attachment style*. They found that couples with different attachment styles may actually antagonize each other, escalating aggression with violence. Kesner and McKenry's (1998) research adds detail to this finding: not only did they find that attachment factors are unique predictors of male violence towards a female partner but that these partners were more likely to have insecure adult attachment styles. Thus it could be productive to discover if Kelly and Mark had different or similar attachment styles; in view of Mark's early childhood experiences of physical and (possibly) sexual abuse, he may well have developed an avoidant attachment style. With refinements to the Adult Attachment Interview, more distinctions have been made about the form violence may take: *dismissing husbands* have been found to be the most controlling and distancing, their violence being related to instrumental violence to assert their authority and control; *preoccupied husbands* tended only to precipitate violence when their partners threatened withdrawal, their emotional and physical violence being related to expressive violence in response to abandonment fears (Babcock et al., 2000). Attachment patterns are also predictive of elder abuse, the links between poor childhood experiences and poor relationships between elderly parents and their children established by Cicirelli (1991) also being found among Chinese families in Hong Kong. In this study of 464 families, a high level of childhood experience of abuse consistently emerged as the single most salient predictor for participants' endorsement of proclivity to elder abuse (Yan and Tang, 2003).

A word of caution is necessary. The Babcock and colleagues study (2000) makes an important point that 74 per cent of the violent husbands (out of a sample size of only 23) were likely to be classified into one of the insecure categories on the Adult Attachment Interview, but there were six violent husbands who were classified as secure. As the authors comment:

> Clearly not all men who engage in repeated physical aggression against their wives have attachment patterns that differ from other men. It is likely that there are many different pathways to becoming maritally violent and a route involving insecure attachments and dysregulated affect is *only one* of them.
>
> (Babcock et al., 2000, our emphasis)

The reader also needs to bear in mind that the correlation between abusive parents and insecure attachment style is not the only correlation revealed. For example, the abusing mothers in the Crittenden study (1988) were also those who had the least education, were likely to be unsupported by either partner or extended family and contained the largest number of women with learning difficulties. Crittenden (1999) argues that these disadvantages were a result of their own childhood experiences resulting in them having severe difficulties in sustaining interpersonal relationships. Equally Fraiberg (1980) suggests that insecure attachments are detrimental to cognitive functioning, but it is dangerous to dismiss the effects of hardship on effective parenting (see, for example, Howe, 1995). An example of these complexities is the case of Kirstie, a young mother of a toddler and new baby who referred herself to a Domestic Violence programme for help with her anger. At least this anger involved her in slamming doors (a frequent occurrence), and at worst in assaulting her partner (this had happened twice) and trashing the house (once). She also had difficulty in meeting both her sons' needs simultaneously. As she had an appalling history of childhood physical and emotional abuse; of violent, drug-using boyfriends in her teenage years (one of whom beat her so badly that she was admitted to intensive care with injuries that were so severe that her eight-month-old foetus died); and had also experienced the deaths of a cousin and brother in separate car accidents (one in which she was a passenger), and the death of another brother from cancer, it would be easy to explain her anger in terms of grief and loss. However, she could respond to the needs of either son sensitively when not stressed by the demands of the other, she was currently in a supportive relationship, she had devised strategies which helped her cope with her mourning, and she only slammed doors when she was under severe external stress. For example, she reported a slip back (more door slamming) at one session, but it emerged that this happened after she had been without a water supply for two weeks and then the expected plumber had cancelled his visit.

Belsky and Nezworski (1998) maintain that although the association between poor quality insecure relationships in childhood and later social and behavioural difficulties is not inevitable, it is probabilistic. But by no means do all parents with poor childhood experiences go on to become abusing parents. Our experience of working with adults who have been sexually abused as children is that they are incensed when their abusers claim their own childhood abuse as a mitigating factor.

Interventions

McLeod (2003) makes the interesting point that Bowlby's ideas on attachment have not resulted in the creation of an 'attachment therapy', although it could perhaps be argued that Fahlberg (1988) has come close to doing so. This is perhaps because the therapeutic tasks outlined by Bowlby (1988: 138–40) are similar to those of psychotherapy, which remains influential in psychiatry, psychology and social work despite numerous critiques and revisions. The central feature of psychotherapeutic work with people who are violent in intimate relationships is helping people to recognize that their internal working models of relationships may not be appropriate to their present and future; that is, 'to modify old representational patterns, to change old inner working models of self and its relationship with other people' (Howe, 1995: 220). To accomplish this, the therapist needs to provide a *secure base* in which it is 'safe enough for members of the family to reconnect with old memories that are resonating with current themes' (Byng-Hall, 1991: 211), or enhance and support secure relationships with non-abusive care-givers. Fonagy (1999) argues that it is the capacity to learn how to **reflect** on experiences that lies at the heart of effective therapy, helping individuals develop the ability to think about and talk about painful past events. Kennedy (1997) divides assessment of outcome in his work with violent parents into hopeful, doubtful and hopeless, dependent largely on parents' capacity for self-reflection. Those who can reflect on their own abuse and show evidence of change in their parenting capabilities are most likely to be classified as 'hopeful'.

Because the repetition by the service user of old child-like patterns of relating to significant people, such as parents, is transferred to the therapist, transference and counter-transference interpretations are a vital component of the psychotherapeutic relationship. Quoting Winnicott, Jacobs says:

> He [the therapist] can never make up to the client for what he has suffered in the past, but what he can do is repeat the failure to love them enough ... and then share with them and help them work through their feelings about failure.
>
> (1988: 14)

Although Bowlby (1988) also viewed transference as a means by which the therapist can link the client's expectations about the therapeutic relationship to experiences with parents, the Stockholm Outcome of Psychoanalysis and Psychotherapy Project shows that this is much more effective in intensive psychoanalysis (four sessions a week) than it is in psychotherapy (one session a week). Overly-analytical psychotherapists were considerably less effective than those who offered less interpretations and were more supportive and involved (for an overview, see McLeod, 2003:101–2). The problem with psychoanalysis as intervention is that it is time consuming, expensive and of limited effectiveness; for example, Bateman and Holmes (1995) consider that people who are unable to control their aggression are unsuitable for this form of intervention, although Hodge and colleagues (1997) cite the Dartington Research Unit's comparison of the benefits of psychoanalytically based intervention with cognitive behavioural models, which shows that outcome of treatment across a wide range of offenders tends to be better with the former. Psychodynamic social work interventions have been demonstrated to be consistently unpopular with adults who are violent (see, for example, Mayer and Timms, 1970; Milner, 2004; Scourfield, 2003), mainly because service users become frustrated with a focus on the past when they locate their concerns in the present. Gallwey acknowledges, for instance, that when parents lose a child following a child protection assessment, 'it may well be that they become paranoid and persecutory and it can be very unfair to pick up the projection and suggest that these are necessarily long-term psychological problems' (1997: 139).

Limitations of psychodynamic interventions

A practical difficulty in using psychodynamic theory as a base for interventions is that the theory is top heavy in content (Butt, 2003); that is, it provides an explanation for the causes of violence but it is less successful in developing interventions that are effective in terms of either costs or user friendliness. The implications of the theory – that violent people are required to admit what they have done; empathize with the victim; and alter their internal working models of attachment – have become part and parcel of folk psychology, even though there is no detailed research evidence to support this. Butt makes the point that psychological expertise and therapeutic potency have become magnified with theories being selectively 'raided' for those components that seem to explain the phenomena under scrutiny: 'The lesson that seems to have been taken from a century of therapy, rightly or wrongly, is that emotions are better out than in' (2003: 164). This echoes only part of Bowlby's claim about effective therapy: 'that a patient not only talks about his memories, his ideas and dreams, his hopes and desires, but also expresses his feelings' (1988: 156).

Storr (1966) cautioned that expressing feelings is only one valuable feature of the psychoanalytic process; that many people do **not** show an improvement as a result of expressing feelings. More recently, Bonanno's research found little evidence that getting people to 'open up' actually helps, and Wessley's study of people suffering from post-traumatic stress disorder found that they actually do best if they suppress their worst memories (reported by Baxter and Rogers, 2003). Encouraging people who are violent to express their feelings is positively dangerous as catharsis (and, by implication, uncovering work too), and actually makes people more aggressive (Bushman, Baumeister and Stack, 1999). Sadly this sometimes is interpreted as evidence that the 'uncovering' therapy is working. For example, a young woman received weekly psychotherapy sessions to explore her experiences of being sexually abused as a means of helping her understand her current physical and sexual abuse of peers. She protested that she did not want to talk about her own sexual abuse and, when this was ignored, she became silent. When this too was ignored, she began protesting more aggressively: writing 'slag' instead of doing the prescribed art work; telling her therapist that she was useless; and playing up in the car going home. The therapist saw this behaviour as evidence that she was engaging with therapy. The young woman saw it as a refusal to listen to her protests.

It is also worth noting that how people express their feelings varies from culture to culture and age to age. As Butt (2003) points out, being 'in touch with one's feelings' is a relatively recent construction in the

United Kingdom. Storr (1966: 66) states that the idea of cure in psycho-analysis raises fundamental problems of philosophy, such as what constitutes human happiness and what sort of person one should be. This argument has been taken up by feminist psychotherapists, who redefine relational bonds in terms of mutuality between mothers and daughters (Jordan, 1997), and view dependency as being able to count on the help of others rather than a pathological state (Stiver, 1991).

The second main working hypothesis that has emerged from attachment theory – that the past inevitably influences the present and the future and may need to be modified (see, for example, Howe, 1995: 190) – has become axiomatic in a wide range of professional interventions, despite it not being particularly well supported by the literature (see, for example, Dogra et al., 2002), or by prominent psychoanalysts. As Rycroft commented, the idea that children should be treated lovingly and humanely does not require any psychological backing; loving is not an activity that can be engaged in on advice, since its essence is sincerity and spontaneity; and much of the trauma and suffering endured by children is inevitable (1966: 16). In the same volume, Gorer (1966: 32) argues that psychologically tinged explanations are invoked for failures, not for successes, so the research base of attachment theory is necessarily skewed. More recently, Kennedy (1997) stresses that although an advantage of the hermeneutics of suspicion theory ensure that professionals do not neglect the 'destructive side' of people, it is counter-productive to focus on the negative aspects of behaviour.

Using psychodynamic interventions effectively

Despite the reservations listed above, there are several points at which the theory can be utilized to inform effective interventions with Mark and his family. Mark may be sufficiently psychologically minded to benefit from long-term, intensive psychoanalysis. The fact that this would be expensive should not rule it out, although difficulties in ensuring Kelly's safety might. If he is not psychologically minded enough to engage with psychoanalysis, then he would resist such an intervention. As the theory links partner abuse with damage to children's emotional development, it might also be useful to consider offering psychoanalytically informed play therapy for Luke and Billy. Such therapy is well developed in the literature and more accessible to a wide range of professional activity (see, for example, Bannister and Huntington, 2002; Fahlberg, 1988).

The most effective use of the ideas described in this chapter, however, is the one proposed by Bowlby: prevention. It is worth remembering that his ideas inspired the original Homestart programme. Howe (1995) describes how interventions informed by attachment theory and delivered alongside practical support can benefit families. Although he is writing about social work, it is perhaps professionals in the health context who can use the approach most effectively. Dangers to Kelly can well be picked up in accident and emergency (A and E) departments (see also, Kingston and Penhale, 1995, for a discussion of the importance of understanding childhood links and violence in elder abuse as well as child and partner abuse). Should Kelly not present at A and E, her midwife could alert the family's health visitor who is best placed to establish the nurturing relationship that Crittenden (1999) considers essential for families with insecure attachment styles.

Summary

- Violence is explained in psychodynamic terms as an essential part of human experience, the 'dark side' of people.

- Attachment theory is invoked as an explanation for all forms of interpersonal violence from child to elder abuse. It is the most enduring theoretical model in contemporary policy and practice, and the most dominant model in child-care practice.

- Bowlby links violence to experiences of grief, loss and fears of abandonment.

- Research has identified links between insecure attachment style and a propensity to violent behaviour, but the majority of people with an insecure attachment style do not go on to be violent. Thus the theory has only limited predictive value.

- Interventions informed by attachment theory have value where they are delivered alongside practical support for new families; e.g. Homestart.

- Psychodynamic interventions can be time-consuming and expensive, with only limited effectiveness. Expressing violent feelings can actually increase violence.

To aid critical reflection we invite you to consider the theoretical frameworks and questions outlined below.

A definition of splitting (from Kreisman and Straus, 1989: 10)

The world of a B[orderline]P[ersonality], like that of a child, is split into heroes and villains. A child emotionally, the BP cannot tolerate human inconsistencies and ambiguities; he cannot reconcile another's good and bad qualities into a constant coherent understanding of another person. At any particular moment, one is either Good or EVIL. There is no in-between; no grey area ... people are idolized one day; totally devalued and dismissed the next.

Normal people are ambivalent and can experience two contradictory states at one time; BPs shift back and forth, entirely unaware of one feeling state while in the other.

When the idealized person finally disappoints (as we all do, sooner or later) the BP must drastically restructure his one-dimensional conceptionalization. Either the idol is banished to the dungeon, or the BP banishes himself in order to preserve the all-good image of the other person.

Splitting is intended to shield the BP from a barrage of contradictory feelings and images and from the anxiety of trying to reconcile those images. But splitting often achieves the opposite effect. The fraying in the BP's personality become rips, and the sense of his own identity and the identity of others shifts even more dramatically and frequently.

Questions

■ Compare this description of Borderline Personality Disorder with Kleinian theory briefly outlined in this chapter.

■ What are the implications of this explanation, outlined in the box above, for assessment and devising an intervention plan?

Read the following extract from Chapter 12 by David Howe in Horwath (2000: 17–18).

PATTERNS OF ATTACHMENT

Based on empirical findings, four combinations of the way self and others are mentally modelled within the parent–child relationship have been identified:

1. Secure attachment patterns: children experience their care-giver as available, and themselves positively.

2. Ambivalent patterns: children experience their care-giver as inconsistently responsive, and themselves as dependent and poorly valued.

3. Avoidant patterns: children experience their care-givers as consistently rejecting, and themselves as insecure but compulsively self-reliant.

4. Disorganized patterns (often associated with children who have suffered severe maltreatment): children experience their care-givers as either frightening or frightened, and themselves as helpless, angry, and unworthy.

Each pattern is associated with a characteristic set of emotional and relationship behaviours across the lifespan. Recent work on adult attachments and the care-giving behaviour of parents recognizes how internal working models and their associated attachment styles continue to affect behaviour, emotions and social relationships, particularly the demands of intimate relationships experienced in romantic partnerships and in parenthood. Insecure attachment styles in themselves are not pathological (indeed in some circumstances they can be highly functional), but most children and adults experiencing social, emotional and behavioural difficulties typically display pronounced insecure attachment behaviours of one kind or another. Each attachment style is an adaptive response to the care-giving situation in which the child finds himself or herself. The behaviours make sense within the context of the particular care-giving relationship. The behaviours adopted are a defensive strategy developed by children to help them cope with feelings of distress and anxiety. Whatever the quality of the relationship, the attachment system is designed to bring children into proximity with their attachment figure, where ideally they will be comforted and understood.

Even when care-givers are rejecting, neglectful or abusive, children have to develop behavioural and psychological strategies that attempt to ward off anxiety or in which they try to seek alternative ways of psychologically securing the attachment figure. It therefore has to be understood that even children whose parents are violent and abusive develop and show attachment behaviour, albeit of a distinctive, insecure kind. It is the type and quality of attachment behaviour that is of interest, and not its perceived presence or absence, strength or weakness. Only in extreme, special cases (institutional nurseries, profound neglect, multiple serial care-giving) might we expect to find children who show no attachment behaviour under conditions of distress and anxiety.

Questions

- How does attachment theory assist you in assessing risk?

- What attachment patterns can you identify in the case study 'Mark'.

- How does the guidance assist you in forming a coherent and effective intervention plan with service users?

CHAPTER 4

'Wrong-Thinking': Cognitive Behavioural Approaches

We now explore the use of an approach that is based on the notion that people learn particular behaviours and can re-learn in order to change. This chapter will outline how the theory explains violent behaviour; how it is used in the prediction of violence and the various forms it takes in managing violent behaviour. This theory has become an increasingly influential one in the development of policies, protocols and practices to tackle violence and has made claims to be the only effective approach (Cullen and Freeman-Longo, 1995); the most effective (Baldock, 1998; Kemshall, 2000) or the most favoured (www.youth-justice-board.gov.uk). Cullen and Freeman-Longo encapsulate this position by stating that: 'The only way you can change this [violent] behaviour is by observing your patterns of thoughts, feelings and behaviours, understanding your cycles, learning the skills and practicing new responses' (1995: 8).

We suspect that most readers will be familiar with some of the principles and practices of this approach, particularly those who are currently working with people who are violent. The development of cognitive behavioural approaches will be outlined, including the move from behaviourism to an increased awareness of the role of cognition. There are several strands to this approach and this chapter will look at the relevance of them to working with violence.

Cognitive behavioural explanations of violence

Cognitive behavioural approaches have developed from clinical psychology and can be grouped into two main strands: the 'traditional' behaviourism of Pavlov (1960), the operant conditioning of Skinner (1958) and the social learning theory of Bandura (1977); and the growth of cognitive approaches with the work of Beck (1967) and Ellis (1962). All these approaches share the central premise that behaviour is learned and can therefore be modified; that it is dynamic and can be subject to change. The focus of concern is the observable behaviour and the thinking (cognition) associated with this, rather than any speculation on unconscious processes, and Sheldon (1995) usefully describes cognitive behavioural approaches as a separation of mind and behaviour. Underlying feelings are considered to be less important than exploring the way people think and process/make sense of situations and their behavioural responses. Unhelpful patterns or cycles of behaviour are identified and strategies are generated with the client to modify them. The approaches make claims to be in partnership with clients, where the client has a voice and is central to setting goals and having some responsibility in achieving change. We will now outline some of the key theoretical strands.

Early behavioural theorists such as Pavlov developed the concept of *classical* or *respondent conditioning*, whereby a Stimulus (S) elicits a Response (R). Pavlov's dogs have entered into popular consciousness and the experiments he undertook that demonstrated how a bell could be associated with the appearance of food are familiar to many people. The dogs salivated at the sound of a bell when they linked this to feeding; the stimulus was the bell and the response was the salivation. Further to this, when the bell was subsequently rung but no food arrived, the dogs gradually ceased to salivate at its sound as the link was extinguished. This in itself may seem benign; however, this approach led to experiments by others such as Watson (McLeod, 2003) where a child ('Little Albert') was induced to have a fear of small animals by the introduction of a loud noise when he held them. Experiments such as this demonstrated that the principles of Stimulus–Response were applicable to human circumstances, although we may raise ethical questions about their nature. The film 'A Clockwork Orange' contains scenes that can be described as classical conditioning, when the young man with problematic aggressive behaviour is shown repeated scenes of violence whilst being subjected to physical pain, thus in future he becomes physically ill when faced with situations containing violence, reducing his capacity for violent behaviour. Elements of classical conditioning have been used with people who commit sexual offences, for example the notion of *extinction*, whereby the link between the stimulus and the response is weakened. Salter (1988) outlines the use of masturbatory satiation with offenders who are encouraged by the therapist to masturbate to their deviant sexual fantasies until they are physically incapable of orgasm, therefore weakening the link between their offending thoughts (Stimulus) and the physical pleasure (Response).

In *operant conditioning*, which is more often found in responses to violence, behaviour is learned through reinforcement of the consequences of the behaviour, that there is a 'reward' of some kind attached to the behaviour. In understanding this process it is useful to consider the ABC model as a linear way of making sense of a particular behaviour. The *Antecedents* (A), *Behaviour* (B) and *Consequences* (C) of a particular action are explored; what led to the actions, what happened and what were the responses/outcomes. In this model there tends to be a concentration on the consequences of actions; however, Stuart (1974) identifies the need to explore antecedents in detail to effectively understand the linear causality of behaviour. Antecedents can support problematic behaviour and therefore it is useful to consider the significance of circumstances in the build up to the behaviour. Thus in our case example, Mark and Kelly 'picking' on each other requires exploration as this is clearly an antecedent to the actual violent, problematic behaviour. It is probably useful to consider removing potentially offensive weapons such as the hammer from the scene.

This approach requires a detailed outlining of all the elements of the behaviour in order to be clear about how it is constructed. Sheldon (1982) says that this should be descriptive rather than analytical, simply stating what is known about the behaviour rather than offering explanations or pre-existing labels. Mark's problematic behaviour would be mapped, outlining the physical reactions he has (the increased heartbeat), the triggers to the 'explosion' of actions, the content of his shouting and threats, and the detail of his physical violence. In this model there is a resistance to placing labels on the behaviour, for example we could easily speculate that Mark is psychopathic, say that he has a low threshold to aggression, has violent tendencies, is acting out previous violence or place other values on his behaviour. A behaviouralist approach would argue that this complicates and confuses the matter at hand, which is the presenting of problematic behaviour.

Operant conditioning in practice has a prime focus on the links between the Behaviour and the Consequences, viewing all behaviours as having consequences that either strengthen or weaken the behaviour. A consequence that rewards behaviour can be a *positive reinforcer*, strengthening that behaviour by gaining or giving something that the person views as wanted, which could include material (e.g. money), emotional (e.g. feelings of power) or social (e.g. status) reinforcers, or it can be a *negative reinforcer*, removing unwanted consequences ('if you behave well you will not go to jail/lose contact with your children/ partner'). Consequences that weaken behaviour are known as punishments, and can also be positive or negative. A *positive punishment* directly responds to the behaviour by aversive methods, such as being arrested and jailed for violence. A *negative punishment* removes something valued by the person, which in our case example may be contact with the children. This very much depends on the specific person, as one person's reward can be another's unwanted consequence and vice versa. If imprisonment holds little fear for people, then it is of minimal reinforcement use. Sheldon makes the point that when assessing what are rewards and punishments, 'It is a good general rule that the "customer knows best"' (Sheldon, 1982: 113).

Reinforcement of any type is most effective when it is closely linked in time to the behaviour and when it is consistent in its application and nature. This may vary in time, for example in *Token Economy* systems, where behaviour is charted during a set period, recognition is given for acts of desirable behaviour, and then this is tallied to generate appropriate agreed rewards. Based on Skinner's work on reinforcement schedules, this method of reinforcement can begin with the acknowledgement of simple behaviours, then progress to more sophisticated, demanding and long-term behaviours, with rewards being spaced at longer intervals. The aim is to assist the development of wanted behaviour and reducing unwanted behaviour to a point where the gaps between the 'artificial' reinforcements become so large that they are no longer required; behaviour is reinforced or punished by usual social processes. In sexual violence Wolf (1984) identified that most offenders do not get caught following their actions and that this acts as a negative reinforcer, removing the unwanted consequences of disclosure and criminal sanctions. When working with boys who have sexually offended, it is important to remember that due to gendered expectations of sexual behaviour their actions can be supported and reinforced by the social status given to male sexual prowess, a situation not available to girls. In our case example we can see elements of reinforcement at work. When Mark threatens Kelly, she tells him to leave, which may be seen as a positive punishment for Mark. However, operant conditioning would be concerned to utilize all the elements of the theory, particularly positive reinforcement which is often forgotten when focusing on problematic behaviour. Although punishments, whether positive or negative, are seen as useful, there is a tendency to concentrate on these to the detriment of reinforcers of wanted behaviour. Reducing unwanted behaviour in itself may be a good outcome, but as Payne points out this '... gives no control over the behaviour which might replace the undesirable behaviour; it might be equally undesirable.' (1997: 118).

Bandura's (1977) Social Learning theory is the third 'traditional' behaviouralist approach, which is premised on the notion that we learn our behaviour through the observation and imitation of others. This is a development from more 'mechanical' approaches to understanding people, as it has a clear focus on change and presumes that people are heavily influenced by social interactions. Again, this is a popular notion supported by everyday discussions around the need for 'positive role models', usually for boys and young men who are exhibiting poor behaviour, where it is felt that they have lacked the influence of men due to the single-parent status of their mothers. It has also been used specifically to address the perceived needs of young men of African-Caribbean descent. In the United Kingdom, the Youth Justice Board has actively promoted the use of mentoring (Youth Justice Board, 2000) with young people 'at risk', whereby adults are encouraged to form mentor–mentee (*sic*) relationships with young people:

> A volunteer mentor from their own community is someone they can rely on, who is not associated with other adults in authority in their lives (police, teachers, social workers, probation officers, even parents), with whom they may have had difficult relationships. Mentors can provide mentees with extra support and a positive adult role model.
>
> (2000: 4)

Clearly this is heavily influenced by Social Learning theory, although there is a more directive approach within the guidance that focuses this modelling on producing 'a reduction in offending behaviour, an increase in young people's awareness of their motivation for offending and the impact of their offending on others' (ibid.: 7).

The theory holds that if someone who the person respects or can identify with is receiving reinforcement for their behaviour, then this behaviour will be imitated. This can lead to the development of poor behaviour including aggression, but can also be modified by the introduction of new, more pro-social role models. The wanted behaviour and associated rewards must be achievable for the person wishing to change, even if this is in a diluted form from, say, a football icon.

Returning to Mark, we may wish to investigate who he has learned his behaviour from and who may be supporting it, raising questions about his background and whether he has seen his father treat his mother in this way, or whether arguments were resolved in this fashion, or whether he has friends who consider such behaviour to be usual and acceptable, thus reinforcing his problematic behaviour. Indeed, his friends (male and female) may consider that any other less aggressive approach is a slur on his manhood, contributing to his violence and locating it within a construct of masculinity. Any assessment of Mark would consider looking at the past and current influences on his behaviour, exploring the significance of influential characters on the development and maintenance of his behaviour. It may, then, be helpful to introduce Mark to figures he respects, but who do not respond in violent ways to situations. Modelling may take place during intervention through working with Mark in ways that demonstrate more constructive gendered relationships, for example through the use of co-working with male and female workers.

All the above approaches require a focus on the detail of the behaviour and to this end there are several models that assist in the collation of information. Cullen and Freeman-Longo (1995) suggest the use of an Anger Log that identifies those times when the client felt angry, then suggest a checklist of associated physical and emotional symptoms, actions and consequences to allow insight into the specifics of the behaviour. This allows for a clear collation of the information required to make sense of the behaviour in order to devise strategies to manage it. Logs and charts are common tools in behavioural work and Schwartz and Goldiamond (1975) proposed a straightforward model that has been replicated in a variety of different settings:

Time	Activity	Where?	Who was there?	What you wanted	What happened
07.00					
08.00					
09.00					
10.00					
11.00					
(and so on)					

A similar version is offered by Cullen and Freeman-Longo to chart patterns of anger. The purpose is to illuminate the links between aspects of the behaviour and to understand the mechanics of the linear antecedents, behaviour and consequences.

It is important to establish what behaviour is wanted, and how things need to be different. In Mark and Kelly's case, there are indications that they both wish for a less stressful relationship without the anger and violence. A behavioural assessment would require more specific detail about their preferred relationship, including: clear behavioural goals that they want to achieve; specifics about what this behaviour would look like and when it would happen; agreement about what achievement would look like; how others would see the difference in their behaviour; what the benefits of this new behaviour would be and how this would be different from the current problems. Underpinning this is clarity about how the achieved changes would be measured.

Utilizing the problem behaviour charts, it should then be possible to decide whether the difficulties are due to too much unwanted behaviour or too little wanted behaviour. This can be analysed by exploring which behaviours need to be increased or decreased; how unwanted behaviour is being positively or negatively reinforced; what alternative behaviours need to replace it; what the antecedents are and whether there are models that are reinforcing unwanted behaviour. Mark and Kelly may consider that decreasing their 'picking' behaviour as an antecedent to violence will be helpful, and Mark may need to explore how his actual violence is being reinforced, possibly through the release of the anger that is building up inside him.

Once an understanding of the behaviour has been achieved and agreement has been reached about preferred behaviour, it is then possible to agree strategies for change. To develop the wanted behaviour, the required antecedents need to be identified and generated; reinforcers need to be agreed along with who provides them and when they are provided; or appropriate role models should be identified. Mark may choose to have kind words from Kelly, to reinforce the times when he is achieving the preferred behaviour, if this is what he feels is useful. It could be agreed that this is done consistently, perhaps with the assistance of a chart of his behaviour. Of course, Kelly has to agree to this as she has a clear responsibility to reinforce his wanted behaviour, which begs questions of gendered expectations. In strengthening some of the existing wanted behaviour, it may be helpful to identify how this works in terms of antecedents and consequences, enhancing these elements to maximize the potential for consistent positive behaviour. Is there any way in which his current rewards can be increased and made more effective? Mark may also be encouraged to spend more time with a friend who deals with conflict in a less aggressive way, learning from him, and Kelly may have someone she can identify with to develop her skills in negotiating problems.

The more traditional behavioural approaches are generally recognizable and often 'fit' with popular notions of how people work. Behaviour modification is common in most child-rearing practices and is found professionally in residential care, where there is the opportunity to have a managed environment where the full complexities of the approach can be controlled and monitored. Clearly there are more problems where the antecedents to behaviour cannot be consistently modified and where behaviour and its associated consequences cannot be effectively monitored. This model requires consistency over time if it is to achieve change and, as life is rarely entirely stable, there can be a multitude of factors that may occur that prevent the pure application of this approach. It would be difficult to claim success (or failure) for the approach if other variables or influences cannot be assessed, so although a programme of work may appear to be helping Mark change his behaviour, it may actually be influenced by a new set of friends he has coincidentally met.

Cognitive approaches

The behaviouralist approaches above have in common their dismissal of internal processes as unquantifiable, unknowable and unnecessary for modifying behaviour, with a focus on the observable behaviours and actions of people. However, there has been an increasing interest in the thinking patterns that cause or influence people's actions. The work of Ellis (1962), the founder of Rational Emotive Therapy (RET), and Beck (1967), who founded Cognitive Therapy, has been influential in this, viewing thinking as a form of behaviour that had been learned and therefore susceptible to reinforcement and change. Behaviour is heavily influenced by thought processes, similar to the notion of stimulus discussed earlier. The term cognitive behaviour is used to denote the emphasis on changing how a person interprets or views the world, as this way of interpreting can lead to and maintain problematic behaviour. There is still a focus on current problems, rather than on past events (Cigno, 1998) as it is the immediacy of the interpretation, the way someone is 'wired up' to respond to a given situation that is part, if not the whole, of the problem. This actually allows for some personal agency on the part of people rather than the more deterministic underpinnings of traditional behaviouralism. It accepts that people think about their actions and have the capacity to make sense of them and to respond in different ways. Cognitive behaviouralism views people as

having 'faulty wiring', where some of their thinking processes and perceptions of the world are wrong, leading to problems with their
responses. As Sheldon states: 'irrational thoughts or disturbances in perception lead us to process our view of the world incorrectly' (1995: 185).

This premise of irrational, wrong or dysfunctional thinking has led
to responses that seek to change the way that people make sense of situations, challenging current thinking patterns that lead to problematic
behaviour (Robinson and Poporino, 2001). It assumes that people are
in essence rational and can make choices, even though these will have
been limited or influenced by their upbringing and social environment. The role of feelings is acknowledged, although Werner encapsu-
lates the cognitive behavioural understanding of these when he states
that 'emotion is a feeling a person experiences after estimating what an
event means to him' (1970: 254). Thus feelings may exist for whatever
reason, but it is the way we process these cognitively that is the key to
understanding (and changing) our behavioural reaction. In this context violent behaviour can be seen as a specific outcome of a thinking
process whereby people have learned to link certain reactions to particular situations or feelings, often expressing their anger in inappropriate
ways. The notion of a *cycle of abuse* is a cognitive behavioural construct
and has two different meanings: one, that behaviours/responses are
learned from past experiences (if you were abused/witnessed abuse as a
child, then you may replicate this in adulthood) and, two, that people
may enter into a cyclic pattern of behaviour. The significance of this in
terms of assessment and intervention will be discussed later in the
chapter.

Cullen and Freeman-Longo (1995) apply a cognitive behavioural
approach to understanding anger and violence by describing such
behaviour as being the result of 'stuffed' feelings, based on the analogy
of a pressure cooker whereby normal emotional feelings build up, but
have an outlet that is measured, reasoned and socially acceptable. When
these outlets (pressure valve) become dysfunctional or blocked, then
the pressure (emotions) build up and explode in inappropriate ways.
Allowing people to recognize their feelings that are building up and
their lack of coping mechanisms to deal with this is a key to making the
pattern of anger visible, therefore keeping a log of feelings, thoughts and
responses is a central assessment issue. In our case example, Mark would
be encouraged to explore how the arguments develop, what he was thinking, how he felt both physically and emotionally, what he did and how
he reacted afterwards to the events. So, the nature of the 'picking' would
be outlined, the sick feeling and clenched hands identified, and the rapid

escalation into violence linked. This 'anger log' is a useful analytical tool to assist in identifying the processes involved in the problem behaviour and provides the material to assist in change.

The role of *defence mechanisms* has been incorporated into cognitive approaches but with a rather different emphasis than in psychodynamic ideas, looking at behaviour instead of underlying motivations. Thus Cullen and Freeman-Longo identify six defence mechanisms and their associated behaviours that people need to consider in understanding their anger: Rationalization, Intellectualizing, Denial, Religiosity, Justification and Blame. For example, *rationalization* is the process of making excuses for poor behaviour, even though you know it to be wrong. In *denial* (which is a commonly used concept within work with violence) they identify several forms which this may take, including denial of responsibility (I didn't do it), denial of intent (I didn't mean to do it), denial of harm (What is the problem, I didn't hit her with the hammer), denial of frequency (It only happens occasionally/is an exception), denial of premeditation (It just happened/was an accident), denial of intrusiveness (I didn't break down the door, just tried to) and minimization (I only shout. I don't hit). In this approach, defence mechanisms need to be identified to allow for responsibility taking and for someone to begin work on their problem behaviour. Briggs (1998) discusses the importance of denial to many practitioners working with sexual violence, where high rates of denial are seen as indicating resistance to treatment and a higher risk of re-offending. However, denying may simply be an understandable act of lying to avoid adverse social consequences rather than reflecting a psychological state.

Ellis (1962) developed a model of conceptualizing behaviour that has been used in the management of violence, particularly within the Probation Service (Raynor, Smith and Vanstone, 1994). In operant conditioning, the ABC model of Antecedents–Behaviour–Consequences is used to understand the problem behaviour. Ellis changed the emphasis within this ABC model to Activating Event–Beliefs–Consequence, where an event can trigger beliefs (understanding) about the event that lead to consequent behaviour. Ellis maintained that people often act as though the Activating Event leads straight to the Consequent behaviour, and people are unaware that it is their beliefs, or the way they make sense of the event, that lead to the behaviour. These beliefs are influenced by a whole set of learning experiences that construct the way an event is processed. Ellis felt that it was important to enable people to understand that the consequences or responses are due to this belief system, not simply the event. So, in this model people act as though A leads directly to C, whereas the key to understanding and change is recognizing that B leads to C. Cullen and Freeman-Longo state that this is in essence learning to think before you act and describe *Situation Perception Training* as a method of doing this through considering alternative explanations for events. Rather than leaping from event to reaction, people are encouraged to stop and consider explanations other than the ones that lead to a problematic reaction. This emphasis on 'thinking through' actions in a rational manner is in contrast to what Ellis called the 'irrational' A–C responses.

When faced with criticism from Kelly, Mark responds quickly with 'exploding' anger that further compounds the problems. Situation Perception Training would encourage Mark to consider the sense he is making of this criticism; whether he has an automatic over-reaction to criticism that may have developed through his previous experiences, and whether there are other interpretations he could consider. He would be invited to consider his perceptions of these criticisms and perhaps to consider that, rather than a personal attack on him, Kelly is expressing her frustrations about a difficult situation and could need some love and support, rather than harsh words.

Beck (1976) developed the above model further with the notion of cognitive distortions, where someone under pressure (threat) is not able to use their rational thinking processes and resorts to more basic, emotional responses that are unhelpful. McLeod (2003) compares this to Freud's primary process thinking (emotionally led, developmentally immature) and secondary process thinking (rational, logical, 'adult'). Ellis identified certain specific ways of thinking as being unhelpful, such as *awfulizing*, the tendency to see relatively minor events as catastrophic, and *musterbation*, having unreasonably high expectations of performance or gain. Beck's cognitive distortions added to this list, including: *over-generalization* (totalizing conclusions drawn from little evidence); *dichotomous thinking* (seeing the world as only constructed of extreme opposites); *mental filter* (only seeing or validating negatives); *magnification/minimization* (belittling your strengths, exaggerating others' strengths); *personalization* (taking individual responsibility or blame for bad events despite clear indications that circumstances beyond their control have contributed to this). Both Ellis and Beck felt that it was imperative to challenge cognitive distortions, although this could take different forms and be of different strengths. Ellis preferred a more direct and almost aggressive approach that confronted the client with the irrationality of their thoughts, insisting on change and testing the reality of those ways of thinking. Beck promoted a more gentle approach, although rigorous in its confrontation of these unhelpful modes of thought. This drive to challenge cognitive distortions can be seen in several manuals of practice and guidance. However, in conceptualizing violent behaviour as being based on cognitive distortions, we may inadvertently provide an excuse for someone to avoid responsibility for the choice to be violent. To understand that you have cognitive distortions which lead you to behave in a certain way is to distance yourself from the moral decision to hurt someone.

Cycles of abuse

As alluded to earlier, the notion of cycles of abuse has become a key professional and lay discourse in understanding violent behaviour. In one sense this is common sense, as people who have been badly treated may well learn to express behaviour that reproduces their experience, albeit projected on to others. It provides an easy to understand explanation for unwanted behaviour, based on learning theories. It has been used as an explanation for a range of violences including sexual abuse, elder abuse and domestic violence. Cullen and Freeman-Longo state that: 'The repeated pattern of being abused, stuffing your feelings, and then abusing others is a cycle of abuse that is unfortunately very common.' (1995: 20)

Mark may well be performing aggressive behaviour in a way that reflects his upbringing, perhaps having experienced abuse himself, unable to manage the consequent feelings and replicating the behaviour with Kelly. However, this raises questions of responsibility as cycle of abuse theorists are faced with the dilemma of emphasizing the past to explain the present therefore potentially providing an 'excuse' for the violence. Any cursory glance at the media reporting of criminal cases will elicit examples of previous abusive experiences being presented as mitigating circumstances for poor current behaviour. If someone believes that their behaviour is determined by their previous experiences, how does this promote current and future responsibility?

There is a further consideration in this approach. Cullen and Freeman-Longo warn that: 'Unless you intervene, the cycle of abuse continues and your abusive behaviour patterns are passed on from one generation to the next, from the abuser to the victim' (1995: 20). Thus Mark has responsibility not simply for his own behaviour, but for potentially creating other offenders, perhaps his children Billy and Luke, increasing the imperative to change his behaviour.

The determinist element of this approach needs caution in its application. Cycle of abuse notions are almost always qualified by statements that previous experiences *may* rather than *will* lead to future problems, yet this qualification is often minimized. It is perfectly reasonable to consider that someone who has had abusive experiences will seek to *avoid* replicating these in future and empirical links between the past and present behaviours are not always demonstrated in research. For example, a child who has been sexually abused is not destined to become a sexual offender (Caldwell, 2002), and seeking previous abusive experiences as causality reduces the complexity of a wide variety of interacting factors.

In terms of understanding violent behaviour, a second, more immediate type of cycle model is often used to gain insight. In essence, this model views behaviour as a series of interlocking thoughts, feelings and actions that feed into a cyclic pattern. Thoughts about a precipitating incident or 'trigger' can generate feelings that lead to actions, which in turn reinforce the thoughts about events. Cullen and Freeman-Longo describe *thoughts–feelings–actions* as behaviour chains that can link up to form cycles. Illustrating this with our case example, Mark would be encouraged to explore the thoughts he has about the 'picking' arguments they have and to consider the feelings this generates in him, both physical and emotional (heart racing; clenched hands, perhaps feelings of failure). The consequent actions/behaviour would then be linked to these precursors. There are variations on this cycle; however, they generally follow a pattern of:

■ build up to the behaviour, including triggers;

■ expression of the behaviour;

■ feelings of guilt but tempered with defence mechanisms that minimize the harm;

■ superficially 'normal' phase, but where planning and fantasizing about 'the next time' take place, leading back to a build up of the behaviour.

A cycle of abuse model

This cycle has also been used to explain sexual violence (Longo, 2002; Wolf, 1984) and is helpful in demonstrating to offenders that their behaviour does not 'just happen', but is the product of a structure that can be identified and changed. Indeed, some assessment protocols for

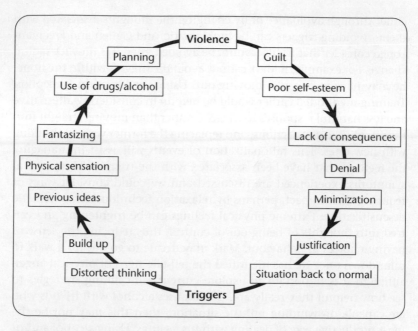

Figure 4.1   Example of a cycle of abuse

violence suggest that inability to understand the cycle of abuse increases the risk that person poses. However, presumption of a cycle can lead to problems. Hackett (2000) describes work undertaken with a child who has sexually abused that was focused on enabling him to understand his cycle. This proved to be difficult as the child did not have a recognizable cycle but was fortunately able to articulate the mechanisms of his individual behaviour in a coherent way that was acceptable to the workers, thus avoiding an increased perception of 'riskiness' through his 'denial' of his cycle. Presumptions of pre-existing conditions or factors can lead to a narrow emphasis on elements that limit a full understanding of the behaviour. Expert knowledge (the factors to look for) is imposed by the worker that restricts the autonomy of the service user to speak their own story and consider the local circumstances of the behaviour.

Once the cycle has been identified (and the cycle can take many forms unique to that individual), then strategies can be developed to change the habitual behaviour, exploring the component parts to break the links. The automatic responses to 'triggers' can be modified, either through avoidance or by changing the thoughts associated with them. Avoiding triggers can be problematic, and Cullen and Freeman-Longo consider that if they cannot be avoided, then it is time for radical change. For example, if Mark cannot avoid the triggers within the home he may have to consider moving out. Using the Situation Perception Training mentioned earlier would be helpful in considering alternative and less harmful responses to triggers, rather than moving straight into the established connections, and replacing the former ways of thinking with new ones. This rationalization of events will assist in managing the feelings that have been associated with the triggers. The physical symptoms experienced are discussed and we could consider ways of reducing their impact, perhaps by relaxation techniques or systematic desensitization. Extreme physical feelings can be frightening and can feed into thoughts of being out of control, thus reducing the sense of having choices in behaviour. Mark may decide to go out for a walk to calm down once he has identified the tell-tale signs of physical anger, although it is important to explore current self-calming strategies to see how helpful they really are. If Mark uses alcohol with friends who are capable of 'winding up' the situation, then this may not be the most productive way of dealing with his feelings. Using alcohol and/or drugs can be seen as a form of self-abuse that feeds into existing negative self-images, thus further limiting the capacity to take positive control of behaviour.

Once the cycle of abuse has been identified and strategies developed to break the chains supporting it, vigilance needs to be maintained to avoid 'switching on' the cycle. The notion of *Relapse Prevention* is a key element in this. Understanding the triggers and responses will allow for the development of future skills in managing potentially difficult situations that may begin the cycle. Utilizing tried and tested strategies to defuse the links is an important part of remembering that circumstances are within your control. This means that there are certain risk factors that may lead into abusive behaviour which need to be guarded against. The assumption within this model is that there must be vigilance against the pro-offending 'hard-wiring' of the mind through self-awareness and self-policing. Once the cycle has been identified, then the strategies can be put in place as a lifelong control for someone's propensity for violence.

Cognitive behavioural programmes specifically designed to respond to violence have grown during the previous decade, encouraged and supported by institutions that have responsibility for managing this behaviour. Kemshall (2001) identifies that these approaches have had two main objectives: first, to change cognitions that support violence; and, second, to change violent behaviour. Anger management techniques including cyclic concepts have been used to change cognitions, and social learning theory has informed behaviour change. An example is the Vermont Cognitive Self-Change programme developed by Bush (1995: 142–8). This targets the:

- distorted cognitions of the offender;

- deconstruction of the 'anti-social logic' of offenders, particularly the logic of self-justification (the 'victim stance') for violence and victim blaming;

- reinforcement and reward for violent behaviour;

- promotion of alternative/pro-social thinking patterns; and,

- teaching of problem-solving skills.

Challenging cognitive distortions is a key element of practice, with an emphasis on confronting the pro-offending beliefs that people may have. There are potential difficulties with this, as there may be a tendency for the worker to be aggressive, utilizing their powerful position to enforce change (Jenkins, 1990). Indeed, the use of language such as 'breaking through', 'confronting' and 'challenge' can replicate styles of behaviour that have been identified as unhelpful in clients mandated for violent offences, and have an air of masculinity about them.

Risk assessment

Cognitive behavioural approaches are focused on the connections between thoughts, feelings and behaviour that arise from triggering situations. In thinking about risk of recurrence of the violence, it is important to explore the factors that have led to previous poor behaviour in order to guard against future problems. These factors can be broad, such as poverty (e.g. Klassen and O'Connor, 1988); age (see, for example, Swanson et al., 1990); being a man (see, for example, Genders and Morrison, 1996) or more specifically about the person, such as having cognitive distortions that support violence or minimize harm to victims (Bandura et al., 1975). Research in this field tends to take an explicitly positivist approach, usually based within psychology, that explores the deficits/cognitive distortions of people who exhibit problem behaviour.

This focus on the problems in people's lives or personalities allows for the construction of common risk factors to be found in like populations. Cognitive behavioural approaches lend themselves to the creation of risk-factor tables and checklists, and we may find that Mark has certain traits that are commonly found in other people who are violent. Examples of these checklists/assessment instruments include the Violence Risk Assessment Guide (VRAG) (Quinsey et al., 1998) discussed in a previous chapter.

The effectiveness of cognitive behavioural approaches

Although popular in responding to violence, the research evidence for the effectiveness of cognitive behavioural approaches is mixed. Meta-analytic reviews of offending behaviour programmes have indicated a small but significant reduction in re-offending of about 10 per cent (Hollin, 1999). The claims for effectiveness are supported by the application of natural scientific research methodologies, such as the Randomized Control Trial, as these approaches locate themselves within a rational scientific discourse. Indeed, claims for the superiority of these approaches over other methods are often made on the basis of the rigour of the research (Sheldon, 1995). However, there are inherent limitations to such research methodologies which are minimized by those who have an attachment to such ways of thinking. One of the key difficulties is comparing like with like, as the participants **have** to be compared with people who have not received the intervention. Agreeing what constitutes a comparison group may be problematic, as trying to create a coherent group out of disparate individuals is not easy and this approach relies on the identification of a limited number of key factors, often the lowest common individual denominators, to generate similarity. These tend to be categorizations such as type of offence, length of sentence, ethnicity and estimation of the risk of re-offending. This categorization excludes factors that are complex and difficult to measure such as the social context in which people are situated, leading to a biased understanding of the effectiveness of interventions (Tilley, 2001).

The integrity of the programmes is also a factor, as making a rational-scientific assessment of effectiveness requires that the programme is delivered consistently to all participants, following a predetermined structure that cannot be deviated from. A method of ensuring this is to video record all sessions and be assessed by evaluators. Unless the participants receive the same 'treatment dosage', it is hard to make rigorous comparisons. Deciding on what constitutes success is also problematic, as measurement of re-convictions does not necessarily reflect re-offending and the length of time following intervention can influence outcome studies. For example, Farrington and colleagues (2000) found that re-offending within one year of a programme was significantly reduced, but that after two years monitoring the re-offending rates matched those of the non-treated group. Outcome studies tend to include only those participants who have completed the whole of a programme, on the basis that they have received the required 'dosage', and those who have only taken part of the treatment cannot be included. This leads to the exclusion of 'drop-outs' from effectiveness studies, so that if 100 people begin the programme and 50 do not complete, then the effectiveness will be determined through the follow-up of the 50 who do complete. It is reasonable to presume that those who complete are more motivated than those who do not, yet motivation is rarely seen as a factor, partly because it is hard to measure. It also raises questions about the efficacy of programmes if there are high drop-out rates (if the medicine is so unpleasant that many people will not take it, then what is the point of prescribing it?), plus there is evidence that those who do drop out of cognitive skills programmes may well be made worse by the experience (Robinson, 1995).

Evaluating outcomes in offender cognitive and behavioural programmes is not straightforward and reductions in reconviction rates are variable (Bonta, 2002). Falshaw and colleagues studied the effectiveness of Cognitive Skills programmes within prisons in the United Kingdom and found: 'no differences in the reconviction rates for a sample of adult male offenders who had participated in a programme [n = 649] and a matched comparison group of offenders who had not [n = 1947]' (2004: 11). They speculated that factors that may defy measurement could be significant, such as the enthusiasm of staff in engaging with people and the institutional expectation that offenders attending programmes may improve their chances of parole, thus: 'While current participants may have been motivated to attend a programme, they may not necessarily have been equally motivated to change.' (ibid.: 10). Of participation in the 14 programmes accredited by the National Probation Service for use in the community, the increased number of referrals and completion rates (outputs) are listed as improvements in 2004, but the profile of those who drop out, which remains static, is only briefly mentioned. As research into cognitive behavioural programmes has developed, the outlook appears even gloomier for claims of effectiveness, with no statistical difference in re-offending between those who have attended these programmes compared with a matched sample. This appears to be the case for adult men (Falshaw et al., 2003), young offenders (Cann et al., 2003) and women (Cann, 2006).

Research claiming success for cognitive behavioural programmes has tended to make global claims through application of a particular form of methodology. However, the studies may well inform us what has worked for a specific group without acknowledging the context within which it was delivered. The impossibility of replicating the exact conditions (the different individuals; the group dynamics and composition; the social environment) to reapply the 'successful' programme will be obvious; therefore a judgement has to be made about which conditions are significant. This is difficult to untangle and often ignored, denied or marginalized by the natural scientific approach (Tilley, 2001).

Summary

- Cognitive behavioural approaches are the most common way of understanding and responding to male violence.

- They lend themselves to a clear and purposeful way of working.

- Claims are made for their effectiveness supported by some research evidence.

- They take a rational approach, viewing people as having learned 'wrong-thinking' (cognitive distortions) which can be changed to the 'correct' way based on normative assumptions.

- They tend to locate the problem behaviour as 'hard-wired', thus creating an identity based on the behaviour.

- Models of understanding and responding to violence are imposed on people, with acknowledgement of the model by the person being central to managing change.

- They tend to psychologize the problem behaviour and pathologize the individual.

- They lend themselves to measurement within a limited evaluative framework.

- The worker role is to assist the person to understand their deficits and propose a predetermined strategy to correct them.

To aid critical reflection we invite you to consider the frameworks and questions outlined below.

National Probation Service information on 'Think First' cognitive behavioural programmes

What is Think First?

Think First is a General Offending Groupwork Programme – one of several independently accredited programmes for use in England and Wales. Accredited Offending Behaviour programmes are part of the Probation Service's What Works initiative, which aims to reduce general reconviction rates by providing types of supervision for offenders which are based on research and sound evidence. These approaches or 'programmes' are effective in changing the way offenders **think** and **behave**.

Think First consists of:

- 22 intensive groupwork sessions

- 4 structured pre-group sessions and

- up to 6 post-programme sessions.

Who is it for?

Think First is aimed at offenders within the **medium/high** risk of reconviction group because available evidence indicates that it is most effective with these groups.

Programme content

Think First is a cognitive skills programme, based on the premise that thinking is the basis of all behaviour, so in order to affect or change criminal behaviour the underlying thoughts and attitudes of offenders must be addressed. Research shows that many offenders have not acquired the skills of thinking in certain areas such as problem solving and critical reasoning. Offenders may not always see things from other people's points of view and can also have a poorly developed sense of values. The 'Think First' programme aims to tackle:

- **Lack of problem solving skills.**   Often offenders do not recognize or anticipate problems or fail to consider alternative forms of action. This programme can challenge these rigid thought processes. The programme approaches problem solving as a skill which everyone can learn and which can be applied to different situations. It enables offenders to see how their behaviour often works to their own disadvantage in the long term, how it can harm their families and the victims of their crimes.

- **Poor social skills.**   A large proportion of offences either occur in groups or are perpetrated by groups acting together. Poor social skills often result in inappropriate behaviour which can be manifested in aggression, violence or hostility. The programme can teach the offender how to counter or resist pressure from others.

- **Poor personal control.**   Some offences appear to have been committed on impulse. When such offences are examined carefully, it is often possible to identify the thinking that allowed someone to behave in such a way. Think First can tackle these problems and teach self-management skills to enable offenders to think about things differently.

Diversity

The National Probation Service recognizes that women, minority ethnic offenders, those with a disability or other special needs may have additional issues. These issues will be fully addressed in order that they derive maximum benefit from Think First.

The programme is approved as an additional requirement of a Community Rehabilitation Order or a Community Punishment and Rehabilitation Order in accordance with the Powers of Criminal Courts (Sentencing) Act 2000. Supervision of the order will begin immediately and commencement of the groupwork programme will be with the first available place following appearance in court. Attendance at the full programme, which includes the 22 groupwork sessions, four pre-group sessions and up to six post-programme sessions, is monitored in accordance with Home Office standards. Any breach of attendance or conditions will be dealt with appropriately and may see the offender returned to court.

Questions

- How might the 22 sessions address the individual requirements of the participants?

- What 'additional issues' do you think women, minority ethnic offenders, those with a disability or other special needs may have? What assumptions are being made about the 'normal' offender here?

- Can you identify any 'rigid thought processes' that you may hold?

- To what extent do people choose to offend within this approach?

- To what extent are the social circumstances of the person addressed in this model?

CHAPTER 5

Challenging Men, Supporting Women: Feminist Approaches

This chapter examines how men's violence to known women and their children is understood in terms of patriarchy (the structural dominance by men within society); how this theory influences risk assessments; and the implications for prevention and intervention. As the term patriarchy is used mostly in feminist research and theorizing, the various forms of feminism will be briefly explained. The impact of 'second wave' feminism on professional practice (supporting women; challenging men) and government policy will be explored, particularly the work of Dobash and Dobash, and Pence and Paymar. The limitations of this theory as an explanation for all family violence is also discussed, with reference to elder abuse, same-sex violence, female sexual abuse, and female-on-male violence.

Feminist understandings of violence

Feminist theories view the power wielded by men as the underpinning basis for their violence, therefore explaining the ways in which power operates and is maintained is central to this approach. Whilst the broad aim of all feminist theory is concerned with understanding and transforming the subordinate position of women in society, the second half of the twentieth century saw the emergence of a wide range of feminist theories with different, and often competing, understandings of male power. Liberal and Marxist feminisms have developed the focus of women's rights in the public sphere, emphasizing political action and reform as the key to addressing inequalities between men and women. Radical feminism is more concerned with developing an analysis of women's role in the private sphere of the family, emphasizing the links between the private and the political. Patriarchy is the key concept of radical feminism, contesting Marxist and liberal feminisms in that unequal gender divisions are seen to serve the interests of men rather than of capitalism: 'there is more that joins men across class and disability, and even race and sexual orientation, than divides them' (Cordery and Whitehead, 1992: 29). Black feminism contests this, arguing that there is more solidarity between white men and white women than there is between white men and black men (Joseph, 1981), thus theories of patriarchal power are seen as neglecting the effects of racism. For example, the Southall Black Sisters suggest that black women have to struggle against cultures and traditions that keep women weakened and without power to determine their owns lives; Mama (1989) views the under-reporting of domestic violence by black women as part of the racism black families experience, such as the atti-tude of acceptance of family violence within the black community, and the brutalization of black men by state repression. Psychoanalytic femi-nism looks more at the mutualities between women, particularly mothers and daughters, in terms of strengths to resist the oppression of men; for example, 'dependency' is seen as being able to depend on the help of others and thus an empowering rather than as a weakened state (Stiver, 1991). Similarly postmodern feminism, and many mas-culinisms, emphasize the importance of differences within the category of 'woman', such as class, sexuality, race, age and disability as important influences on women's experiences (see, for example, Messerschmidt, 1993; Poon, 1995).

Hearn argues that rather than 'reifying a particular definition of vio-lence as absolutely the most important ... it is more important to appre-ciate the changing definitions of violence through time and place' (1998: 14). The changing definitions of violence analysed in postmodern femi-nism reflect the social and economic changes in women's lives (see, for example, Featherstone, 1999), and the impact of feminism on men (see, for example, Milner, 2004); but it is radical feminist explanations that have most significantly informed practical agency interventions (see, for example, Teft, 1999), and the development of policy (see for example, Department of Health, 2004; Home Office, 2003b). Therefore we describe radical feminism more fully below, first in terms of heteropatriarchal explanations of men's violence, and second in terms of the interventions this analysis has inspired.

Heteropatriarchy

Radical feminism locates men's violence to known women (and their children) within the context of structural inequalities, the key mechanism of which is the heteropatriarchal exercise of power and control over women. This is not to say that men are violent all the time or that it is only men who are violent, but that it is men who dominate the business of violence. Female violence is seen as an aberration from the category of 'woman', whereas violence is more routine for men, being constitutive of the category of 'men' (Hearn, 1998). As every avenue of power within patriarchal society is in the hands of men, the threat of violence as a means of controlling women is sufficient to remind them of their subordinate place. This means, say Stanko and colleagues (1988), that all women must be continually on their guard to the possibility of men's violence. Thus radical feminism is interested in analysing patriarchal control at all levels of society, both public and private spheres. On a broad level, Corrin (1996) argues that the violence of war involves a coming together of patriarchal and militarist systems that can be fatal for women. Boric and Desnica (1996) also view war as an extreme form of patriarchy that minimizes the effects of both civil and war violence on women; for example, they explore how the use of 'strategic rape' as a means of ethnic cleansing in Croatia was manipulated for political reasons; the increased violence brought home from war was silenced; and women's solidarity disrupted by displacement from their homes. In a less extreme example, most state agencies are controlled largely by men and thus influence how men's violence is defined and managed (see, for example, Langan and Day's, 1992, analysis of men's domination of child protection services). And the violent acts of individual men, including violence against children, young people, mothers and elderly people, can also be best understood as gender class distinctions of men over women within differential contexts of patriarchy (see, for example, Hearn, 1990, 1999, Hunt and Martin, 2001).

Over the past two decades radical feminist analyses of men's violence have centred on listening to women and validating their experiences as a necessary counter to the male 'objectivity' of existing research (see, for example, Bograd, 1990; Hearn and Parkin, 1987). At the same time pro-feminist men's research of men's violence focused explicitly on men's subjectivity in order to problematize the traditional association of knowledge and objectivity (see, for example, Hearn and Morgan, 1990; Morgan, 1981). The very nature of this research, and the populations researched, means that radical feminism has been most successful in terms of impact on policy and professional practice in exposing the prevalence and nature of men's violence to known women *within* the home (and the resulting costs to the state), rather than violence in other contexts, such as the street or workplace (Gilchrist, et al., 2003; Mullender, 1996). At the same time men's violence to children was linked to their, and their mothers', subordinate position in the home (see, for example, Scourfield, 2003) and, increasingly, links were made between what had previously been regarded as separate forms of family violence: child abuse and domestic violence. For example, research demonstrated that at least one in three of all pregnant women have been subject to violence within the home, it commencing or escalating with pregnancy; with post-partum women being particularly susceptible (for an overview, see Hunt and Martin, 2001). Other research establishing the links between the physical and sexual abuse of children with the domestic violence of their mothers (Humphreys et al., 2001; Waugh and Bonner, 2002) meant that children were viewed as victims in the same way as their mothers.

The impact of this research was to broaden the original intention of listening to and supporting women in strategies to prevent violence. The implications of this conceptualization of unequal power relationships in the home and, therefore, the need to challenge men, is promoted by the Home Office, which says that programmes 'based on the premise that domestic violence is about the abuse of power and control on male–female relationships ... is an approach we recommend' (Home Office, 2003b: 3.7). Professional practice based on this premise is also promoted as 'good practice' within agencies (see, for example, Humphreys, 1999; Mullender and Burton, 2001), thus practice has become dominated by programmes aimed at challenging men in the work of probation (Teft, 1999) and child protection (Scourfield and Dobash, 1999), underpinned by zero tolerance police responses (Cosgrove, 1996). These responses and interventions have developed largely from the Duluth Domestic Abuse Intervention Project (DAIP) in the United States (Pence and Paymar, 1985, 1990) and CHANGE and the Lothian Domestic Violence Probation Project (LDVPP) in the United Kingdom (Dobash et al., 2000).

Power and control

The Domestic Abuse Intervention Project emerged from an audit of services in Duluth following the murder of a man by his partner, a woman who had asked in vain for help for many years. Aided by the fact that Duluth is a relatively small city, with a commitment to community

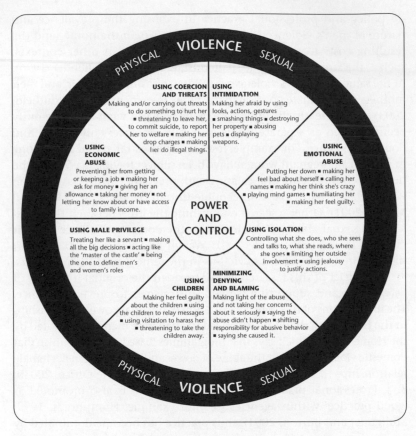

Figure 5.1   Power and control wheel (Duluth Domestic Abuse Intervention Project)

action, and the existence of skilled feminist activists, a number of institutional and organizational changes made Duluth a beacon of good
practice worldwide. The feminist activists, many already working in
refuges, sat down with women who had been subject to domestic violence and asked them to construct a pictorial image which summarized their experiences. Out of this came the *Power and Control Wheel*
(Figure 5.1), and then the women constructed a wheel that would explain
what a respectful and equitable relationship would look like – the *Equality
Wheel* (Figure 5.2). These images are widely used in work not only with
victims and perpetrators but also professionals (see also, Hunt and Martin,
2001: 151, 153, for examples of *Medical Power and Control* and *Advocacy
Wheels*). Whilst the power wheel provides a simple way to explain and

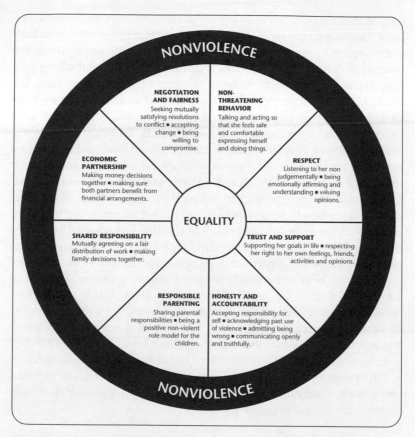

Figure 5.2 Equality wheel (Duluth Domestic Abuse Intervention Project)

understand domestic violence, it was largely the coordinated approach to domestic violence that was remarkable. Each element of the Duluth project (Pence, 1983; Pence and Paymar, 1985, 1990) has been replicated in the United Kingdom in the following ways:

1 Reducing the screening out and diversion of cases of violence in the home from the justice system

The good practice advocated by government (Home Office, 2003b) includes a pro-arrest policy on the part of the police, taking the burden of prosecution off the victim, provision for vulnerable or intimidated witnesses, the deployment of civil support workers in police stations to follow up police responses, and dedicated domestic violence courts. This has

necessitated a fundamental change in police responses to domestic violence. Drawing on the work of Hoyle's re-conceptualization of 'cop culture'
(1998), Grady's research (2002) demonstrates the influence on the development of police officers' working assumptions of radical feminist conceptualization of domestic violence as a crime committed by men. She
charts how, first, social attitudes have changed within the police force
so that not only are men viewed as the assailants but, where women are
violent, this is viewed as fighting back (Counts, Brown and Campbell,
1992; McGibbon, Cooper and Kelly, 1989;). Second, force policy has been
amended via the establishment of dedicated domestic violence units,
where staff are trained in the Duluth analysis, and all incidents of male-on-
female violence are recorded and followed through. Thus police officers
have no discretion in their responses, 'no further action' being no longer
an option. More recently many police forces have also adopted a policy of
reporting all such incidents to the child protection services. Having been
previously severely criticized for its response to domestic violence, police
practices have been influenced by the zero tolerance promoted by feminist
activism originally launched in Edinburgh in 1992, which, as Cosgrove
(1996: 202) stated, 'insists that men take responsibility for their violence'.
However, Cosgrove also argued that this in itself was insufficient, as the
feminist initiative 'also insists that the political, social and cultural contexts in which it occurs and is allowed to continue must be changed'.

These responses may not be sufficient to meet the needs of children
living with domestic violence, with some studies showing that such
children are critical of police responses:

> though they may be quick to arrive, their intervention is rarely effective,
> because the man is not removed or is soon allowed to return, and that the
> police do not talk to them, even when the children are present at the inci-
> dent or at the police station or even where it is the child who has rung 999.
> (Mullender et al., 2002: 221)

It would be helpful if police officers could be trained in talking with
children so that the overriding needs of children to be safe and have
someone to talk to can be met.

2 Shifting responsibility for the violence away from the victim and onto the state and the assailant

Once identified, the response to victims and assailants is deliberately
asymmetrical, reflecting what is viewed as the asymmetry of power
relationships between men and women. Dobash and colleagues (2000)

assert that the fundamental principles are that men's violence stems from the unequal relationship between men and women in marriage and society; and that abusive behaviour is learned and intentional. Similarly:

> At the most basic level, preventing violence against women in the home involves two components: increasing the safety of women and their children in the short term and ending the man's violence in the longer term – in short, *supporting women* and *challenging men*.
>
> (Burton, Regan and Kelly, 1989: vii, our emphasis)

Supporting and empowering women to make choices for themselves is underpinned by state policies and practices that give them accurate information, advice and advocacy about their legal rights, support and access to refuge and community services, and the encouragement of mutual self-help and support (see, for example, Debbonaire, 1994). Practice is developed through consensus decision making so that not only are women residents involved in the running of refuges, but they also have a say in how services are further developed (see, for example, Mladjenovic and Matijasevic, 1996, for a description of how a refuge provided the space where many ideas originated and many activities started). The twin principles of empowering women to make their own choices and holding men responsible for their abusive behaviour (especially challenging their attempts to shift responsibility on to their female partners) means women victims are not always seen as capable of making informed or rational choices. For example, Alcock (2001) says that she begins her counselling of survivors of domestic violence by affirming their experiences, but that this involves challenging every minimization of their experiences of abuse. And, because men's programmes are not always run on Duluth principles, their effectiveness is viewed as necessarily suspect (see, for example, Mullender and Burton, 2001); therefore there exists a powerful subtext about which choice is a right choice. For example:

> Though women who leave as soon as violence starts are in a minority, we may perhaps hope that as the message about the damage to children of staying in the abuse could be spread more widely and if effective help to women could be better funded and politicized, this number would grow.
>
> (Mullender et al., 2002)

This is a very strong message to women that the only sensible choice for them as mothers is to leave their partners, due to their moral duty to protect their children. Supporting women is, then, about re-educating

them to become aware of 'the patriarchal forces that shape their identity and their interactions' (Hunt and Martin, 2001: 175), thus in our
case example the support offered to Kelly would focus on how her, and
Luke's, safety could best be ensured, but the discussion would be slanted
in favour of her separating from Mark. In order to do this safely, she
would probably need to take out an injunction against him visiting the
home, the locks and telephone number would need to be changed, she
may need an alarm, and the ongoing support of an aid worker. Contact
between Mark and Luke would need to be arranged at a safe place. The
problem of what should be done about Billy would be rather more difficult as his mother would have to decide whether to maintain or cease
his contact with Mark. The research is less clear here as it shows that
children are not necessarily as afraid of their fathers as their mothers may
be, and that many of them feel both love and fear (Mullender et al., 2002).

The re-education process is also a central feature of shifting the responsibility for the violence back on to the abuser, the Duluth model asserting
that the only safe, ethical option is for men to be seen in men-only
groups where their behaviour, attitudes and thinking can be challenged:

> Any interventions directed at stopping the violence would need to address
> the problem that men do not see it as a problem; do not believe it truly
> harms others; imagine that there are no effects beyond immediate
> injuries; and harbour the notion that once the violence stops everything
> is immediately solved, all is forgotten, everything repaired.
>
> (Dobash et al., 2000: 23)

The key words in working with violent men are 'retribution', 'reparation'
and 'reformation'. Although the challenges made to violent men are
meant to be 'respectfully retributive' rather than combative, the assumption is that it is necessarily both painful and challenging. Past violence
is remembered because 'one must look back at what was wrong and
harmful to others as a necessary part of moving forwards to the elimin-
ation of such behaviour' (Dobash et al., 2000: 51). The insights gained
from this way of working are meant to form the foundation of new
ways of thinking and acting. Both the CHANGE and LDVPP programmes
work in close cooperation with Women's Aid agencies and stress to the
female partners of men accepted on to the programme that the programme is for men only; that she is not responsible for his violent
behaviour; that there is no promise to keep the relationship together;
and that it is important for her to continue with her personal safety plans.
As Mark has not been convicted of an offence, he is not eligible for

re-socialization in a men-only group reinforced by legal sanctions. He may not be expected to make sufficient changes to his thinking if he voluntarily attended a programme where his attitudes and behaviour were not overtly challenged nor supported by the threat of sanctions. 'Couples work, anger management or mediation are not an appropriate setting in which to address men's abusive behaviour towards women' (Home Office, 2003b: 3.7)

3 Imposing and enforcing increasingly harsh legal sanctions on the abusers who fail to stop

The Duluth programme began by working with court-mandated offenders; these men, convicted of assault on their partners, are required to attend 12 weeks of counselling sessions followed by 12 weeks of Batterers' Anonymous, where their attendance is monitored and reported by probation officers. Three unexcused absences resulted in return to court, where they could have a jail sentence imposed or be mandated to continue in the Batterers' Anonymous group. Attendance on CHANGE and LDVPP programmes is also court mandated – as a condition of probation orders for a period of not less than six months. They must not only attend but also actively participate; refusal to do either being considered grounds for referring the men back to court for alternative or additional sanctions. Repetition of the behaviour in whatever form could constitute a breach of the order and precipitate a prison sentence or further programme attendance.

4 Creating policies and practices that provide specific deterrence for individuals and general deterrence for the wider community

Humphreys and colleagues (2000) conclude that domestic violence policies and guidelines are fundamental because they provide a consistent framework for the work to be undertaken, recommending the adoption of the practice principles and minimum standards set out by Respect (2000). Future policies and practices are spelled out in detail in *Living Without Fear* (Home Office, 2003a), including resource packs for schools; making communities safer through crime prevention initiatives and exploring how public transport can be made less dangerous, but perhaps the most effective deterrence has been the increased media focus on domestic violence and a cultural shift in attitudes. Popular television programmes depicting domestic violence as damaging and unacceptable have great potential to provide a most effective challenge to men's attitudes. This is identified by *Living Without Fear* as a key influence on social attitudes. We have small-scale evidence of this from our work with men who are violent: one man commented, 'it was getting embarrassing watching the telly. I thought, like, I do stuff like that', whilst another reported that his wife felt brave enough to challenge his behaviour when they were watching a soap opera in which a character was violent to his partner. Seeing their behaviour portrayed on television led both these men to refer themselves to the scheme. Indeed, we find that many boys and men are able to name their behaviour as 'sexist', which although requiring exploration illustrates a questioning of the notion of entitlement over women.

5 Achieve these aims by improving interagency communication and cooperation to secure a consistent and uniform response

As the primary considerations in work with men who are violent include: parallel work with women; building women's accounts into evaluations; increasing safety for women and children; and challenging and changing men's attitudes to violence while reducing the risk of re-offending (Humphreys et al., 2001), multi-agency work is essential. These agencies will include: the voluntary agencies who provide much of the support for women; child protection workers (for safety checks); and links with the police, probation and the courts so that there are consistent sanctions for men who fail to complete programmes (Mullender and Burton, 2001). Without a consistent focus between agencies which holds men responsible for their behaviour, says Respect (2000), women and children will be disempowered and lose access to options other than continuing to live with violence. It is worth noting that not all women's organizations welcome a multi-agency focus. Gupta (2003) is concerned that giving centrality to (male) community leaders can deligitimize more radical voices and disempower women in minority communities, suggesting that agencies need to recognize the often competing interests of differences within communities.

How feminist ideas inform risk assessment

Following on from the establishment of the Sex Offenders' Register, the Home Office discussed creating domestic violence registers in its consultation document *Safety and Justice* (June 2003b), and the Department of Health is planning a register of the names of people judged unsuitable to work with vulnerable adults (under the provisions of the Care

Standards Act 2000). Whilst the latter would prevent agencies from off-loading unsuitable staff (for a discussion, see Valios, 2003), a register of convicted domestic violence offenders is of more limited usefulness. Women who are already in a violent relationship know only too well that their partner is violent and women embarking on a new relationship would hardly be likely to check out their new partner. The simplest point at which risk assessment can be undertaken is when a vulnerable woman or child makes contact with the health services, not only for the treatment of actual injuries (Stanko, Crisp, Hale and Lucraft, 1998) but also because domestic violence has diverse and wide-ranging effects on women's health. Domestic violence has been shown to be linked to anxiety, depression, and sleeping and eating disorders (Butler, 1995; Campbell, 2002), low birth rates and miscarriage (Johnson and Sacco, 1995; Mirlees-Black, 1995), and psychological symptoms such as intrusive memories, nightmares, and low self esteem (Richardson and Feder, 1996). The World Health Organization cites domestic violence as one of the principle factors in gender inequality (2000). A substantial majority of women experiencing domestic violence not only seek help from the health services (Abrahams, 2001), but the research shows that they expect health professionals to bring up the subject, take time to listen and give advice (Schornstein, 1997).

The influence of feminist analyses of the abuse of male power is evident in the literature on Accident and Emergency (A and E) unit nursing (see, for example, Davies and Edwards, 1999; Mortlock, 1996). The research shows that not only do women seek medical attention for physical injuries sustained as a result of domestic violence but they also account for at least one in four suicide attempts by women (Abrahams, 2001), thus A and E staff are in a strategic position to make an early risk assessment, including elder abuse. Kingston and Penhale (1995) suggest that the A and E nurse offers the older woman victim a private interview where she can be asked such questions as: 'we know that violence is a problem for many women in their lives. Is it a problem for you in any way?' Shepherd (1998) suggests that casualty department computers could be standardized so that an annual report on violence could be compiled to complement the British Crime Survey.

As Kelly did not suffer physical injury and her experience of domestic violence would not have been picked up at the antenatal clinic, the person best positioned to assess risk is her health visitor. Women say that they would most easily turn to their health visitor for advice (Abrahams, 2001) and, like the midwife, she has the opportunity to spend time with women and listen, ask intimate questions, and undertake a physical examination

(Hunt and Martin, 2001). A problem for these professionals is what to do with Mark. If he agrees to attend a programme, he is ineligible for those most approved in the theoretical approach outlined in this chapter due to the voluntary nature of the circumstances. Schornstein (1997) cautions that there is no quick fix and often significant dilemmas; whilst the woman should be given options, she is the only person who must face the prospect of divorce, loss of her home, child custody battles and the fear of retaliatory violence. Ensuring safety is not without costs to the children either; the research shows that children appreciate the help of professionals, but they suffer many losses once they accompany their mothers to refuges (Mullender et al., 2002). These losses range from separation from familiar objects, such as toys and photographs, to separation from significant others, such as friends and fathers. Thus early risk assessment does not necessarily make decision making any easier for victims of domestic violence.

Another problem for health professionals is that of being saturated by change; required by the Department of Health to become knowledgeable about, and intervene effectively in, cases of domestic violence (Department of Health, 2004), their workloads are increased at a time when the health service is already coping with a massive extension of its role in many areas. Their vulnerability in responding to domestic violence is well documented (Frost, 1997; Ramsey, Richardson et al., 2002). Schornstein (1997) recommends that health professionals recognize that women who have experienced domestic violence will not be 'perfect patients', so a change of expectations and definition of success is needed, such as looking for small victories. She also cautions against the danger of imposing assessments used in the United States to identify either women at risk of being killed, or of killing her partner (see, for example, Hart and Gondolf, 1994) as these assessments are based on retrospective research identifying the factors associated with homicide and relate to correlates not to causative factors (see, for example, Campbell, 1986, 1995).

Risk assessment at later stages of the violence can also be problematic for women and children unless they are truly offered choices and appropriate support is offered. Research into child protection and domestic violence shows that assessment not infrequently restricts women's choices. Scourfield (2003) found that social workers expected more of non-abusing women than they did of violent men and that if a woman failed to make the 'right' choice, that is, to protect her children, she risked having her children's names placed on the child protection register if she didn't agree to leave a violent partner. This can be couched in terms of needing her 'consciousness raising' in order to accept the essentialist

explanations for male violence before she can 'move on' and truly a
the reality of the situation. Paradoxically this approach considers a woman
to have distorted beliefs about the nature of men, that 'blame' her for her
lack of enlightenment, and consider her 'in denial' if she questions this
explanation of her specific situation.

Interventions for women and children

Interventions premised on the principle that men's violence to known
women is largely about the misuse of power and control in the context
of male dominance are necessarily separate and asymmetrical for victims
and offenders; and work with women is prioritized to prevent the risk
that developing men's programmes may direct attention and resources
away from women's projects (Mullender and Burton, 2001). As services
for women have been largely provided by voluntary women's organizations, which are chronically under-funded, this section will begin
with interventions that support women. The voluntary sector has
played a major role in the development of support services for women
experiencing violence because of the failure of professional organizations to address this issue in a way which meets women's needs; they
seek help from other professionals only when they have exhausted other
sources of help and the violence has become frequent and severe
(Dobash et al., 1995). The first step for any professional organization is
to 'name' the problem by asking about it routinely and monitoring it
effectively; Mullender and Burton (2001) regard this as Good Practice
Indicator 2.

As noted above interventions for children need to avoid heavy-handed
child protection approaches which can result in both children (and their
mothers) having to make harsh choices about which parent (partner)
to stay in touch with, as well as the dangers of incurring other losses.
Refuges recognize children's needs, promoting particularly play and other
child-centred activities to provide a setting for promoting mutual support
between children, and between children and their mothers (Debbonaire,
1994). Play, outings and activities also provide children with a more
relaxed and informal opportunity for children to express their fears and
problems (see also, Bannister, 2000); the opportunity to be listened to
being a major finding of the research (Mullender et al., 2002). Refuges
often provide a specialist children's support worker who also ensures
that children's rights are respected and their lives are disrupted as little
as possible by maintaining school places wherever possible.

Arranging safe contact between women and their partners, and between children and their fathers, is also a major consideration. Mediation is inappropriate, and even dangerous and abusive to women, in situations where mediators do not ask about domestic violence (Hester, Pearson and Radford, 1997). The way in which men use contact with their children to continue controlling their partners is well documented (Hester, Pearson and Harwin, 1999; Humphreys, 2000), so all agencies concerned with contact need to make effective safety plans. Refuges can provide a 'safe' space through anonymity within the community (although it is almost impossible to maintain any secrecy) and through rules about the exclusion of men from the premises, as well as providing useful data to inform safe contact where appropriate.

Women's organizations, particularly refuges, are evaluated positively by women (for an overview, see Mullender, 2002), so the lessons learned from these organizations are vital to the successful development of interventions. Direct work with women who have experienced violence needs to recognize the typical process through which help is sought and bear this in mind when talking with women. The Women's Aid network offers a range of services to enable women to determine their own futures, in their own time. This may involve a stay in a refuge, which is offered on an open-door policy, so any woman seeking refuge, for however long or short a time, can be referred on to any refuge with space. During her stay, she will be provided with legal advice about her rights and assisted to secure permanent accommodation. At the same time she will be given opportunities to take part in the running of the refuge. Should she choose to stay with her partner, she will receive help and advice from a support worker within the home, a service that would be helpful for Kelly. These services are in stark contrast to typical local authority residential provision with its waiting lists, 'gate keeping' through detailed assessment procedures, lack of flexibility about length of stay, and paternalism. Mullender (2002) argues that because the problem of domestic violence thrives in isolation and intimidation behind closed doors, groupwork is the most powerful way of challenging its impact. Although she acknowledges that individual feminist counselling can be helpful, she views groupwork as more effective; groups have the capacity to aid healing and growth because of their educational content. They focus on helping women understand that the abuse is not their own fault and that the abuser must take responsibility for his behaviour. Naming the abuse enables women to rebuild self-esteem and independent life; using women's own stories highlights not only the causes and effects of men's controlling tactics and women's enforced submission, but also builds on their survival strategies. Group work with abused women evaluates well in the United States (see, for example, Tutty, Bidgood and Rothery, 1993) although there is no evaluation of women's experiences and satisfaction when they drop out of such groups. Our experience is that women do value the support they are given by Women's Aid workers, but that they also bend the rules to increase their options; for example, they frequently continue to see their partners on 'the quiet', despite expectations that they should sever all contact (for more details, see Milner, 2004). Those who have dropped out of groups give as their reasons that the group discussion is stuck in the past, a typical comment being: 'it was as though I'd never left. Five years, and they were still going on about the same old things'.

Interventions for men

Interventions for men who are violent to their partners are basically educational groupwork programmes aimed at re-socializing these men. Using broadly cognitive behavioural techniques, the men's attitudes and beliefs about how men and women should be – their root expectations – are challenged. A programme curriculum is designed around these attitudes and beliefs, divided into modules, with weekly sessions of a minimum of two hours. The Camberwell Domestic Violence Programme typically takes 22 two and half-hour sessions to complete, not counting initial assessment and final evaluation sessions. Some programmes are based on a 'two tier' system whereby a man can progress from a physical abuse group to a non-physical abuse one if he has not been physically violent for the duration of the first group. Such a length of time is considered necessary for a man to make a 'difficult journey from abuse to intimacy' (Teft, 1999). Equally he can be asked to repeat the first group should he become physically violent during the second group. An example of a typical curriculum is that of the Lothian Domestic Violence Prevention Project, which devotes three to five sessions to the following modules:

■ Power and control wheel

■ Minimizing, denying and blaming

■ Using children

■ Using male privilege

■ Using economic abuse

■ Using isolation

■ Using emotional abuse

■ Using intimidation

■ Using coercion and threats/physical violence (five weeks)

(Dobash et al., 2000)

Men are screened for suitability: they must acknowledge that they have been violent, indicate willingness to participate actively and accept that their partners will be informed of their progress or, more importantly, their lack of progress. This latter Good Progress Indicator is not always held to consistently in practice (Mullender and Burton, 2001). Programmes vary as to whether they are willing to accept men with alcohol or substance misuse problems.

Each session is organized in such a way as to decrease men's overt resistance, this client group being considered to be 'notoriously manipulative and evasive' (Teft, 1999) and, therefore, likely to minimize and deny their behaviour (see, for example, the experience of Johnstone, 2000; Jukes, 1996). Blaming others, such as their partners, their own experiences of abuse or alcohol, is expected behaviour in need of challenging, the Duluth model explaining this in terms of the psychology of colonialism – the dominant group needs to find justification for its need to dominate (Pence and Paymar, 1993). Hearn, too, warns of the dangers of 'separating' violence from the person: 'this is itself part of the form of violence and part of the way in which it is perpetuated – as being a thing that can be talked about separately' (1989: 196).

In our case example, Mark would be expected to attend the group sessions (if mandated to) and to accept the premises on which this is based. His non-gendered explanations for his behaviour would be challenged as minimizing and denying his male power, the assumption being that his motivations are based on the male propensity to control women, whether he recognizes this or not. His behaviour would be framed within this construction and he would have to accept these explanations in order to 'progress'. There is a strong possibility that if Mark raises questions about the applicability of this model to the totality and complexity of his behaviour, then he will be seen to be minimizing his responsibility. Service-user explanations for their behaviours are to be treated with suspicion if they do not conform to the theoretical assumptions.

The focus of the group work always remains on violence as intentional as a means to obtain and maintain power and control. This means that women who are violent to their male or female partner and men who are violent to their male partners are ineligible for these programmes. A central principle of CHANGE, for example, is that violence within same-sex relationships or from women to men is neither the same as – nor symmetrically opposite to – men's violence to women. In the case of the latter, violence is considered to be the violence of resistance. Respect (2000) takes the view that projects that do not have a clear understanding of the different dynamics at work should not undertake perpetrator work with women or perpetrators in same-sex relationships.

Dobash and colleagues claim that these programmes are 'generally acknowledged to be one of the most successful community-based projects for violent men anywhere in the world' (2000: 48), but the research shows the results to be rather more equivocal (for an overview, see Mullender, 2002). Drop-out rates are high; Burton, Regan and Kelly, (1989) reported a drop-out rate of up to 70 per cent in self-referrals; Dobash and colleagues (2000) experienced a drop-out rate of 50 per cent in those mandated to attend, with a higher drop-out rate of younger men and self-referrers; Mullender and Burton (2001) found that some groups had completion rates of only 30 per cent; and Taft and colleagues (2001) found that race was the strongest predictor of drop-out rates, particularly black men. There is some evidence that the groupwork process rather than the educational format obtains the best results; having an opportunity to 'talk things through', was statistically linked with a third of women who reported a 'great extent' of change in their partners (Gondolf, 1998); in other words, when the central working hypothesis of challenging is not rigidly held to. Similarly, findings emerging in sex offender treatment programmes show a confrontational style to be negatively related to behavioural change (Marshall et al., 2003); and the M.A.P Initiative (2003) found that, freed from a confrontational dynamic, men were able to see that the victim bears no responsibility for the abusive behaviour without the need to talk about their own victimization.

Limitations of feminist approaches to domestic violence

Like attachment theory in child protection work, a feminist theory of domestic violence has become the dominant discourse across agencies working with domestic violence. It had been established as the dominant definition, based on men's expectations of power and control over their female partners, as Good Practice Indicator 1: 'it is essential to work within an agreed definition of domestic violence and its causes ... [to] avoid sliding into a more blurred model of anger management' (Mullender and Burton, 2001: 261). The privileging of one definition of domestic violence has had major benefits to women's safety, but it has also had the effect of providing limited and essentialist explanations of how women and men should be. As we have seen above, this necessarily undermines the central principle of supporting women in making their own choices. Women do not usually want to leave their partners (Lipchik and Kubicki, 1996); and only one-third of them want the offender arrested. Of the others, some act out of fear of retaliatory violence but most do not want the relationship or family to break up and consider the sanctions imposed inappropriate and undesirable (Hoyle, 1998). They call the police more for help with the immediate incident rather than as a desire for prosecution, so a blanket approach to prosecution (based on an assumption that women retract allegations through fear) is unhelpful. As one woman told us, 'it's awful. It's like the police are running my family. I'd rather have a beating.'

There is an irony, too, in the reality of programmes for men. These have only limited success in changing the attitudes of a population that is largely white and economically disadvantaged (Scourfield and Drakeford, 2002) who are the very people most likely to construct a masculine identity that is anti-social (Howell and Pugliesi, 1998). Handing over power to male-dominated agencies to manage the violence of subordinated males can unintentionally reinforce gendered power relations through confirming that male authority is natural and expected. Jenkins (1996) refers to this as operating a therapeutic tyranny.

In producing it own universalizing discourse (Blakemore, 1999), this feminist perspective has prioritized heterosexual, white women's voices at the expense of distorting and silencing the voices of all people who experience domestic violence. This has been increasingly recognized within postmodern feminist theorizing. Research shows that violence is not necessarily asymmetrical:

■ Women do abuse men (Aitken and Griffin, 1996; Mirlees-Black, 1999).

■ Women-on-male violence can be as severe as male-on-female (McKeowan, Haase and Pratschke, 2001).

■ Women can minimize and deny their violence in much the same way as men do (Henning, Jones and Holdford, 2005).

- The incidence of same-sex violence is equal to that of male-on-female violence (Chandler and Taylor, 1995; Island and Letellier, 1991; Leventhal and Lundy, 1999; Renzetti, 1992).

- Lesbian violence can be more severe than heterosexual violence (Turell, 2000), perhaps because of lesbian fusion and isolation (Waldron-Haugurd, Gratch and Magruder, 1997).

Faced with these forms of violence in practice, workers whose assessments and interventions are based on working hypotheses about the misuse of male power are helpless to act.

> How do we name woman's behaviour, when there are voices saying we should be supporting her? And if you do name, acknowledge the abuse, confront the women with their [abusive] behaviour, they leave and you've lost them.
>
> (Fitzroy, 2002)

An example of how current understandings of violence limit responses is a referral to a domestic violence project. A lesbian couple was being extremely violent towards each other including performing this in front of their children. The response in a male-on-female situation would have been an automatic referral to the police and social services, based on the potential harm to those children in witnessing this violence. However, the confusion created by who the protagonists were (women-as-aggressors) meant that this procedure was not followed, potentially increasing the danger to the children.

In terms of intervention, Cayouette (1999) found that lesbians were resistant to groupwork services predicated on challenging (which as we have seen is the dominant approach to domestic violence), thus raising questions about the applicability of current services. Also we have found that in our direct practice with girls who sexually abuse other children they are often either over- or under-reacted to due to people's struggles to 'fit' their behaviour into theoretical (and emotional) frameworks of sexual aggression. Particular readings of feminist approaches are thrown into disarray when the assumptions about how women behave are challenged by women's actual behaviours.

Men who are abused by men are particularly isolated because their abusers can use the homophobic context as an additional strategy of control and domination (Russo, 1999). HIV positive men are even more vulnerable: 'who's going to want a sick old fairy like you?' (Hanson and

Maroney, 1999: 105). The different masculinities in society make global assumptions about male violence problematic. Simply because there is a dominant cultural story about maleness does not make this an absolute for every man, and there are consequences of holding such assumptions about men. Heteronormativity ensures that men are graded hierarchically according to norms of how they are expected to be, with consequences for not being a 'real' man. For example, research shows that the working hypotheses held by the police about the victims of domestic violence lead them to under-record incidents of violence against men: 'the police do not tend to see domestic violence against men as a serious crime, but rather see male victims, if they see them at all, as rather pathetic figures of fun' (Grady, 2002: 96). One man we worked with told us that the police responded to his 999 call with amusement, telling him he was 'a bit of a wimp', despite the fact that his female partner had thrown him down the stairs to prevent him from leaving the home whilst she continued to batter him. Sullivan's work, based on counselling with male survivors of sexual assault, identified that 'Feminist theory ... hides male victims and females as perpetrators' (2005: 84) through emphasizing a limited notion of male power and female powerlessness, with severe consequences for men who have been subjected to domestic violence.

The major limitation of a strictly gendered analysis of domestic violence is that it assumes a stability of gender identity across ethnicity, place and time that does not exist (for a detailed discussion, see Mangan, 2003). For example, Yick's study (2000) of 262 Chinese American families found that, contrary to the feminist literature, gender role beliefs were not related to violence. Margolin, John and Foo (1998) found that negative life events, marital dissatisfaction and employment status were as important variables as attitudes towards the acceptability of violence, that they fluctuated over time as well as co-occurring, with poor employment status tending to increase violence most. A shift in women's economic power is likely to have more protective power against men's violence than any other factor.

Using feminist interventions effectively

As there is a danger that operating from this model may lead professionals to develop their own dominating practices, it is important that they remember that a principle laid down by Respect (2000) is that of applying the principles in their own lives, both in and out of work. The advocacy wheel (similar to the Equality Wheel, Figure 5.2) described by

Hunt and Martin (2001: 153) includes respect for a woman's autonomy: the right to make decisions in her own time, when she is ready, and recognizing that she is an expert in her own life. Thus whatever hypothesis a worker holds about domestic violence, it is important to hear and value the individual service-user's perspectives. Kelly's current reality is that she contributes in some way to the arguments with Mark and this story can be respected at the same time as she is offered support to keep herself safe. To tell her she ought to leave Mark may well be the safest option, but it also tells her she is a fool for choosing Mark in the first place and a bigger fool for allowing him to separate her from her family. Undermining her experience of her life is not a sensible way to set about building a therapeutic alliance.

Similarly respect is the key word in working with men who are violent. Dobash and colleagues (2000) emphasize the need to be respectfully retributive and this involves a delicate balance. It does not mean vigorously challenging every utterance as this is counter-productive as well as disrespectful. In a counselling session with the authors about his violence, Gary complained bitterly about his probation officer's 'attitude' to him. Gary was violence free and back with his wife, who was feeling safe enough to give vent to old resentments; a situation that Gary was not enjoying, but one he felt he deserved after what he had done to her earlier. He began to explain this to his probation officer with the statement, 'I'm still having a bit of bother with my bird …', only to be interrupted with, 'listen to you! Bird! Can you hear yourself?' As his probation officer had also kept him waiting for the appointment without explanation or apology, Gary found this treatment disrespectful and announced that he would 'just sit there, and nod and smile in future'. Challenging does not need to be so combative; it can be surreptitious, gentle and engaging whilst still exerting a powerful impact.

Equally, the emphasis on always challenging men's minimization of their violence does not necessarily mean that they are inherent liars. They often have good instrumental reasons for not admitting all immediately, not least being the possible legal and financial consequences. It is not helpful to view men who are violent as 'notoriously manipulative and evasive', as Teft (1999: 12) does. Such a view makes direct work very difficult as how could someone ever be trusted? There is no reason why workers should not be polite, punctual and considerate, modelling the behaviours they are hoping to inculcate. This would also include paying attention to the physical environment in which they are seen. As the National Task Force on Violence Against Social Care Staff research shows (Department of Health, 2004), creating a good care environment reduces the level of assaults on staff, in which male social workers and probation officers are eight times more likely to be abused than other workers.

A further way in which the power and control model can be used effectively is by remembering that domestic violence is linked to other violences through patriarchy. As we noted earlier, war is an extreme form of patriarchal power, collective violence is associated with increases in other civil violence (WHO, 2004) so men's experiences of violence are relevant to their behaviour in their families. Allocating funds to men's programmes which enable them to live more peaceful lives adds to women's safety and ought not necessarily be ruled out on the grounds that they take resources away from services for women.

Summary

- Feminist thinking views men's violence as the exercise of male power and control over women and children.

- Challenging men about their misuse of power and supporting women is seen as the central feature of professional practice.

- Supporting women is intended to promote choice but often has the effect of limiting women's choices to that of leaving their male partners, especially where there are children in the home.

- Challenging men is based on the premise that men deny and minimize their violent behaviour, therefore they are viewed as needing to be re-educated in male only groups.

- As much domestic violence begins when a woman is pregnant, the role of midwives and health visitors is increasingly seen as important in safeguarding women and children from violence.

- Interventions based on challenging men have high drop-out rates, especially with self-referrers.

- Feminist approaches can prioritize heterosexual, white women's voices at the expense of other victims, such as gay and heterosexual men and lesbian women.

To aid critical reflection we invite you to consider the frameworks and questions outlined below.

Statement of Principles and Minimum Standards
(from Respect, 2000)

Principles and Philosophy for Working with Men's Violence to Partners and Ex-Partners

1. Domestic Violence is unacceptable and must be challenged at all times.

...

- Physical violence includes all forms of aggressive or unwanted touch, including sexual violence and witnessing physical violence.

- Non-physical violence includes verbal, social, racist, mental or emotional violence, neglect, economic and spiritual violence

Although only physical, sexual and some forms of racist violence are illegal and attract criminal sanctions, other forms of violence can also have very serious and lasting effects on one's sense of self, wellbeing and autonomy.

2. Men's violence to partners and ex-partners is largely about the misuse of power and control in the context of male dominance.

RESPECT believes that all attitude and behaviour change work with men must be done with an awareness of the social context of men's violence to partners and ex-partners. ... [O]ur social history has largely been one of male dominance in all spheres of public life, reinforced by and allowing male dominance in the family. Gender socialization of girls and boys to accept and continue gender roles has further reinforced male dominance. In this social context until recent times men's violence to family members was largely hidden and private and surrounded by shame and secrecy and this is still often the case. ... People outside the family have been reluctant to intervene, and the response of the police and the legal system has often further disempowered women by failing to offer them the equal protection of the law.

3. Violence within same sex relationships or from women to men is neither the same as – nor symmetrically opposite to – men's violence to women.

RESPECT believes that ... unequal power relations account for the fact that the vast majority of domestic violence is from men towards women rather than vice versa. For this reason the primary focus of RESPECT and the work of its members is men's violence towards women.

RESPECT is aware that in the minority of cases, however, domestic violence does not reflect conventional power relations. ...

In the case of women's violence to men in relationships, RESPECT takes the view that this violence runs counter to conventional power relations. The violence may be the violence of resistance – where a woman who does not hold the balance of power in the relationship and is not the primary abuser, occasionally fights back. This is not 'domestic violence' in the sense of the systematic abuse of power by the woman over the man. Or, the power relationship between the man and the woman may run opposite to societal gender relations and the woman both holds the power, and systematically abuses that power.

RESPECT believes that all of the above cases must be treated differently to each other and differently to male to female domestic violence because they may differ in any or all of the following respects:

- They are not similarly supported by conventional power structures.

- They will not be experienced as the same by the persons involved (in the same sense as racist violence does not constitute the same experience for perpetrator or victim as violence between persons of the same ethnicity).

- There may be different access for victims to social networks of support.

- There may be different institutional responses to the violence and different institutional resources available for both perpetrators and victims.

RESPECT takes the view that these perpetrators and victims should therefore not be in groups with perpetrators and victims of men's violence to women. Projects that do not have a clear understanding of the different dynamics at work should not undertake perpetrator work with women or perpetrators in same-sex relationships.

RESPECT recognizes that further exploration needs to be done in order to develop appropriate and specific interventions along with minimum standards for working with domestic violence in these different groups.

4. Men are responsible for their use of violence.

The use of violence is a choice for which each man is responsible and for which he should be held accountable. Although a man may have been socialized to believe in his right to control women and children, or even have been trained to use violence, he can still choose to take responsibility and learn non-violent ways of relating. Some men who seek assistance with stopping their use of violence have also experienced violence themselves and may use this as a justification for their own violence. Workers need to keep separate at all times the issues relating to a man's own experience of being violated and his responsibility for his own use of violence against others. Any excusing, condoning or minimizing of this use of violence on the basis of his own pain and difficulties reinforces his use of violence rather than challenging it.

5. Men can change.

Men can change their attitudes and behaviour and learn positive, equal and non-violent ways of relating. ... [M]en who use violence ... report a range of negative effects for themselves. These include shame, guilt, hating themselves for what they do and frustration at not having the kinds of relationships with their partners and families they would like to have. Often they feel powerless themselves and use violence to try to increase their sense of power. ...

Workers can challenge men with the nature and consequences of their violence and the fact that they choose to use it. They can then invite men to take responsibility to stop using violence and learn non-violent ways of relating with others. Projects should embark on this work with an active commitment to wider social change to end oppression on the basis of gender.

6. We are part of a community response, which needs to be consistent and integrated at all levels.

RESPECT supports the ongoing work of many people working for change at all levels. This includes work to challenge and change gender socialization, to provide services to support and empower women and children, to improve community awareness about domestic violence and to improve the response to domestic violence on the part of health and community support agencies and the police and legal system. The long term prevention of domestic violence requires a clear and consistent message from all individuals and social agencies that domestic violence is unacceptable and will not be tolerated.

Men need to know that their use of violence will not be condoned by anyone and that everyone will respond to protect the rights of others to safety and autonomy. ... Women and children need to know that they will be taken seriously and that their rights will be enforced. ...

There should be a consistent focus between agencies which holds men accountable for their violence and expects them to address their behaviour. Without this, women and children will be further disempowered and lose access to options other than continuing to live with violence.

7. Everyone affected by domestic violence should have access to support services which address their needs.

...

Projects and practitioners must demonstrate a commitment to anti-oppressive practice and respecting difference. Projects should have an active commitment to meeting the needs of the communities they serve. Projects should have a commitment to child protection and have an active child protection policy and procedures, ensuring that the needs of children are incorporated into all aspects of their work.

8. Promoting positive relationships.

In addition to working to prevent the negative and destructive behaviours and beliefs associated with men who perpetrate domestic violence, RESPECT believes all work with perpetrators and victims of domestic violence must actively promote an alternative, positive and constructive model of human relationships, based on the following principles:

- Respect for the autonomy and self-determination of all individuals.

- Belief in the fundamental equality of all human beings.

- Willingness to negotiate and compromise.

- Acceptance of power as a shared and negotiated commodity.

- Determination to seek and apply non-violent ways of relating.

- Refusal to accept, tolerate or practice beliefs or behaviours which breach the above principles.

Questions

- What models 'gave cause for anxiety to activists and practitioners', and why?

- What is the evidence for the claim that the Domestic Abuse Prevention Programme is 'best practice'?

- If you were devising a groupwork programme for men who are violent to known women, how would you decide on the content and length of each module? What evidence have you to support your choice?

CHAPTER 6

'Mad and Bad': Mentally Disordered Offenders

Increasingly mental health services have had to engage with responding to and managing violence and the potential for violence with people that they work with. This has been influenced by political and media representations of violence associated with those who have mental health problems, with legislative initiatives that have raised questions about civil liberties and how we view people who commit violent offences. The responsibility placed on practitioners in mental health services to prevent violence by their service users is a taxing one, and these demands can be impossible to meet in any absolute way.

Traditionally violence has been explained, predicted and managed within mental health services in terms of the links established between violent behaviour and specific mental disorders. Thus the emphasis has been on the accurate diagnosis of the relevant disorder so that treatments, especially those involving drug regimes, can be delivered effectively. Although many violent offenders are diagnosed as psychopaths (now more commonly referred to as personality disordered persons), they are rarely offered inpatient psychiatric care on the grounds of their 'untreatability', although the category has been retained for the assessment and prediction of seriously violent offenders whose management requires long-term incarceration in secure units (Ramon, 1986; Rose, 1985). Under current mental health law, patients are defined and treated differently depending on which category of mental disorder is diagnosed. Under current legislative proposals in the United Kingdom, the government proposes to introduce one broad definition of mental disorder, which means that personality disordered people will no longer be excluded from compulsory treatment on the grounds that they are 'untreatable' (Department of Health, 2004; National Institute for Mental Health in England [NIMHE], 2003). This involves a radical modernization and reform of mental health services which will challenge much established practice, particularly how mental health professionals assess the risk of violence both for people before the courts and in treatment. The consult-ation on the Bill raised questions that have led to a reconsideration of the content; however, it is likely that key elements will be retained. There are differences in the way Mark will be regarded under the current and proposed 'systems' but, as it is unlikely that new practice will be imple-mented smoothly (and there are commonalities in theoretical under-standing), this chapter discusses the implications of both diagnostic systems in terms of his access to mental health services.

Traditional approaches

Despite advances in molecular genetics and the identification of neuro-chemical pathways, it has not proved possible to delineate the psy-chopathology of mental illness, yet mental disorders are regarded as discrete entities that can be defined categorically into distinct conditions with recognizable symptoms (Everett, Donaghy and Feaver, 2003). This is largely because of the historical prominence of the medical profession within mental health practice, although it is increasingly recognized that the pharmaceutical industry exerts a strong influence on the identification of diagnostic categories (see, for example, Shorter and Tyrer, 2003). Diagnostic definitions are made through scientific consensus by a small committee of experts in the World Health Organization and the American Psychiatric Association, with the aim of achieving more precision in diag-nostic methods for effective treatment, and to allow more accurate com-munication between professionals (Gibb and Macpherson, 2000). There are two systems of classification currently in use, the International Classification of Disease (ICD-10) and the Diagnostic and Statistical Manual of Mental Disorders – Fourth Edition (DSM-IV). The former is the more commonly used in clinical practice in the United Kingdom, but both will be briefly outlined here as the DSM-IV is frequently referred to in the psychiatric literature and influences research and theory. Diagnostic categories also influence those examined for psychopathology in psycho-logical tests, such as the Minnesota Multi-Phasic Personality Inventory-2 (MMPI-2) and the Millom Clinical Multi-Axial Inventory – third edition (MCMI-III). The former is designed to differentiate between those with a psychopathology as compared with 'normal' individuals, providing 'a broad-based test to assess a number of major patterns of personality and emotional disorders' (Butcher et al., 1989: 2); the latter aims to pro-vide an integrated model of functioning considering the behavioural, cognitive, interpersonal and psychodynamic realms of expressions of psychopathology. Both inventories are commonly used in the psychological assessments of violent offenders requested by criminal courts prior to sentencing and family courts where decisions have to be made about the risk the offender poses to his/her family.

DSM-IV

The DSM-IV defines a mental disorder as:

> a clinically significant behaviour or psychological syndrome or pattern that occurs in an individual and that is associated with present distress (e.g. a painful symptom) or disability (i.e. impairment in one or more important areas of functioning) or with a significantly increased risk of suffering death, pain, disability, or an important loss of freedom.
>
> (DSM-IV, American Psychiatric Association, 1994: xxi)

The DSM-IV uses a multi-axial diagnostic system in which the practitioner uses five axes to ensure that information needed for treatment planning, prediction of outcome and research is provided:

Axis I   Clinical disorders and other conditions that may be the focus of attention (psychiatric diagnoses).

Axis II   Personality disorders and mental retardation (developmental problems).

Axis III   General medical conditions (concurrent physical factors).

Axis IV   Psychosocial and environmental problems (social stressors).

Axis V   Global assessment of functioning (the degree of the effect of the disorder on adaptive functioning).

Thus the DSM-IV attempts to bring in the best features of both phenomenological and psychodynamic diagnostic systems, allowing a holistic understanding of an individual's difficulties resulting from the psychiatric disorder. Assessment on Axis V is important to treatment planning, particularly the assessment of the likelihood of treatment success, so past as well as current functioning is often reported.

Even with the small amount of information available in our scenario, Mark meets the criteria for several disorders on Axis I. For example, he meets sufficient of the criteria for a diagnosis of *conduct disorder* developing in his childhood to have been made: he is aggressive towards people in that he bullies, threatens and intimidates others (shouting and swearing) and he has used a weapon (the hammer); he is destructive towards property (hammering on the door); and the disturbance causes clinically significant impairment in social, academic and occupational functioning (he is unable to hold down a job or get on with his in-laws). Equally, he could be examined under 'other conditions that may be the focus of clinical attention', such as V61.10 (partner relational problems), or V61.12 (physical abuse of partner). Other disorders on Axis I that are linked to violence include schizophrenia and substance abuse. People with schizophrenia are slightly more likely to be violent than other members of the population (Walsh, Buchanan and Fahey, 2002), and the research shows that the frequency of interpersonal violence and criminal damage rises after the onset of the illness (Taylor, 1993). Prins (1995) suggests that although the incidence of schizophrenia in relation to violent crime is low, it may be of considerable importance in particular cases, especially where there are delusions of a sexual jealousy nature. Substance-related disorders are closely linked with violence (Royal College of Psychiatrists, 1996), and drug use also increases mental illness (Rey and Tennant, 2002), so it would be important to assess Mark for psychotic symptoms (perhaps his explosive behaviour), and ask him about any drug use.

However it may be that Mark's behaviour is indicative of an enduring pattern or personality trait that is sufficiently inflexible and maladaptive that he meets the diagnostic criteria on Axis II for personality disorder, particularly those on Cluster B: anti-social, borderline and histrionic personality disorders. Whiston (2000) suggests that where the symptoms and behaviour appear florid, the practitioner would be directed to Axis I disorders, but where the problem appears to be more pervasive, long-standing and trait-like, then Axis II disorders would be examined – although under this system of classification it is possible to diagnose on both axes. Symptom disorder and personality disorder co-morbidity is common, but the former is considered more 'treatable' than the latter, largely because personality disorders involve enduring patterns of behaviour and thus personality disordered people find it difficult to perform the role of patient because they 'see the maladaptation as part of themselves and see the situation as just being the way it is' (Whiston, 2000: 301). As we noted above, personality disorder is strongly linked with violent behaviour (Royal College of Psychiatrists, 1996; Tardiff, 1989,) but a diagnosis of this disorder for Mark would also include a gloomy prognosis for treatment success: since by definition it is an enduring state, how would his 'recovery' be established?

ICD-10

This uniaxial system is more flexible than the multi-axial DSM-IV system and its descriptive approach is more in keeping with clinical practice. Operational criteria are only used in the research version, but guidelines leading to confident diagnoses are given in the standard version. There are several subgroups of personality disorders within the ICD-10, but all share the same diagnostic guidelines, with the symptoms tending to appear in late childhood or adolescence and lasting into adulthood. The following general guidelines have been developed to assess the nature of the personality disorder:

a. markedly disharmonious attitudes and behaviour, involving usually several areas of functioning, e.g. affectivity, arousal, impulse control, ways of perceiving and thinking, and style of relating to others;

b. the abnormal behaviour pattern is enduring, of long standing, and not limited to episodes of mental illness;

c. the abnormal behaviour pattern is pervasive and clearly maladaptive to a broad range of personal and social situations;

d. the above manifestations always appear during childhood or adolescence and continue into adulthood;

e. the disorder leads to considerable personal distress, but this may only become apparent late in its course;

f. the disorder is usually, but not invariably, associated with significant problems in occupational and social performance

In the specific sub-types of personality disorder it is necessary to identify at least three of the collection of symptoms associated with them.

Under this classificatory system, Mark meets the criteria for an Emotionally Unstable Personality Disorder – Impulsive Type (F60.30): a marked tendency to act impulsively without consideration of the consequences (what Fonagy, 2003, refers to as a failure of 'mentalization – the ability to understand others' subjective experiences'); affective instability; minimal planning ahead; and outbursts of intense anger leading to violence, easily precipitated when impulsive acts are criticized by others. Given the wide range of behaviours that could fall within this category, there are different claims about prevalence rates: Sims (2003: 353) comments that 'fortunately this personality abnormality does not occur very frequently in clinical practice', although Norton (1999) estimates that 10 per cent of the adult population has a diagnosable personality disorder, 4 per cent severely so.

In addition to the above, if Mark is viewed as having intense and unstable relationships that cause repeated emotional crises, excessive efforts to avoid abandonment and a chronic sense of emptiness or lack of purpose then he may be diagnosed with Borderline Personality Disorder (F60.31) and may also show indications of Explosive and Aggressive Personality Disorder with his violent outbursts. Mark may also meet the criteria for Dissocial Personality Disorder (F60.2), where he has 'a gross and persistent attitude of irresponsibility and disregard for social norms, rules and obligations; an incapacity to maintain enduring relationships, though having no difficulty in establishing them; very low tolerance to frustration and a low threshold for discharge of aggression, including violence'. Persistent irritability is also an associated feature of this condition.

In considering these conditions, we reflected on our own potential for being diagnosed with some of the above disorders and found ourselves to a greater or lesser extent, in different times and places, dependant on who would be making the judgement and how the thresholds were decided upon, at risk of such categorizations. Most personality disorders take time to diagnose and the 'snapshot' diagnosis required under Mental Health legislation, with a patient whom the psychiatrist may well not have met before, makes the assessment of an enduring disorder particularly problematic. We would invite readers to consider times when they may have been seen to behave in ways that would lead others to view them as potentially 'disordered'.

In their practice guidelines to support the management of violence in mental health services, the Royal College of Psychiatrists (College Research Unit, 1998) identifies the following risk factors identified as associated with violence:

Demographic or personal history

- a history of violence

- youth, male gender

- verbal threats of violence

- association with a subculture prone to violence

Clinical variables

■ alcohol or other substance misuse, irrespective of other diagnoses

■ active symptoms of schizophrenia or mania, in particular if there are: delusions or hallucinations focused on a particular person; delusions of control, particularly with a violent theme; agitation, excitement, overt hostility or suspiciousness

■ poor collaboration with suggested treatments

■ anti-social, explosive or impulsive personality traits

Situational factors

■ extent of social support

■ immediate availability of a weapon

■ relationship to potential victim

A mental health assessment of the risk Mark poses would note that he scores on at least two of the demographic and personal history factors; two of the clinical variables; all the situational factors; and questioning of Mark (and Kelly) may well establish the presence of other risk factors. Having completed an assessment 'based on evidence, which thereby offers the greatest possible probability of non-recurrence' (Hart and Kirby, 2004), how would mental health professionals then manage this risk and what treatments might they offer Mark? If he is assessed as also suffering from an Axis I disorder, such as depression or anxiety, then he may be prescribed medication. Currently his possible personality disorder would not be seen as particularly treatable as only 17 per cent of Trusts have dedicated personality disorder services; regional secure units actively exclude patients with a primary diagnosis of personality disorder because they do not consider this to be their core business; and many practitioners believe there is nothing that mental health services can offer (NIMH, 2003). In those Trusts providing services, there is disparity in the mode of service delivery, many offenders with personality disorders receiving their care from agencies such as Social Services, voluntary agencies and probation, and a disparity of therapeutic approach:

> If patients with personality disorder receive any treatment, it is most likely to be individual supportive psychotherapy. The aim is to improve

the patient's adaptation through diminishing self-destructive responses to expectable interpersonal frustrations. The aim is not to change the person's personality...

(Norton, 1999)

Such treatment would do little to ensure Kelly's safety although should she present to health services with injuries, current guidelines on domestic violence suggest that the NHS has a particular contribution to make. This contribution seems largely of one referral to community services, such as giving advice about local help lines or refuge services (Home Office, 2003).

Should Mark actually be admitted to hospital, any violence on the ward would be managed differently as concerns about violence to staff and patients have increased. A 2002/3 survey of violence, accidents and harassment in the NHS revealed high levels of violence: staff in acute, primary, ambulance and mental health trusts experienced 11 violent incidents per 1000 staff per month in 2002. It is worth noting, however, that research into violence in ambulance services does not identify the same risk factors as outlined above. For example, Suserund, Blomquist and Johansson (2002) found that violence experienced by ambulance service staff was slightly more likely to be an attack by a female, and three times more likely to involve admissions to geriatric wards than emergency compulsive wards for mental patients. Violence in Accident and Emergency (A and E) units has some features in common with the risk factors identified by the Royal College of Psychiatrists in that the offenders are mostly young, male and substance misusers, but the situational factors are different. These included incidents mostly occurring at night and relating to long waiting times (Stirling, Higgins and Cooke, 2001). Dealing with overcrowding and reducing waiting times in A and E units therefore has potential significantly to reduce the number of violent incidents (Derlet and Richards, 2000; Schneider and Marren, 1995).

Aggressive behaviour towards staff is likely to occur in psychiatric hospitals simply because violent behaviour often leads to hospitalization (Williams, 2003), and there has been an emphasis on identifying the 'trigger phase' in violence (Breakwell, 1995) as specific episodes of violence can sometimes be predicted by observing prodromal behaviour (Musker, 2000). People have been found to communicate their intention to assault up to three days prior to the actual incident by threatening gestures, verbal abuse, abnormal activity and threatening stances (Whittington and Patterson, 1996) so Mark could expect his behaviour to be defused through management of his environment: reduced noise stimulus, greater privacy and increased personal space – 'people who are aggressive are known to require up to four times the normal interpersonal space' (Musker, 2000: 459). Probably Kelly is already expert in this; it is our experience that victims of ongoing violence tell us that they know when they are going to 'get a beating' by the expression on their attacker's face, and that the violent person often reacts to arguments by going outside for more space to calm down. Another problem is that although mental health professionals are slightly better at predicting inpatient violence than community violence (McNiel and Binder, 1991), they consistently over-predict and get their predictions wrong 60 per cent of the time (Menzies, Webster and Sepejak, 1985).

Gibb and Macpherson (2000) argue that despite the rigidity of classificatory systems, they should be retained because they help to understand clusters of symptoms as distinct diagnostic entities. This facilitates research into the aetiology of the specific disorders, allowing redefinition; and helps the development of management plans and prognostic indicators. This argument would only be useful in Mark's case if he were diagnosed with a 'treatable' disorder, such as depression or anxiety contributing to his violence. However, Shorter and Tyrer (2003) argue that drug discovery for mood disorders has been slowed down by the need for pharmaceutical companies to develop drugs for diagnoses. These diagnoses are of questionable relevance as most mood disordered people suffer from *both* depression and anxiety. Before classification systems were devised, treatments tended to be for symptoms, not diseases. When linked to specific diseases, antipsychotics, anxiolytics and antidepressants reinforce discrete medical categories. These then allow for the testing of new drugs in large clinical trials. Shorter and Tyrer raise ethical questions about this process, suggesting that these trials are not unbiased and that the pharmaceutical industry exerts a major influence through the publication of sponsored supplements to journals, which are often poorly peer reviewed and promote unapproved treatments. Altman (a professor of statistics in medicine at the Institute of Health Sciences, Oxford) found that there was pressure to omit negative results in clinical trials, particularly from journals anxious to publish positive findings and keep the length of papers down (Matthews, 2004).

The inflexibility of the DSM-IV and ICD-10 is particularly evident in explanations, prediction, and treatment of violence. As we have shown above, the clinical risk factors account for only a small part of the explanation; prediction is often inaccurate; and treatment regimes are flawed – whether this be for an Axis I disorder, which will limit treatment to a specific disorder (which turns out not to be as discrete as the system suggests) – or an Axis II disorder – which is considered untreatable (except in so far as personality disorders can be ameliorated through psychotherapy). Nowhere are the limitations of the classificatory systems more exposed than in the reality that mental illness and personality disorder coexist in a heterogeneous way (Kendell, 2002). Where this intersects with violent behaviour, the influence of drug misuse and mental disorder, dual diagnosis has become an increasing area for concern, study and treatment development.

Dual diagnosis

As noted above, Mark exhibits several of the risk factors for violence identified by the Royal College of Psychiatrists, and it is not unlikely that he also drinks and/or uses drugs. As alcohol and cannabis are the drugs most frequently used by individuals with mental health problems (Department of Health, 2002b), it might be that a psychiatric assessment would consider that he is a patient with *complex needs*. This term was used originally to describe patients with a combination of substance misuse and mental illness (Rassool, 2002) but is now more commonly referred to as dual diagnosis (see, for example, Healey et al., 1998; Wake, 2004). Following the discovery that increasing severity of substance dependence increases both psychological and psychiatric problems, particularly risk taking behaviour, but that treatment of the substance problem often ameliorates psychiatric problems, and treatment of psychopathology improves prognosis (Crome, 1999), the Department of Health has published good practice guidance on dual diagnosis (2002b) in which Local Implementation Teams are charged with implementing policy requirements in partnership with Drug Action Teams:

> Substance abuse is usual rather than exceptional amongst people with severe mental health problems and the relationship between the two is complex. Individuals with these dual problems deserve high quality, patient focused and integrated care. *This should be delivered within mental health services* ... Patients should not be shunted between different sets of services or put at risk of dropping out of care completely ... Unless people with a dual diagnosis are dealt with effectively by mental health and substance misuse services these services as a whole will fail to work effectively.
>
> (Department of Health, 2002: Executive Summary, original emphasis)

The guidance is focused on people with severe mental health problems and problematic substance misuse, including alcohol, acknowledging the variety of complex ways in which the two problems coexist: a primary psychiatric illness precipitating or leading to substance misuse; substance misuse worsening or altering the course of a psychiatric illness; intoxication and/or substance dependence leading to psychological symptoms; and substance misuse and/or withdrawal leading to psychiatric symptoms or illnesses. Crucially, the guidance insists that people with personality disorders are included:

> It is not acceptable for services to automatically exclude people with personality disorder ... which can coexist with a mental health problem or a substance misuse problem – or both. A diagnosis of personality disorder does not necessarily predict poor treatment outcome.
>
> (Department of Health, 2002: 1.2.3)

and

> Most clients can and will achieve positive outcomes with the right treatments and support.
>
> (Department of Health, 2002: 1.5.3)

Unfortunately the guidance does not offer any research findings in support of this assertion, although it does cite references supporting the effectiveness of treating substance abuse in schizophrenic patients (Bellack and DiClemente, 1999; Carey, 1995). And there is support for the assertion in the work of drug agencies (see, for example, Crome, 1999) and the anecdotal reports of patients published in *Dialogue*, the publication of the *Virtual Institute of Severe Personality Disorder* (for more information, contact the Henderson Hospital, London).

Although the dual diagnosis guidance calls for a full risk assessment for all service users, regardless of their location within the health service, the assessment focuses on a person's treatment needs as much as the risks they pose to others:

> Identification and response to any emergency or acute problem
>
> Assessment of patterns of substance misuse and degree of dependence/withdrawal problems.
>
> Assessment of physical, social and mental health problems.

Consideration of the relationship between substance misuse and mental health problems.

Consideration of any likely interaction between medication and other substances.

Assessment of carer involvement and need.

Assessment of harm minimization in relation to substance misuse.

Assessment of treatment history.

Determination of individuals' expectation of treatment and their degree of motivation for change.

The need for pharmacotherapy for substance misuse.

Notification to the National Drug Monitoring System.

Other than the assessment of physical, social and mental health problems, this sort of assessment offers little scope for use of either DSM-IV or ICD-10 classificatory systems. Indeed, the guidance recommends assessment instruments that specifically focus on substance misuse (see, for example, Maisto et al., 2000). Risk to others is included in terms of 'Exploration of the possible association between substance misuse and increased risk of aggressive or anti-social behaviour ...' (ibid.: 3.1.4). Both Mark and Kelly could be more optimistic about their treatment options under this guidance; not only could Mark expect to receive a thorough and wide-ranging assessment of his needs and any risk he poses, but Kelly's needs as a carer would also be assessed.

The most significant difference between this approach and more traditional ones is in the treatment approaches. Mark would not only receive treatment, but he would receive motivational work where it was assessed as necessary to ensure his engagement in treatment. Similarly, relapse treatment programmes are specified although should Mark be a cannabis user, there would be problems in supporting his withdrawal as there currently is no substitute prescribing available. Otherwise, Mark could expect an integrated treatment programme, such as that offered by the Kingston CDAT Dual Diagnosis Service (Department of Health, 2002: 25). This service is proactive in outreaching clients in partnership with mental health services and follows a four stage approach of assessment, education, harm reduction and abstinence and relapse prevention. Similarly COV-AID (control of violence – anger, impulsivity and drinking), a programme for intoxicated aggression and violence in personality disordered offenders is currently being implemented in maximum and medium secure hospitals and mental health service outpatients (McMurran, 1999/2000). This programme has three components: anger control intervention (Renwick, Dunbar and Davidson, 1983), problem-solving skills for impulsivity, and teaching controlled drinking skills (McMurran and Hollin, 1993).

New legislation

The good practice with people who are violent and have complex needs outlined in the Department of Health guidance on dual diagnosis and people with personality disorders is an example of the thinking behind government plans to reform mental health services. The draft Mental Health Bill published in June 2002 claimed to be a landmark in legislative reform; the first major overhaul of mental health services in 50 years, and one that would bring the current system up to date with new patterns of care and drug treatments. The new focus was on the needs of individual patients rather than the dictates of classificatory systems, although these systems are not entirely discarded (see, for example, NIMH, 2003: 9). The draft bill introduced one broad definition of mental disorder, and one tight set of conditions to govern the use of compulsory powers. This did not constitute a return to the hospitalization of patients, rather it recognized that patients need both acute and community care. The draft legislation was intended to ensure that people with personality disorder, including the small number of people who are dangerous, would no longer be excluded from treatment. The implementation guidelines (ibid.) proposed the development of specialist multi-disciplinary personality disorder teams, specialist day care in areas with high concentrations of morbidity, and extensive training opportunities (ibid.). However, the contentious nature of some of the proposals has led to a rethinking of the required legislation and the matter is currently under review.

Despite the rhetoric about recognizing modern forms of treatment and providing individualized care, it is more likely that this proposed legislative reform constituted a reaction to the fall-out from various scandals, where dangerous patients were refused inpatient care on the grounds of their 'untreatability' and were discharged into what proved to be inadequate community care. As Ryan (1996) pointed out, larger organizations must be seen to be doing something to protect the public, and current policy relating to mental health services is particularly concerned with those people who are dangerous. This was reflected in the draft Mental

Health Bill press release (www.doh.gov.uk/PublicationAndStatistics/ PressReleases), where Jaqui Smith talked much more about dangerousness than she did about new treatments:

> Some people, however, because of their illness can be a danger to them- selves, whilst a very few can pose a risk to others. In these cases govern- ment has a responsibility to ensure that treatment can be provided to these patients in the most appropriate way – to protect them, their fam- ilies and the wider public.

The 'tight set of conditions' for compulsory admission did not neces- sarily indicate a lessening of compulsory treatment; the same press release reported that 500 extra secure places have been provided, more than 320 24-hour staffed beds and 180 outreach teams. Smith comments that this is a good start, but it is difficult to see how all this will benefit the 'average' person with a mild to moderate mental illness; all these places are for people who may be dangerous – through personality dis- order, substance misuse, mental illness, or a combination of all three. It can only be good news that people are no longer to be labelled as 'untreat- able' psychopaths (it is hardly surprising that such patients are also found to be depressed when they read gloomy prognoses about themselves in court reports), but it is worth remembering that very little is known about the successful treatment of personality disorders in mental health services: 'personality disorders are conceptually heterogeneous ... information about them is limited, and [that] existing knowledge is largely derived from unrepresentative clinical populations' (Kendell, 2002). No one thera- peutic method is advocated in government guidance: a combination of psychological treatments, reinforced by drug therapy, being recom- mended – as long as the therapy is well structured; devotes effort to achieving adherence; has a clear focus; is theoretically coherent to both therapist and patient; is relatively long term; is well integrated with other services; and involves a clear alliance between therapist and patient (NIMH, 2003: 23). As dynamic psychotherapy, cognitive analytical therapy, cognitive therapy, dialectical behaviour therapies, therapeutic community treatments, antipsychotic and antidepressant drugs and mood stabilizers are all listed as possible treatments, it would impossible to predict quite what would be offered to Mark should he be diagnosed as having a personality disorder. Government may have decreed that such a condition is treatable, but it does not seem clear about effective treatment – other than a firm hand being needed: 'Staff need a high degree of personal resilience and particular personal qualities that allow them to maintain good boundaries, survive hostility and manage conflict (ibid.: 440)

Another worry is that government seems implicitly to be talking about *men* who are potentially dangerous due to them having been diagnosed as having a personality disorder; although between 10 per cent and 13 per cent of the population is estimated to have a personality disorder, equally distributed between men and women, anti-social personality disorder is most likely to be diagnosed in men and borderline personality disorder in women (NIMH, 2003: 11). The Department of Health guidance on women's services (Department of Health, 2003) has very little to say on women who are dangerous, other than commenting that there are distinct differences in the social and offending profiles of men and women, their experience of mental ill health, patterns of behaviour, and their care and treatment needs. Commenting that women are generally less of a risk to the public than men, it dismisses women with a diagnosis of personality disorder in one sentence: 'Women's secure services need to incorporate a range of in-patient settings for women who need intensive care; have challenging behaviour; or who receive a personality disorder diagnosis' (Department of Health, 2003: 11). Women who are diagnosed as having Borderline Personality Disorder are not viewed as potentially dangerous at all, only that they have 'a compulsion to engage in abusive relationships' (ibid.: 8.6). Women who misuse substances are mentioned only in terms of their needs, on the grounds of, for example, their more likely experience of sexual, physical or emotional abuse as children (ibid.: 8.7). Whilst it is excellent that women's special health needs are receiving consideration (Kelly might well benefit from this emphasis), it is nonsense to ignore women's violence. Women's violence is already hidden in a number of ways: police reporting of incidents, the labelling of women as victims; and the dismissal of lesbian violence as different from heterosexual women's violence (for an overview, see Milner, 2004), but this does women a disservice. It denies violent women access to services and it limits the services available to women and men who are the subject of violence. The emphasis on men's violence, and adult men's violence at that, also has the effect of denying appropriate mental health services to other adults who are violent.

Outcomes

Although government guidance on mental health services commonly cites outcome studies, inadequacies in classificatory systems combined with a very wide range of treatment options and different modes of service delivery, makes it impossible to comment with confidence on any particular approach to people who are violent and may have a mental illness:

> Since much criminal behaviour is somewhat arbitrarily defined, and there are arguments about the existence and definition of mental abnormalities (disturbances), it is hardly surprising that we experience difficulty in trying to establish connections between these two somewhat ill-defined and complex behaviours.
>
> (Prins, 1995: 89)

Categorization can have advantages, however, as service users can ask for a range of therapeutic options at an early stage, delivered in specialist services rather than as part of general mental health services. They may well have to be classified as suffering from a discrete mental disorder to access such services, but it is worth remembering that service users request that they are neither labelled as just the diagnosis, nor treated in a patronizing manner. If the new legislation empowers mental health service workers to be creative in their practice and in managing the mental disorder label, it is possible that people who are violent may benefit from categorization.

Summary

- Traditionally mental health professionals have attempted to define links between mental disorders and violent behaviour

- The diagnosis most used to define people who are violent is that of personality disorder but this has been of limited usefulness as it has been considered an enduring pattern of behaviour that is largely untreatable.

- Classificatory systems such as the DSM-IV and the ICD-10, are too rigid to encompass the complexities of violent behaviour, especially as mental and physical disorders frequently coexist.

- Dual diagnosis is increasingly being considered since treatment of substance misuse often ameliorates psychiatric problems and the treatment of psychopathology improves the prognosis in substance misuse.

■ Recent government proposals were moving towards only one broad definition of mental disorder; people with personality disorders will no longer be excluded from treatment.

■ A range of therapies such as dynamic psychotherapy, cognitive therapies, and drug regimes are recommended interventions.

■ Government guidance prioritizing gender minimizes women's violence, and may restrict women's access to mental health services.

To aid critical reflection we invite you to consider the framework and question outlined below.

Mental Health Implementation Guide; Dual Diagnosis Good Practice Guide (from DoH, 2002: 17–18)

3.1.3 Specialized Assessment

Specialized assessments are undertaken to determine the nature and severity of substance misuse and mental health problems, and to identify corresponding need. The more comprehensive and focused the assessment the better the understanding will be of the relationship between the two disorders. Since substance misuse can itself generate psychological and psychiatric symptoms, assessment of this relationship should be longitudinal and open to revision. Box A presents the necessary components of a specialized assessment.

Box A Assessment components

■ Identification and response to any emergency or acute problem.

■ Assessment of patterns of substance misuse and degree of dependence/withdrawal problems.

■ Assessment of physical, social and mental health problems.

■ Consideration of the relationship between substance misuse and mental health Problems.

■ Consideration of any likely interaction between medication and other substances.

■ Assessment of carer involvement and need.

■ Assessment of knowledge of harm minimization in relation to substance misuse.

■ Assessment of treatment history.

■ Determination of individual's expectation of treatment and their degree of motivation for change.

■ The need for pharmacotherapy for substance misuse.

■ Notification to the National Drug Treatment Monitoring System.

3.1.4 Risk Assessment

Routine risk assessment protocols need to address specific factors relevant for individuals with a dual diagnosis. The severity of substance misuse, including the combination of substances used, is related to the risk of overdose and/or suicide. Exploration of the possible association between substance misuse and increased risk of aggressive or anti-social behaviour forms an integral part of the risk assessment, and should be explicitly documented if present.

Question

■ Section 3.1.4. specifically instructs you to explore the possible association between substance misuse and aggressive behaviour. Consider the assessment components in Box A in the box above.

CHAPTER 7

Safety Building: Solution-Focused Approaches

This chapter outlines a very different approach from the preceding ones in that it does not attempt to explain and categorize violent behaviour at all on the grounds that it is not necessary to understand a problem to arrive at its solution, and it is more profitable to concentrate on competencies rather than deficiencies, strengths rather than deficits, and safety rather than risk. Thus there is very little in this chapter on the similarities between people who are violent and even less on the prediction of risk. Instead, there is a great deal on solutions and signs of safety. The basic principles and techniques of solution-focused practice are described, followed by a detailed discussion of assessment and intervention using a signs of safety approach. As the approach has been extensively evaluated, outcome research is detailed, plus examples of how solution-focused practice 'works' in a variety of service-provider settings.

Solution-focused theory

This approach shares some of the values of the humanist models of counselling and has some features in common with cognitive behavioural therapies in that it uses cognitive and behavioural questions and frequently leads to tasks to be carried out (for an overview, see Macdonald, 2007). However, the focus is quite different; other approaches focus on understanding *problems*, classifying them, and identifying each category to match up treatment models. Solution-focused practice focuses on understanding *solutions*.

This approach originates mainly from work developed at the Milwaukee Centre for Brief Therapy by Steve de Shazer and his colleagues. In a succession of publications, de Shazer (see 1985, 1988, 1991, 1994) set out the solution-focused approach, which can be described as postmodern

and constructionist. His philosophy is largely based on the psychotherapeutic ideas of Milton Erickson (1959), and on the theories of language
and meaning of Derrida (1973) and Wittgenstein (1980). This philosophy is set out more fully in Parton and O'Byrne (2000), Milner (2001);
and Milner and O'Byrne (2002). The image of the person in the social
constructionist approach is that of the person as a social agent, one who
has to be seen in a cultural context. This leads solution-focused practitioners to:

> explore not what is *within* (intrapsychic) people, as if there was an inner
> world divorced from a cultural, anthropological context, but to examine
> what lies *between* people, i.e. an interactional perspective. Feelings,
> thoughts and actions always take place within the linguistic negotiations
> in which people engage. Meanings are always open for renegotiation.
>
> (O'Connell, 2001: 29)

At its simplest, solution-focused practitioners hold a belief in the
capacity of service users to discover their own workable solutions to
their problems. Although by no means a solution-focused practitioner,
Winnicott (1971: 84) identified that 'I think I interpret mainly to let
the patients know the limits of my understanding. The principle is that
it is the patient and only the patient who has all the answers.' Solution-
focused practice claims to assist in seeking these answers.

De Shazer looked at problem patterns and how attempted solutions
often served to maintain them, in the process becoming interested in
the inconsistencies of problem behaviour. However serious or chronic a
problem, it was never possible to obtain a truly accurate picture because
nothing ever remained quite the same. Thus whatever the problem
behaviour, there will always be exceptions, times when the problem is
less apparent or even absent altogether. Examining in great detail 'what
worked', de Shazer's team perfected a set of economical techniques that
form the foundation of the approach. Many of the techniques will be
familiar to practitioners adopting different approaches, particularly the
Socratic questioning of Frankl's logotherapy or Beck's cognitive therapy (for a more detailed discussion, see Colledge, 2002), but solution-
focused practitioners use them to explore futures, not to understand past
events. Solution-focused practice also has a strong foundation in research,
testing its assumptions and discarding anything which is not backed
up by the evidence, so we can say that the theory grew out of effective
practice. None the less the practice itself is atheoretical in that it uses
the 'local knowledge' of service users (which is theoretically limitless),

rather than depending on 'professional knowledge'. Practitioners avoid hypotheses on the grounds that, however well they are constructed, they do not necessarily shed light on what a violent person needs to do to make progress.

Thus solution-focused practice embraces one-half of evidence-based practice development, effectiveness, remaining cautious about the evidence-based practice which makes generalizations about the nature of people. It is deeply sceptical about the ability of the 'grand' modernist theories and explanations to deliver truth; holding to a plurality of truths, especially including those contained in the 'local' theories of service users. It avoids any form of diagnostic labelling and sees professional categorization of people as disempowering. For example, the Finnish psychiatrists Furman and Ahola (1992), reframe 'depression' as 'latent joy' and 'borderline personality disorder' as 'a search for a new direction in life', in order to broaden possibilities for change. As people are viewed as essentially capable, there is a constant search for competencies; for example, although a young person with sexually concerning behaviour was considered a particular risk by his teachers because he had been diagnosed as suffering from Asperger's syndrome, and *de facto* was unable to show victim empathy, he was viewed by his solution-focused practitioner as having special strengths: his tendency to 'intellectualize' his behaviour meant that he had the ability to analyse it thoroughly and develop a solution.

Solution-focused practice takes a deliberately not-knowing stance towards people's problems, preferring to remain curious about people's stories and views, about their strengths and potential, about occasions when the problem was less, and about how that happened – curious about the seeds of solution. Rather than seeking to understand (based of some grand theory or research findings), it merely seeks more helpful 'misunderstandings'. There is a preoccupation with difference, but this is a preoccupation with what was different when things were better and what needs to be different for them to be better again. Each problem-free aspect of the person is utilized to this end. The therapeutic relationship is built by engaging in problem-free talk, engaging the person rather than the problem. Sharry, Madden and Darmody (2001) comment that though this superficially resembles social chitchat, problem-free talk is a skilled process involving the practitioner in looking always for service-user strengths and resources that may be helpful in resolving the problem, however tangential they may at first appear.

Solution-focused practice sees the problem as outside the person: the person is not the problem; the problem is the problem. The practitioner joins with the service user *against* the problem and thereby gets a different story. Therefore this approach eschews pathology and the identification of deficits. This solution-focused approach seeks to find the seeds of solution in a service user's current repertoire, seeking those occasions or *exceptions*, however small or rare, when the problem is less acute in order to identify when and how that person is doing or thinking something different that alleviates the problem. This involves listening carefully to, and then *utilizing*, what the person brings to the encounter, focusing on problem-free moments, constructing an envisaged future when the problem is no longer there, and getting a very detailed description from the service user of what will be different then and whether any of that is already beginning to happen. In partnership, the service user and the practitioner build a picture of a possible future without the problem. For example, the foster-carer of a young woman who was both sexually and physically violent with her peers reported that despite an incident free summer holiday, the young woman had 'gone back to square one' on return to school and been temporarily excluded. Examining the problem-free holiday period revealed that she had handled her upset feelings by ignoring wind-ups and seeking private space to settle herself. When asked if any of this happened at school, she could identify periods of up to two days at a time when she could 'do this'. Analysing these exceptions was much more fruitful in terms of solution building than analysing the problem's reoccurrence.

Emotions are not ignored but they are validated through what O'Hanlon (1995) has referred to as 'empathy with a twist', adding a word that implies a possibility of difference. For example, if a service user says he feels suicidal, the practitioner would reply, 'that must be scary, have you felt suicidal *before*?' If the answer is affirmative, the follow up question would be, 'how did you recover *last time*?' (Lipchik, 1994). Service users need to be heard; rather than attempting to understand their emotional experiences as separate; emotion, cognition and behaviour are viewed as interdependent and the focus is on engaging at an emotional level (Lipchick and Turnell, 1999). Hence the service user is asked how they *do* depression, happiness, being calm and so on (actions over which they can gain some control), rather than how they *feel* them (emotions over which they have little control).

Talk (language) is seen as powerful enough to construct life; talk of life with the problem constructs a problem-laden life; talk of life without the problem constructs a problem-free life. Talking in detail of what will be happening, what people will be saying, what effect this will have on relationships and so on, provides the experience of a glimpse of that life; that life then becomes a possibility and the person experiences a sense of personal agency in setting out to construct it. The new story can even include a changed or different self, especially an accountable self. Assessments that fix people's identities, conflating the person and the problem, are avoided as new possibilities become visible. For example, a person who could be classified as suffering from Obsessional Compulsive Disorder, when viewed from a solution-focused point of view, would be seen as being a person with many strengths – tenacity, conscientiousness, concern for possible harm to others and the like – all of which can be used in solution finding.

This approach thus has a view of assessment different from most others. Rather than assuming that information about a problem will help to find its solution, the assumption is that we can understand a solution without necessarily knowing a great deal about the problem. Searching for an understanding of a problem usually leads to a laundry list of deficits or negatives, whereas this approach says that what is needed is a list of personal strengths, resources, and exceptions to the problem. Lists of deficits often risk overwhelming both service users and the practitioners, engendering hopelessness and a tendency on the part of the practitioner to use such expressions as 'unmotivated', 'resistant' or 'not ready to change'. In solution-focused assessments, 'resistance' is regarded as an inability on the part of the counsellor to recognize the client's 'unique way of cooperating' and an indication that more careful listening needs to happen.

Durrant (1993) identifies that psychological assessment tends to assume that qualities are measurable entities, that there are 'normative' criteria for determining healthy functioning and that we need to identify deficit and fault before planning intervention. He contrasts this with the solution-focused approach, which assumes that the meaning of behaviour and emotion is relative and constructed, that psychological and emotional characteristics are partly a product of the observer's assessment and interpretation, that intervention need not be directly related to the problem, and that practitioners should build on strengths rather than attempt to repair deficits. This approach therefore develops an apparently 'atheoretical, non-normative, client determined view' (Berg and Miller, 1992: 5) of difficulties in which change is regarded as constant and inevitable. As a result, it makes sense to find what bits of positive change are happening and to use them to develop a solution. If practitioners do not look carefully for what the client is doing when the problem is not happening, or is not perceived to be a problem, these exceptions will go unnoticed. The most striking example of this is the 'pre-session change' question. Because de Shazer's team believe that change is constant, that no problem, mood or behaviour happens all the time or to the same degree, new service users are asked what has changed since the appointment was arranged. The team found that a considerable proportion of people reported some change. By then asking 'How did you do that?', they quickly got a solution-focused assessment under way.

Solution-focused explanations of violent behaviour

Quite simply, the solution-focused approach does not have an explanation for violent behaviour, nor does it attempt to predict dangerousness. This is in part because it considers that diagnoses provide extremely limited perspectives of individuals' capacities for change. It is particularly concerned with the negative effects of labelling; for example, Turnell and Edwards (1999) argue that violence in families usually accounts for no more than 5 per cent of the family's behaviour and that focusing solely on this ignores 95 per cent of family competence. Concentrating on the signs of danger not only gives an unbalanced picture but engaging with risk leads to defensiveness, engendering an adversarial and hostile relationship (Berg, 1994; Lipchik and Kubiski, 1996).

By not holding one, or more, explanations for violent behaviour, the solution-focused practitioner is acknowledging that, despite a strong interest in assessment, *accurate* prediction of violent behaviour is out of our reach. Lee, Sebold and Uken, (2003) review the research into domestic violence, illustrating the incomplete and contradictory findings. For example, although research has identified links between violent behaviour and psychopathy, Gondolf and White's study of 840 male participants in batterer programmes in the United States (2001) found that the evidence of psychopathic disorder was relatively low, particularly in 'repeat assaulters', of whom 60 per cent showed no serious personality dysfunction or psychopathology. Also, whilst the 'repeat assaulters' were likely to be younger, have substance abuse problems and to have been arrested for other criminal offences (similar in findings to the Royal College of Psychiatrists' study, 1998), the extent of difference in these problems was small and not clinically significant. The differences between re-offenders and other participants are not substantial enough to help professionals predict or identify high-risk offenders. Any assumption that people who are violent are similar to each other and different from non-violent people is, therefore, fatally flawed. Additionally, negative assumptions about the meaning of the offender's behaviour means that situational and complex variables that might be significant are ignored (Lee, Sebold and Uken, 2003).

This is not to say that accountability is either denied or minimized in a solution-focused approach to the assessment of, and intervention in, violent behaviour; what is avoided is blame and confrontation. In the first place, 'acknowledgement, whilst preferable, is neither a sufficient nor a necessary condition of safety' (Turnell and Edwards, 1999, p. 140); we all know of heavy drinkers who acknowledged the mantra: 'I am an alcoholic', but went on drinking, or the serial sex offender who acknowledges his crimes during a prison sentence but re-offends on release. The motivation of a violent offender to acknowledge culpability and guilt may be to avoid a long prison sentence or obtain parole, while denial may be due to shame, the desire to maintain an interpersonal relationship, or a way of avoiding humiliation. Many violent offenders are not able to discuss their violence in detail until they have gained some confidence in their ability to be different (Milner and Jessop, 2003; Milner, 2004). Equally, the idea that confrontation will help offenders see the error of their ways and that accepting responsibility for past behaviour is the first step before they can move forward is not particularly effective. It takes considerable effort and usually results in the creation of significant resistance. This has the potential to turn the therapeutic relationship into an adversarial one and, perhaps, explains the increased use of motivational interviewing in the Probation Service as a means of preparing offenders for programmes in which they will be challenged and confronted (see, for example, Fuller and Taylor, undated). Here there is an assumption that violent offenders are in denial (see, for example, Teft, 1999), or ambivalent about making changes in their lives (Miller and Rollnick, 1991, 2002). Importantly, being accountable and taking responsibility for past behaviour does not necessarily help service users to ascertain what they need to do differently.

The solution-focused practitioner holds violent offenders responsible for finding their own solutions to their behaviour, particularly what their futures will be like when they are violence free. However, there is no assumption made that this will be easy; De Jong and Berg (2002) describe a solution-building process that requires discipline and effort. The role of the solution-focused practitioner is, therefore, one of helping the offender define a goal that is achievable, measurable and ethical; helping them find exceptions to the violent behaviour, and solution behaviours; and then amplifying, supporting and reinforcing these. Exceptions are not discovered simply to be praised, nor are solution behaviours regarded as 'positives'; rather they are examined as possible competencies that the person can utilize in the search for a satisfactory and enduring solution. For example, a teenage boys' group working on developing respectful behaviour towards women teachers were asked where and how they were able to show respect (they all said they respected their grandmothers), and could they do it again.

Thus a solution-focused assessment of Mark would include problem-free talk to identify his strengths and resources; for example, has he ever done anything that took a lot of effort, is there something he is proud of doing, can he list the good things about himself? He would also be asked about any times he could have lost his temper but didn't, any times he could have argued with Kelly, but didn't, and so on to discover exceptions to his violent behaviour. These may be quite small; for example, he may only be able to tell of a relatively short argument or one that took place out of earshot of the children. This would not matter, the important aspect of the work being to discover, and amplify, any exceptions. He would also be asked how he preferred to be as a man, a father, a husband, including his best hopes, and whether any of this was happening already. He would also be asked what Kelly, his children and other people in his life would notice differently about him when his preferred future started to become a reality. Kelly would be asked similar questions if she wished to join in the therapeutic endeavour; contrary to assumptions in the feminist model of working with violence, solution focused practitioners have found that conjoint therapy does not increase danger for the partner and that the majority of partners do wish to be involved at some level (Lipchik and Kubicki, 1996; Milner and Jessop, 2003; Milner, 2004). Whether or not Kelly wished to be involved, her safety would be assessed and any discrepancy between her estimation of her safety and Mark's estimation would be the focus of future sessions, as would any discrepancy between other agencies' goals and Mark's goals.

As can be seen from this brief outline, assessment and intervention intertwine in a solution-focused approach which is most commonly referred to as a *signs of safety approach*.

The signs of safety approach

This approach accepts that risk assessment defies accurate quantification. Telling a person what they ought not to do consists of nothing more than the absence of something and we can rarely be sure that an unwanted behaviour has ceased. Neither does it help a person who is violent to work out how they will be when they are non-violent. Instead, a signs of safety approach emphasizes identifying existing signs of safety, which are measurable; develops these signs and expands them so that a safe care plan can be put in place. The service user is helped to do this, but is held accountable for their behaviour in the future. The six practice principles developed by Turnell and Edwards (1999) are outlined below.

Understanding the position of each family member

Basically this means accepting people who are violent as people worth doing business with. Jenkins (1996) comments that we treat those who are violent to others with considerable disrespect at the same time as we expect them to learn how to show respect to others. Practitioners working with people who are violent often operate from a position of self-righteousness, therefore the first step in building a partnership approach it to quell one's own 'inner tyrant' and seek to identify and understand the values, beliefs and meanings of the violent person as well as of the victim(s). This does not involve colluding with an offender's mitigating account of the violence; rather it means listening respectfully to accounts of perceived unfairness, encouraging them to explore the meaning of their behaviour to them and the underpinning beliefs. Cavanagh and Lewis (1996) found that this helps offenders to move beyond superficial responses. Respectfulness also involves not reframing people's concerns as poor motivation, denial, victim blaming or resistance to change. A central feature of solution-focused practice is seeking the person's unique way of cooperating. Listening carefully to their accounts of their lives avoids a sullen stand-off often initiated by confrontation.

Practitioners often have firm hypotheses about violence and its causes which make a person who has already been humiliated by the circumstances of arrest only too aware that the damage they have done is disproportionate to the satisfaction or tension release the violence provided in the first place, and worried about the consequences, feel even worse about themselves. For example, Scourfield (2003) discusses how social workers treat sex offenders within a rigid template; one that assumes recidivism and untreatability but that is reading one's own hypothesis into another person's life story, one that ignores the complexity of violent behaviour: Kearney describes this as 'therapy's insufficient awareness of its own narrative process as it sought to unravel and negotiate an extremely sophisticated and unconscious web of history and story'

(2002: 41). At the Barnados Junction project for juvenile sex offenders in Rotherham, the child with sexually problematic behaviour is asked how they would like to be helped, what effect the problem has had on them, how things have changed for them since the problem came to light and so on, acknowledging them as people who have concerns about their own as well as other people's safety (Myers, 2005). It is much easier for a person to begin accepting responsibility for changing their behaviour in the future when they have been listened to and permitted to explore their own beliefs and meanings.

Listening carefully reveals the complexities of violent behaviour (for a fuller discussion, see Milner, 2004) and it is already apparent that Mark knows that he frightened Kelly when he hammered on the door and does not need to be told he was abusing his masculine power. He would be asked about his experience of the violence – how it has impacted on him as well as on Kelly and the children, and how he wishes to be as a man, a father, a husband. Lee, Sebold and Uken (2003) comment that when they meet 'resistance', they keep in mind that they may be out of step with the participants in their groupwork programme for men who have been violent, moving too fast or demanding more than they can deliver at that particular time. They note that feedback shows that participants appreciate that they do not give up on them.

Ensuring that all family members are heard is crucial to this approach and, particularly where the family is remaining together, it is helpful to hear how others view the unwanted behaviour. This can allow for clarification for the violent person about the impact of their behaviour and give a firm and measurable safety plan located with the people most involved in the day-to-day monitoring of change. Partners and children are encouraged to voice their understanding of the situation; consider solutions and think about what is needed to support a change in behaviour.

Finding exceptions to the violence

The occasions when the person was frustrated and angry but was not violent are examined in great detail – when, where and how – so that these abilities can be used in other situations – 'can you do this again?' Asking a person to tell you about a time when they could have been violent, but were not, helps a person who talks about being overwhelmed by violent feelings which 'just explode' to recognize that they do have some control over their behaviour. This control may not be directly linked to the violent context which led to the referral, and it may be a very small exception, but it can be used in solution building. For example, one young man attending the Junction project identified a time when he was babysitting and had the 'chance he had been waiting for a long time' when one young boy pulled down his trousers and invited him to 'do something sexual'. The young man declined the invitation on the grounds that his friend was in the next room and that he was afraid of the wait to be found out. He did not think he would decline a second invitation. As these were not particularly useful exceptions in solution building (they depended on other people's actions), the exception was analysed further, revealing that he had had fleeting feelings that he described as 'right care' because he had built up an emotional attachment to this boy, what he described as 'right love'. Acknowledging that a person cannot help how they feel but that they can take responsibility for how they act, this single exception was used as a basis for developing the young man's ideas about 'right care' and 'right love' in subsequent sessions.

Where exceptions exist and the person can recognize how they did them, they are developed by setting homework tasks that involve 'doing more of them'. Sometimes exceptions are discounted as chance events ('I don't know, it just happened') or the result of other people's efforts ('if she doesn't wind me up, I don't get mad'), and then a prediction task is given. When a person gets a high proportion of their predictions correct about the days when they are going to be non-violent, they are asked if the exceptions are really spontaneous or do they have some control over their behaviour. This control is again analysed in great detail so that they can increase their chances of 'doing it again'. Exceptions are the first signs of safety, although it is not always easy to confirm that they are present. Whilst it is simple to check with other family members that physical violence has decreased, this confirmation is harder to come by when the victims are not known or when a person is reporting exceptions to sexual urges. Here, a tangential approach is needed, checking for allied behaviours which are measurable – such as increased respectfulness to others, responsibility taking over a wide range of situations, truthfulness and so on. Where there is a total lack of exceptions, the person can be given a pretend homework task: pretending not to be angry or frustrated one half of the week and noticing what is different or what other people see is different. This helps to identify possible exceptions. Where there are no signs of safety at all, dangerousness is increased.

Mark may have exceptions that can be easily developed: he may recognize that he can keep his temper with the children if not with Kelly; he may well handle frustration when out with his mates; or he may control his temper at work when faced with men in authority. How he does this would then be used to broaden his capacity for self-control.

Discover strengths and resources that can be used in the problem situation

A focus on deficits discourages people; violent offenders are rarely told what they are doing well (the 95 per cent competence referred to by Turnell and Edwards, 1999), so begin to believe that there is nothing good about themselves – especially when it is written down in psychopathological terms. This does not aid engagement in the therapeutic process as the person will resist hearing bad things about themselves or become depressed; the frequent coexistence of depression with violent behaviour has been noted earlier. Looking at existing strengths validates the totality of people's experiences, places current problems in context (few people are completely evil), and makes contact with professionals less threatening. More importantly, it helps the person develop a more competent self – it is easier to do more of something that is working than to stop doing something that is problematic.

It is not always easy to elicit strengths and resources. Solution-focused practitioners find that when asked to detail the good things about themselves, service users often reply that there aren't any (see, for example, Milner and Jessop, 2003). Where this happens, a series of prompts are needed, such as 'what would your mother say makes her proud of you, can you tell me about a time you were being caring, what is it about you that means you have been able to keep the same friends? With young children a set of 'strengths' cards (http://www.stlukes.org.au) can be used to identify not only what strengths the child already has but also what strengths they would like to develop. Strengths in any area of life can be used as all strengths and resources are transferable skills. From our scenario it not possible to say what strengths Mark has, but there must be some as Kelly does not wish to separate from him. It is the task of the solution-focused practitioner to search for these relentlessly.

Focus on the goals of *all* involved people to ensure the safety of those most vulnerable

The setting of goals is vital to the process of assessment as this enables clarity about the nature of the problem and what can be done about it. In solution-focused practice, goals must be measurable, achievable and ethical. It can be difficult for an offender to develop a realistic goal because other professionals may have predetermined goals. As we have already seen, Scourfield (2003) noted that social workers tended to expect women to separate from an abusing husband in the interests of the children's emotional wellbeing. As most women and children prefer for the violence to stop rather than the family to be split (Lipchik and Kubicki, 1996; Milner, 2004), there are often conflicting goals which hinder the therapeutic process. Similarly child sexual offenders pose particular problems for parents and foster-carers who have a duty of care and love to both the offender and the other children in the family.

Achievable, ethical goals are set through negotiation with all parties with an emphasis on the safety of vulnerable people. Rather than accepting a blanket goal of the violence stopping, what will be happening differently when all parties consider that safety is present is identified. Thus a referring agency that has child protection issues is asked what the offender will be doing differently that would make them confident enough to close the case; a 'victim' is asked what he or she will notice differently about the offender when they feel safe; the offender is asked what they need to be doing differently to ensure the safety of others *and* their own safety from accusations. This latter is especially important in situations where sexual abuse is strongly suspected but denied. Essex, Gumbleton and Luger (1996) make it the responsibility of the suspected offender to devise a safety plan that will ensure the dual safety demands. Thus the emphasis is always on developing a goal that meets everyone's needs and is measurable – the signs of safety that are measurable. For example, Mark's goal may be to ensure that he stays in the family and keeps out of prison; Kelly's goal may be for Mark to listen to her without violent argument; the children's goal may be for him to play with them more without getting cross; and child protection agency goals will be for the children to show evidence that they are thriving and that Mark and Kelly can resolve differences without violent argument. None of these goals are incompatible, but he will need help to work out how these goals can be broken down into doable small steps and what he needs to do to demonstrate that his solutions are working.

The solution-focused practitioner is not surprised if the offender finds it difficult to describe a clear goal in the early stages, not least because they would not have been likely to resort to violence had they already a well-developed repertoire of solutions. Lee, Sebold and Uken (2003) spend time helping people develop goals as this offers choices and aids change. They suggest the following questions to clarify goal setting (ibid.: 57):

> What would we see if you were doing your goal right here today?
>
> What might your wife notice that would be different when you are doing this goal?
>
> How might she respond to you doing this goal?
>
> How do you think it will be helpful to you?
>
> If this goal is helpful, how will you know?
>
> What do you think you might notice that you are doing differently?
>
> When will you do this?
>
> Can you do this goal now?

They will help a person with goal development, but if there is no clear goal after three sessions they will suspend therapy until the person has worked out what the goal is to be – it remains the person's responsibility to work on this for themselves. Goal setting of this kind removes responsibility for monitoring dangerousness and assessing risk from the practitioner. For example, a sex offender may well undertake a variety of courses in prison (victim empathy, alcohol control, etc.) and the probation officer may have put in place a number of monitoring devices in the community but, unless the offender can say what *he* will be doing differently when he is released from prison that will ensure the safety of others, and how this will be measured, then there are no signs of safety. The goal of getting out of prison by being a model prisoner is not an ethical, measurable goal that involves the person in doing something differently to ensure the safety of others.

Scaling safety and progress

Professional risk estimation is often based on the *absence* of risk/danger, which makes quantification problematic, as it is difficult to say that just because something is not happening then it will not happen again. This drive to eliminate risk can lead to practice that does not address the local circumstances of the people involved, imposing professional answers that are not achievable and reducing the potential for safe partnership. For example, if the child protection agency insisted that Mark leave his family home, placed the children on Care Orders to ensure their safety at home with Kelly, and recommended that Kelly attend a groupwork programme for the victims of domestic violence (a common scenario in our experience), no-one's goals would be met. As in most cases, Kelly and the children will probably want to maintain their relationship with Mark, but for the violence to cease. This will leave the agency with a situation where Mark and Kelly continue to meet regularly away from the home and the provision of supervised contact for several hours a week. The children may not see as much of their father as they wish and the couple may incur serious debts as Kelly may not be able to maintain employment without Mark's child-care support. Mark may not be able to find employment that allows him time off for contact with his children, a reality for many working people. The child protection agency is unlikely to be able to provide supervised contact outside working hours for Mark or affordable child care for Kelly. Within this context, they are also left with the impossible task of assessing the degree of risk Mark poses to all concerned.

Solution-focused practice avoids these dilemmas. Quite simply, Mark will be asked how safe he rates Kelly on a scale of 1–10 and his rating will be compared to Kelly's. Then he will be asked what he needs to do differently for Kelly to feel safe. She will be given the opportunity to talk about her safety without Mark being present and provided with ways of communicating any unsafe feelings; for example by means of the provision of stamped, addressed 'help' postcards to alert a trusted professional about her concerns. The older child can be involved in this scaling process too, but simpler ladder scales would be necessary or smiley and sad face charts. Similarly the child protection agency can be asked to scale safety and progress. All parties would be asked for evidence of any changes. In cases where safety is impossible to imagine then more direct preventative action will have to be taken, but this process aids in clarity of decision making for the family.

Using scales makes it possible for people to acknowledge when they are not making sufficient progress without making them feel like complete failures. The range of points on a scale means that they are rarely condemned and recognizes their aspirations to 'do better'. The scales can be constructed in such a way as to make it easier for families to discuss what they need to be doing differently even when the subject is emotionally charged. For example, in instances of child abuse, a mother can be asked to rate her mothering ability on a scale of 1–10 with 1 being Rosemary West and Mother Teresa at 10 (the role models differ depending on current dominant images). When the scale is so wide, the person can readily locate themselves at some point. Where this point is doesn't matter at all as long as what needs to be done differently to move up the scale is identified. For example, 'you rate your parenting at 5 but your social worker rates it at 2. What do you think you will be doing differently when you can agree?' In complex situations where an offender is separated from partner and children and the courts are involved, questions can be asked such as: 'when you are asking the judge for contact with your children, what will you say that will convince him that your child is safe with you?' Again this places the responsibility for developing a safety plan, and putting it into effect, on the person whose violence led to safety concerns in the first place.

Assessing willingness, confidence and capacity to change

Although it is important for offenders to take responsibility for their behaviour in the future, Turnell and Edwards make the point that practitioners have a responsibility for setting the scene so that motivation can be improved. Adversarial relationships with professionals reduce the possibility of this, causing unnecessary frustration and increasing feelings of powerlessness at the same time as the offender is expected to exercise self-control. Willingness to change can be increased by assessing whether the person needs help with motivation or ability to change. This is done by creating separate scales for each of the behaviours: for example, 'if 1 means you can't be bothered and 10 means you will do anything it takes, where are you on this scale?' And 'if 1 means you have no confidence in your ability to change and 10 means you have complete confidence, where are you on this scale?' The lower of the two scores becomes the focus of the work; that is, 'what will you be doing differently when you are one point higher?' It is also important to ask, 'if 1 means you haven't a clue about what to do differently and 10 means you know exactly what to do to change, where are you on this scale?' Mark may be well motivated to change his behaviour, but lacking the knowledge or confidence to make the necessary changes so solution-focused practitioners assume nothing, asking questions to which they genuinely don't know the answer and are keen to discover so that they can remain flexible and creative to opportunities for change.

Limitations of solution-focused approaches

Although the approach claims to be atheoretical, it is influenced by postmodern and constructivist theory and, therefore, has a particular political stance about the concept of self as constructed. Elliott (2002) discusses the complex, and often unintended, ways in which academic study of the self can, of itself, shape local knowledges, thus it is important to remember that the self-reflexivity of postmodernism and the search for meaning making via deconstruction and reconstruction may appear to be neutral, but the practitioner will hold a particular view about how the self can be reconstructed. Elliott also considers the solution-focused emphasis on the interactions between people to be a postmodern intellectual sleight of hand in that it ignores unconscious drives which, he maintains, cannot be created in discourses.

Whilst the danger of the practitioner being solution-forced rather than cooperatively solution building is recognized in the literature, there is less acknowledgement of the politics of solution building:

> There can be a relentlessness in the solution focused approach. It can communicate to the client a message that if she is not an activist for change there is something wrong. This aspect of the model colludes with the contemporary spirit which sets results above process and the outer world above the inner.
>
> (O'Connell, 2001: 101)

This means that practitioners need to be aware of, and explicit about, their values and meanings. They do have influence by the nature of the questions they ask; hence the importance of only asking questions to which one does not know the answer, and not mentally framing 'the next question' until the answer to the previous one has been fully heard and acknowledged. Acknowledging an answer involves using service users' language, the actual words, and not translating them into 'practitioner' language. This is important to avoid feminist criticisms of solution-focused approaches (see, for example, Dermer, Hemesath and Russell, 1998). Language may be culturally determined and infinitely fluid, but it does have a constant theme in that it is basically man-made (Graddol and Swann, 1989; Spender, 1995). O'Hanlon maintains that language and interaction are part and parcel of the therapy and problem, and problem definition, and also part of the solution (Bertolino and O'Hanlon, 1998: 25), but it needs to be remembered that it is possible for both service users and workers to be linguistically oppressive (for a fuller discussion, see Thompson, 2003). The solution-focused practitioner, no less than any other, is in the business of creating coherent narratives with service users and has a responsibility to use their words carefully.

Using solution-focused approaches effectively

Solution-focused practice has been extensively evaluated (for a full and regularly updated list of studies, see the research page at www.ebta.nu). The results show that the therapy is as effective as, or slightly more effective than, other psychotherapies. Benefit is not limited to any specific service-user group or problem type, the outcome research showing that it has been effective with traditionally poor outcome problems, such as substance abuse and mental disorder, regardless of learning ability, age or socio-economic status. There is also evidence that drop-out rates are lower than other approaches and that results are long lasting with solutions being transferred to subsequent problems. Outcome studies of solution-focused practice with people who are violent are relatively recent but encouraging (see, for example, Essex, Gumbelton and Luger, 1996; Lee, Sebold and Uken, 2003; Milner and Jessop, 2003; Myers, McLaughlin and Warwick, 2003). It is most effectively employed when the worker can accept that the approach has a completely different emphasis to problem-solving approaches and is able to let go of existing working hypotheses about people who are violent in order to avoid the possible limitations outlined above.

Summary

- Solution-focused theory has no one explanation for violent behaviour on the grounds that diagnoses provide limited perspectives of individuals' capacities for change.

- Solution-focused practice emphasizes safety rather than risk as this is more measurable.

- Confrontational challenges to people who are violent are avoided to reduce the establishment of defensive or adversarial relationships.

- People who are, or have been, violent are assisted in identifying exceptions to their violent behaviour and encouraged to expand their capacities for non-violent behaviour.

- The safety goals of all people are considered in this approach: the offender/s, victim/s, and involved professionals.

- Drop-out rates are lower in solution-focused interventions, and results have been found to be long lasting as solutions are transferred to other problems.

To aid critical reflection we invite you to complete the Signs of Safety Assessment chart below on a service user you work with (The Junction, adapted from Turnell and Edwards, 1999) and then answer the question below. Although designed for children with sexually harmful behaviour, it can be adapted for use in any assessment situation.

Question

■ Analyse this completed initial assessment form and consider what signs of safety would convince you that progress was being made. What would an adequate safe care plan look like if you were confident that you could close the case?

Evidence Sheet of Safety and Concerns

Name ----------------------------------Date --

CONCERNS   **SAFETY**

◄────────────────────────────────────►

<u>Child/young person's goals</u> <u>Carers' Goals</u> <u>Professionals' Goals</u>

<u>Strengths Scale</u>

0 ◄────────────────────────────────────► 10

Scale the young person's current strengths to control the sexual behaviour

0 = Struggling to control   10 = Back in control

Signed . . . . . .   Signed . . . . . .   Signed . . . . . .

Adapted from Turnell and Edwards 'Signs of Safety', Norton, 1999.

SIGNS OF SAFETY ASSESSMENT AND PLANNING FORM

DANGER -- SAFETY

1. Martin played willy games as a young child 2. Martin sexually assaulted a 7-yr-old-boy 3. Martin touched a vulnerable girl inappropriately 4. Martin had penetrative sex with a 12-yr-old-boy 5. Maisie has been sexually abused 6. Maise is showing sexualized behaviour 7. Barbara can't always protect because of ill health 8. Martin can be dominating	9. Martin understands that young children can't consent to sex play 10. Martin is more respectful than he used to be 11. Martin is beginning to take more responsibility	12. Barbara is being firmer about responsibility taking 13. Barbara and Martin are willing to work on safety 14. Martin can be kind and gentle (esp. with pets) 15. The family are warm, loving and fun. 16. School have implemented safety plans 17. Barbara can work with Carole 18. Martin has support in school from Diane

Safety scale (0 means that children are not at all safe with Martin, 10 means that they are completely safe). Martin and Barbara think SSD would say 4.

Goals: SSD and school want Martin to show that he can behave in a sexually appropriate way; have support for his learning needs; Barbara to have support with her health needs; and Maisie to be safe.

Barbara wants the family to be restored and both her children to be safe.

Martin wants to be able to lead a normal life without allegations being made about sexually inappropriate behaviour, and Maisie home.

Action: Martin will have a go at taking more responsibility. First he will help with the pets more and do his homework without being asked – or arguing. Later they will work with Judith on a safety plan.

CHAPTER 8

Deconstructing Problems: Narrative Approaches

In this chapter we will look at a further approach based within a post-modern framework, that of narrative therapy, and how this can be used to understand and respond to violence. As the term implies, narrative approaches are interested in the stories that people live their lives by and consider that these stories can often be unhelpful and limiting, influenced by the larger and more powerful stories that society has generated in making sense of the world. These powerful stories, or dominant discourses (Foucault, 1965), can have a pervasive influence on how we live our lives and how we are allowed to think about ways of being. Narrative approaches seek to make these ways of being transparent and to develop new stories that are less problematic. Telling and retelling stories of peoples' lives is a key element of this thinking, particularly with a view to developing alternative stories that are more relevant for, and local to, the people involved. Although it shares certain commonalities with solution-focused approaches, it is more interested in deconstructing the past in order to move forward and takes a more explicitly 'political' stance through the recognition of power relations within society and how these impact on people's behaviour and potential for change (Morgan, 2000). Thus gender, sexuality, class and 'race' are central (though not exhaustive) concepts that are considered within any narrative work.

The emphasis within this approach is on collaboration between the worker and the service user, working together to understand current stories and in 're-authoring' new stories. The way the service user makes sense of their world is respected, heard and questioned; seeking to understand how power influences their stories and actions. Looking for times when the person has resisted invitations to behave badly is important and exploring the problem identity they have been entered into assists in making the limitations of this transparent. We have professional experience of young people coming to us to work on their sexual behaviour where they have been labelled a 'sex offender'. Such an identity does not assist in moving forwards and can restrict their view of their capacity for change as it is a powerful statement about who they are. Seeking to explore what this means and in what ways they are *not* a 'sex offender' opens up possibilities for living a problem-free future. The 'totalizing' effects of such labels and identities encourage the person to be seen (and see themselves) as the problem, a pathologizing approach that leads to misery and an inevitably poor prognosis. In assisting to identify the behaviour as a part and not the whole of someone, narrative approaches potentially free up the space to recognize the more helpful qualities, strengths and behaviours that constitute the person, which can assist in promoting a positive outlook and in promoting responsibility.

Narrative theory

Originally developed in Australasia by Michael White and David Epston (1989), the approach is grounded in the work of Foucault (1965, 1973) and other post-structuralists and postmodernists (Onega and Landa, 1996), recognizing the importance of language (Halliday, 1978) and that knowledge is determined by powerful social forces that generate the boundaries of what is allowed to be known about particular subjects. Macleod states that it 'represents an alternative to the pragmatic, empiricist, instrumental therapies and health-care systems that have come to dominate the global psychotherapy scene in recent years.' (2000: 333). It can be seen as part of the 'linguistic turn' (Rorty, 1967) within philosophy and the social sciences to a focus on the centrality of language as generative in its own right; the language of representation rather than simply a descriptor of an event or object. By this we mean that the way we talk about something and the words we use are not neutral, but actually reflect and reinforce a particular discourse that is favoured at the time. These discourses are also supported by powerful cultural understandings that can make claims for the 'truth', but are in actual fact merely ways of sense making that are bound by the social constructions of that culture. Language can distort and 'boundary' the sense we make of our lives through the stories we have, and it can also influence how we feel and think about the world. This is the key to narrative therapy, that the stories we hold about ourselves can be changed through the use of language and purposeful talk. Besley (2002) charts the influence of post-structuralist thinking on the development of narrative therapy in a clear and comprehensive way that is useful further reading.

Structuralist ways of understanding the world are currently the dominant way of understanding violence and responding to it, as can be seen in the earlier chapters, whereby there is a sense of some inner model of how people work that is 'fixed' and requires expert investigation to 'put right'. This idea of the 'self' is the dominant one in Western society and has been seen as a product of Enlightenment thinking (Peters, 1999). Post-structuralist approaches question this assumption and consider that although we may often act as though this is 'true', people's identity is actually multiple, contradictory and in process (Newton, 1988), influenced by the social context in which we find ourselves. Identity is negotiated with the environment and can be very different depending on who we are talking with, where and when we are doing this and how this is done. The postmodern assumption that we do not have an 'essential' identity, character or personality allows for a much more optimistic view of the potential for change. In engaging with violence, the notion that someone 'is violent' may construct an identity based on their behaviour, rather than a narrative assumption that people can be violent in certain situations and at certain times, but are rarely violent *all of the time*. Exploring (deconstructing) how and when someone is violent can firmly place this behaviour in context and create the space for consideration of non-violent ways of being.

The Dulwich Centre in Adelaide, Australia, has a helpful website that outlines how this change can be achieved:

A narrative therapy assists persons to resolve problems by: enabling them to separate their lives and relationships from those knowledges and stories that they judge to be impoverishing; assisting them to challenge the ways of life that they find subjugating; and encouraging persons to re-author their own lives according to alternative and preferred stories of identity, and according to preferred ways of life.

(www.narrativeapproaches.com)

These dominant, unhelpful stories can be accepted uncritically by people, either through the embracing of grand theories of, say, masculinity, or through professional discourses that reinforce the problem behaviour as located within the person. White describes this process as being entered into a story which people begin to believe about themselves. It would be foolish at the beginning of the twenty-first century to say that masculinity is no longer an influence on the way that young men are expected to behave and that this has no consequences that are problematic for themselves and others. Yet this is not to say that these 'big' influences are monolithic in their effects, as despite their power they are also experienced and performed individually, with results that will have benefits and negatives for those subject to them. How people make sense of and act out these influences are of interest to narrative workers as they provide the material with which to raise questions about their usefulness. As an example of how this may work, we have experience of working with one man who was viewed as being 'big and aggressive', particularly towards a woman worker. As contact with him developed, it became clear that he had felt that he was being dealt with as someone who was not respected due to his class and gender, therefore he had acted in ways to confirm the professional (and class) assumptions being made about him. He regretted having done this, as it had delayed his ability to discuss the emotional needs he had following major adverse events in his life. In being invited to act out this stereotyped role he and the worker had co-constructed an identity that excluded any possibility that he may actually need or be able to weep, as this would not fit with the identity of being 'big and aggressive'.

The language used within narrative approaches strives to be respectful through inviting people to tell their story and their understanding of the situation, avoiding pathologizing labels and seeking to develop an open and optimistic culture within the interaction. The focus is on the individual rather than any particular group they may belong to since these groupings are often socially constructed categories that enforce a limiting identity, which blurs the experience of that particular person and reduces any sense of agency they may have. The local knowledge of the person is privileged over broader professionally constructed 'expert' diagnoses. This is in contrast to most approaches where the professional subjects the person to what Foucault (1965) described as the 'clinical gaze'; a stance of knowing what to look for through professional knowledge, how to do this, what questions to ask, and how to interpret the information found. The narrative worker is 'de-centred', performing a role of asking helpful questions and assisting in making current knowledge transparent, thus placing the person at the centre of the interaction.

This raises the fundamental issue of responsibility, as in this approach the person has responsibility for developing strategies away from the problem, rather than having this analysed and prescribed by the worker. The worker can be helpful in assisting to identify strengths and exceptions to the problem that may have been overlooked or devalued by the person, as histories can often be places of misery and defeat for people subjected to structural disadvantage, the location of the vast majority of people we work with. Using questions is a central way of learning about that particular person; their likes and dislikes, the influence of the social on their understanding of the world, how they perceive social events, what sense they make of their behaviour and, indeed, how well the work is going. By maintaining a questioning, not-knowing stance within the interactions, this reduces the tendency for workers to make premature judgements on people (which are usually encouraged and supported by professional knowledge) and develops a richer sense of the complexity of the individual. So, rather than seeking and identifying a 'cognitive distortion' for example, a narrative perspective would ask questions about the belief and the links to behaviour, relentlessly seeking to deconstruct the way this has been developed and to discover when this is less strongly held. Having genuine curiosity about the person is a stance that underpins this approach, where the worker resists the temptation to 'close down' conversations by imposing their analysis or becoming confrontational when faced with beliefs and actions that are difficult to hear, understand or accept. Questions are asked for the person, rather than for the worker's pre-formed ideas of what may be happening and seeking answers that confirm or deny this.

In seeking to deconstruct the problem a key approach is to look for those times when the person has resisted the problem and has contradicted their dominant story, confounding the notion that they are a 'slave' to the behaviour and creating space for difference. Inviting people to consider how they have been recruited into the dominant problem-saturated story when they have more complex ways of being, allows for reflection and the development of distance between themselves and the problem story. If people can see the problem as just one of their 'aspects', then this allows for a separation of the person from the problem and the development of a more complex view of themselves. This separation is called *externalizing* within narrative approaches and is often assisted by giving the problem a name, usually by the person, and then interrogating the problem to understand the influence it has on the individual and vice versa. Understanding the relationship between the person and the problem is a helpful process, partly to develop a sense of distance but also by giving clues for changing it.

This process can also indicate motivation by asking the person how attached they are to the problem; whether they want the problem in their lives; and the reasons for wanting to be rid of it. Violence may well be attractive and functional to some people and the idea of being not-violent may well be difficult, therefore requesting that people justify their claims to a violence-free future can demonstrate just how hard the required change may be. If, when faced with the reality of change, people can still see good reasons for this, then they can be asked what this says about them as people, particularly their capacity for taking hard decisions. This approach leads to people taking steps to reclaim their life from the problem behaviour. The role of the narrative worker is to assist in providing the context for change, asking helpful questions and making exceptions to the problem transparent.

Post-structuralism has been criticized for a lack of moral stance, for a moral relativism where anything goes and anything can be talked into or out of 'reality'. A clear danger within this would be that certain behaviours and ideas would be simply seen as a different way of thinking, therefore there may be a reluctance to pass judgement on them. White (1995) has written about this problem and that some stories are more helpful than others; that some stories can actually be harmful to the person and others. Clearly, within our case study, Mark has behaviours that are a risk to himself and others, and it would be easy to condemn this behaviour out of hand. The desire to punish and control him replicates dominant stories that have contributed to the problem, so confrontational and 'challenging' approaches can be seen to be exerting authority (often patriarchal) which paradoxically supports the problem behaviour. The narrative worker is acutely conscious of the ways in which power may be operating through their actions and language, imposing their external will on the person they are working with and reducing the agency of the person. Workers are as prone to the influence of dominant stories as anyone else, although this may take more subtle forms following training courses and the acceptance of professional cultures.

Jenkins (1996), who has written extensively on working with violence, cautions against approaches that take a stance of self-righteousness and moral superiority. Narrative workers are not objective, neutral experts, but are actively involved with the person in exploring and reconstructing a problem-free future. This is done with curiosity and optimism, respectfully searching for the richer, *thicker stories* that actually reflect the person more than the socially and professionally constructed and limited, *thin stories* that most people are subjected to. If, as White and Epston (1990: 29) say, narrative workers are continually challenging the 'techniques that subjugate persons to a dominant ideology', then exercising these techniques through their contact with people is anathema. In our experience, the imposition of a 'cycle of abuse' model on young people with sexually harmful behaviour is an example of the way in which dominant ideologies (in this case psychological, structural understandings of people) seek to bend people to their will, providing an explanation and response to this behaviour that demands acceptance. When one young man was released from a residential facility following a cognitive behavioural programme of sex-offender work, he was able to say that he was a sex offender with thoughts and feelings that triggered his cycle and could describe the inevitability of this pattern within him and his need to be vigilant about it for the rest of his life. This *thin story* was in danger of becoming his whole being, and provided the focus of all work with him. The narrative work began by exploring with him those times when he was not a 'sex offender', an option he had not been given. This opened up opportunities for a 'sex-offender' free future through exploring a much richer, *thicker story* of his complexity. Yet narrative approaches are not a 'free for all' where anything goes, uncritically privileging the person's story. They are actually directive and purposeful in their use of questioning, empowering people to find their own voice (Speedy, 2000) rather than imposing that of another.

In working with people who have been violent it is useful to be clear about the moral position taken towards violence and responsibility in order to avoid collusion and confusion. As an example of moral positioning, Wirtz and Schweitzer (2003: 193–4) have developed what they call 'Golden Rules for stopping men's violence and abuse, and being more responsible', which underpin the narrative groupwork they facilitate. These are:

- The safety of women and children is always rule number one.

- No excuses for violence – ever.

- If you can't challenge the silence and secrecy about violence, you can't stop the violence.

- Violence is a crime.

- Violence is a choice.

- Violence is about using power and control, not about being out of control.

- If you want to say no to violence, you have to say no to patriarchal thinking.

- It's the man's responsibility to stop the violence and abuse.

- Violence and abuse are no laughing matter.

- If you are responsible, you have the strength to take no for an answer.

- When you are learning responsibility, the women and children judge your progress.

- Being responsible means giving up using force and power to get what you want.

The rules show influences of feminist thinking with their focus on women and children, and to a certain extent do not fit comfortably with a narrative approach which may consider this as being too narrow and potentially limiting, but none the less demonstrate consideration of the desire to take a moral stance. Slattery (2003: 170) outlines the aims of a programme for adolescents who have sexually harmful behaviours in which the moral position is implicit and more clearly within a narrative construct:

- Take responsibility to stop sexual abuse and sexual harassment.

- Make restitution to help heal the harm caused by sexual abuse and sexual harassment.

- Respect others and develop appropriate relationships.

- Build self-respect and confidence.

- Find ways of making sexuality respectful and positive.

Here the focus is on responsibility and developing preferred ways of being that do not make assumptions about the nature of people's violence or how it should be managed, but provide a framework for individual change.

Narrative techniques

Milner (2001) outlines the key elements of a narrative approach, although this is neither prescriptive nor definitive in the way it is constructed as the range of techniques available will be subject to the needs of the specific individual. We will investigate these techniques and relate them to Mark with a view to illustrating how this approach differs from other ways of working.

Deconstructing the problem story

This is a way of beginning to work with people that allows for the varying perspectives on the problem to be made more transparent. Questions would be asked about how the problem first arose and how this affects the view people have of themselves. Mark will be asked questions about the violence in his life and how he makes sense of his behaviour, attempting to encourage the range of explanations that he may have and to explore how useful his current life story(ies) are. Looking for complexity and ambiguity are key to this (White, 1995), with the assumption that Mark may have entered into (or been entered into) a quite limited explanation of his behaviour that does not allow for change or hope. If Mark believes that his behaviour is due to the way he was brought up (parenting styles), then this story can be explored by the worker to question the strength of this explanation, what it is based on and whether this provides a full explanation of all his behaviour, including that which is non-violent. Interrogating dominant stories tends to destabilize them, loosening the ties between the explanation and the 'being' of the person and creating space for responsibility taking. Further questions may ask how useful the current explanation Mark has for his behaviour is and when the explanation does not 'fit' his actions. The powerful story can be contextualized through simply asking how he came to believe such an explanation, inviting reflection on the influences that constructed this way of thinking and enabling consideration of the limitations of this.

Mark has been subjected to powerful stories that he has 'problems', in particular an Attachment Disorder and a Conduct Disorder. The referral form is saturated with information that may story Mark in a limited way with an ascribed problem identity. White (1995) recognizes the importance of how professional documents are written in constructing pathologized identities which are often absorbed by the persons themselves. These labels can have a bearing on how Mark views his capacity for change, as they make absolute claims for who he is, and a narrative approach would consider inviting Mark to explore what sense he makes of them. It is useful to know the detail of the behaviours that have led to the diagnosis, as a construct such as Conduct Disorder is a very broad collection of symptoms that are based on professional interpretation. The diagnosis may well hinder Mark in developing responsibility for both his actions and change, therefore the usefulness of Conduct Disorder for Mark will be explored, as well as those times when his behaviour does not fit the diagnosis. Questions such as, 'When did Conduct Disorder

enter your life?'; When has Conduct Disorder been helpful to you?';
'How does Conduct Disorder help you to develop your preferred way of
being?'; and 'When have you resisted Conduct Disorder?' Kelly may also
be subject to assumptions about who she is, based on notions of gender
where she could be viewed as the passive victim of male violence. In
talking with her, it will be helpful to gain her understanding of what is
happening in the relationship, not simply the problem times. Discussing
how violence has come into their lives, when it is more problematic;
when and how she has resisted it; how Mark can act in responsible ways;
and what a life without violence would look like are all areas to explore
with Kelly. Identifying and validating her resources are important to
avoid providing a professionally led explanation and answer to the violence, as well as providing information for the local strategy to develop
a violence-free future.

Mark may consider that he has to act in certain ways in order to achieve
his role as a father, husband, mate and so on, and the helpfulness of such
expectations can be questioned by the worker through exploring how
Mark came to believe that such behaviours are associated with being a
man, but also in thinking about the limitations this poses for leading a
problem-free life. Inviting Mark to think about what supports his problematic behaviours allows for strategies to resist them. It may be that
the gendered role that Mark is under pressure to achieve is not one that
he feels entirely comfortable with, limiting the range of emotions and
actions he has or would like to develop. The worker and Mark can begin
to think about the times when the masculine story has not been good
for him, but also when it has worked in his favour. Having clarity about
the consequences (for themselves and others) of such stories or ways of
being is to create conditions that allow for change, as it becomes clear
that this is just one story, albeit a powerful and socially accepted one. The
contradictions are explored; for example, it is possible that Mark's violence is actively encouraged by those close to him at certain times and
in certain places, but is frowned upon in others. We have experience of
men's violence being actively instigated by their families to address some
perceived community problem, but railed against when such violence
becomes directed against family members. To ignore such complications
will diminish the credibility of the work with people who are generally
capable of seeing that the world is complex. This is not to accept the
behaviour, but to gain a fuller understanding of the local experience of
it. In narrative therapy, direct challenging is not confrontational, but
done through helpful questioning, inviting the person to reflect on how

they came to act in such a way. The emphasis is always on *their* behaviour, but in a way that does not blame, shame nor ask for justification.

Mark may be asked whether he wishes to continue to have the problem behaviour in his life, an approach taken by Furman and Ahola (1992) that enables clarity on how motivated people are to change, as well as allowing for reflection on the influence the problem has on his life. Mark could reasonably argue that parts of the problem are more 'problematic' than others and that to survive in an environment of masculine violence he needs to retain some of the image of 'hardness' in order to make his way through the reality of *his* life. We have found that clients, particularly men, are often not in a position to make some great leap forward to becoming a complete 'new man', with the inevitable associations with 'femininity', as they live in world that would victimize such an image. 'Giving up' is one side of the work; assisting in the development of 'something else' is the key to sustaining change.

Identifying unique outcomes

The ideas of *unique outcomes* (White, 1995) or *sparkling moments* (Bird, 2000) are helpful narrative techniques in that the person is invited to consider those times that they resisted the problem behaviour or label they have been given. Questions would be asked about how they came to have 'an uncontrollable temper' or were labelled 'violent', seeking to reflect on what influences there were that assisted in the construction of this identity. In itself this is useful as it tends to destabilize totalizing constructs, creating the space for consideration of how these came into being and therefore placing their development within social influences. The creation of these stories can then be placed in a context, illuminating how one story has gained precedence over alternative or preferred ways of being. Looking for the times when the dominant story did not fit, or when the person did not act in ways that followed this script, undermines the claims made by such stories that they are their 'true' way of being (Epston, 1998). These resistances to the dominant story are explored in order to find out how the person did this in the face of such powerful forces, with the intention of validating their qualities in making positive choices and in resisting the seductive invitations of the problem story.

Mark would be invited to consider those times when he had not chosen the route of violence; when there were times that he could have been violent but he found other ways of dealing with his feelings and the situation. His strengths in other areas of his life may be explored, to uncover those times he has resisted behaviour that supports aggression. This can be counterposed against those times when Mark has followed the dictates of the story, an often easy option supported by ideas of being a man. The alternative behaviours and actions are encouraged through asking questions such as 'What does it say about you if you can resist such a powerful problem?'; 'How did you find the courage to say "No" to this'; 'What was it like when you outsmarted the problem?' Unlike many other approaches, the history of the problem is explored not in order to uncover Mark's shortcomings, but to uncover his resources in previous encounters with the behaviour.

Externalizing conversations

Many social and psychological understandings of how people are tend to locate problematic behaviour as a trait or pathology of the person. This is the case with lay people as well as professionals and can be seen in the way that popular culture discusses difficulties; for example, the range of addictions that people experience, such as drugs, alcohol and sex. These are often viewed as located within the person and as some thing they 'are', that people have 'addictive personalities' or genetic pre-dispositions. This is a powerful way of thinking that makes 'the person the problem', which leads to particular ways of understanding and responding to the behaviour. A consequence of holding such views is that it can reduce the capacity for 'personal agency', in that people can feel enslaved to a behaviour that is beyond their control. This can lead to despair in the face of what can appear an overwhelming problem, but it can also lead to a lack of responsibility taking, as the label provides a convenient excuse for either not taking action or for explaining why change is too difficult.

We have encountered situations where the aggressive behaviour of children has been minimized and explained by parents, teachers and the child as due to their Attention Deficit Hyperactivity Disorder (ADHD). This biological explanation (of neurological dysfunction) serves to provide a convenient label that reduces the need to talk further about the behaviour, especially if the child is medicated. There are major questions to be considered about this diagnosis, not least whether it truly exists as a discrete medical condition, but for the purposes of this chapter it is the consequences of the label that are important. The problem is located within the body of the person and the responsibility for the behaviour is reduced to ensuring that the medication is taken to control it. Quite apart from the unknown long-term consequences of the pharmacological treatments available, we have yet to come across a child who has been 'cured' through medication and the problem behaviour still persists, albeit in a modified form. In talking with children with this diagnosis, it is useful to ask them what the meaning of this is for them and how they came to be 'ADHD', exploring what sort of behaviours led to this and looking for exceptions to the behaviour. The times when they have resisted the totalizing label of ADHD are of interest, as well as the usefulness or otherwise of having this diagnosis. By doing this we can begin to break down the sense of hopelessness that sometimes pervades those who have this condition, as the preferred response is simply to take the medication to control the 'programmed' behaviour. In our case example, Mark may well be considered as having Adult ADHD, a relatively recent diagnostic phenomenon that seems to be based on notions of the genetic nature of this condition (www.adhd.com).

'The Problem is the Problem; The Person is not the Problem' is a central part of narrative approaches, which may seem deceptively simple yet it requires considerable skill and self-reflection (and in our experience occasional intakes of breath) to ensure that we do not fall into the professionally sanctioned mode of locating problem behaviour within the person, through their upbringing, ways of thinking or social position. If, as we have seen above, there is a tendency for people to understand problems as being a characteristic of their personality (which is often expressed through the use of totalizing labels such as 'addict', 'sex offender', 'violent person'), then where is the space for change? Traditional interventions tend to treat the label rather than the person, thereby reinforcing this identity rather than promoting comprehensive change. Narrative approaches recognize the power of such ways of thinking and seek to distance the person from the problem through externalizing conversations, hopefully creating what Freeman, Epston and Lebovits describe as '... the space between person and problem, (where) responsibility, choice and personal agency tend to expand' (1997: 8). By separating the person from the problem this reduces the sense of blaming and the feeling of having to justify actions, both of which can generate defensiveness and hopelessness in people. As Besley says, 'Externalizing conversations are aimed to stop people being disabled by the problem.' (2002: 128)

One established narrative way of externalizing which we have found useful is that of *naming the problem* (Payne, 2000), where people are invited to consider what to call the problem behaviour so that this can be used in subsequent conversations. In naming this, the *problem* is given an identity separate from the person, allowing the *problem* to be viewed as an entity that has characteristics and modes of being that can be explored. In working with children with sexually harmful behaviour, we have found that the name can be negotiated through providing choices on cards, as sometimes children struggle to find a suitable concept. One name that has become a popular choice is that of 'The Touching Monster' (Myers, McLaughlin and Warwick, 2003), which can describe a range of sexual behaviours, although others can be chosen as long as they have meaning for the person. This may be as straightforward as 'sexual behaviour problem'; 'child pornography' or 'nasty sexual thoughts', depending on the behaviour and the most meaningful image for the child that 'fits' this. In our case example, Mark may be invited to consider 'Violence', or perhaps 'Temper' as metaphors for the difficulties in his life, or he may describe it as 'relationship problems'. Although naming the problem is helpful, it is not compulsory, and it is possible to talk in other ways that disaggregate the person from the problem.

Once named, the *problem* can then be pondered over, with the worker asking helpful and curious questions about the nature of the *problem*. For example, 'The Touching Monster' will be interrogated to see when it appeared; what it likes; when it is strong; what maintains it; what it does not like; where it lurks; and who it likes or dislikes. In doing this, the worker and the person can gain a clearer sense of the problem, uncluttered by pathological explanations of blame, and begin to understand how the problem works. By exploring those times when the problem was unhappy, thwarted, less strong or not there, or when the invitations of the problem had been resisted, this gives clues for future action in combating the problem. Looking for detail and maintaining curiosity are central to ensuring that the exceptions to the problem behaviour can be found, as often such exceptions are minimized or seen as 'luck', rather than recognizing that we have opportunities and strengths to take some control over our lives.

This approach to understanding the problem does not seek nor presume deficits within the person; unlike, for example, the cognitive behavioural and psychodynamic approaches. Particularly with cognitive behavioural understandings of violence, there is an assumption that the person is motivated through their 'wrong thinking' to behave badly and is in need of assistance in developing their inhibitors through recognition of triggers within cycles of abuse. A narrative approach does not view the person as 'damaged' or deficient, but understands that they have been invited to behave in ways that are unhelpful. Discussions are about how the person can develop their non-problematic behaviours through understanding that the problem is not all-encompassing and can be resisted. This is underpinned by the person's responsibility; the responsibility for giving in to the problem and allowing it to bring difficulties into their lives and others. How the problem gained a hold on people is the focus of talk about the past, including illuminating how seductive some of the stories the problem tells about itself can be.

Mark may have been invited to be violent with the help of those Friends of Violence such as: Expectations of being a Man; Entitlement; Frustration; Difficulty in Communicating Feelings; 'It didn't do me any Harm'; ADHD; Alcohol and a range of other ideas that allow Violence to take a hold of someone. These stories would be explored and undermined, recognizing their role in supporting the unhelpful behaviour. The effects that Violence has on others can also be explored and Mark can be invited to think about how helpful Violence is in developing a preferred way of living with his family. Wirtz and Schweitzer (2003) further develop externalizing conversations with men who have been violent through exploring Responsibility, particularly focusing on the 'Friends' and 'Enemies' of Responsibility, to allow for reflection on what has been helpful or not in developing responsibility.

Developing an alternative story

Externalizing conversations are methods of uncovering those times when the problem behaviour was less of a problem or when the person had actively resisted the invitations to behave in unhelpful or harmful ways. By destabilizing the inevitability of this behaviour we can begin to explore how this came about, with an emphasis on co-constructing a preferred story or way of being. People often believe strongly that they have certain traits or cycles of behaviour that lead inexorably to certain outcomes, a way of thinking that can be supported by professional discourses. People can be invited to consider how helpful this belief is for them and begin to think about how they would like to be. In acknowledging the unhelpful 'traits', it is important to search and enhance those times when the person has acted in a way that contradicts this. These times can form the basis of working towards a problem-free preferred future.

If the story held by the person (and reinforced by others) is one of 'always losing their temper', then finding those times when Temper has not dominated them are useful. The resistances to Temper may be seen as 'heroic' given the circumstances, and developing a story where Temper is put in its rightful place can be a way of making sense to people. Being angry is not necessarily a pathological state and can be helpful at times, particularly when faced with injustice, and it is helpful to explore those times when Temper has been used appropriately. 'Constructive temper' often makes more sense to people than a blanket ban on anger, given the society we live in, plus to expect someone to be compliant is to reduce their agency, as well as being a goal that will seem too improbable to achieve. We have worked with people who have been confirmed as 'violent' when they have expressed anger at their unjust treatment at the hands of Courts and child protection agencies, a totalizing label that denies the specificity of their behaviour.

Internalized discourses of who they are can be very disabling for people, reducing any sense of agency and hampering motivation. People may well be concerned that they are 'violent', or a 'sex offender', labels which reduce opportunities for change due to the power they hold. Dolan (1998) has used a technique of encouraging people to consider how they are different from the story given to them by their family that they are 'just like' someone. In our experience, boys who behave badly are often told they are 'just like their fathers', which leaves their individuality severely compromised. Helping people to consider how they are similar and dissimilar to people or labels has a helpful process. Working with children who have sexually harmful behaviour has sometimes been a struggle to assist the child in resisting the identity of a 'paedophile', a label that has enormous implications for who they are and how they view themselves. Being 'stuck' with this identity is a terrifying prospect that places them on a linear path to being a 'sad, lonely, dirty old man', as one boy put it. The only location for his behaviour was the construct of a 'typical' paedophile, with all the associated negative aspects to it. Work has included exploring what this image is to the child and then testing how similar/dissimilar they are to it, thus questioning its solidity. This helps to reduce anxiety the child may have about becoming a 'paedophile' and also creates space to see how they can use their 'non-paedophile' qualities to develop a more hopeful future.

Alternative stories can be made difficult to achieve through professional practices that support the problem identity. One boy in public care who had behaved sexually inappropriately in the children's home was banned by the caseworker from continuing his promising football career as his love of football was viewed as a cover so that he could gain access to victims in the post-match showers. This view of his sexual misbehaviour created a complete identity for him that left him nowhere to go and severely compromised his future prospects, both social and financial. His sense of injustice was palpable and had serious effects on his commitment to work on his behaviour.

Thickening the counterplot

Through externalizing conversations and the development of ideas about a preferred future, a narrative approach considers how the new ways of being can be made more concrete given the weight of history and powerful forces supporting the old story. Freeman, Epston and Lebovits say that 'Problematic stories have an advantage. They've been around for a while … These problem-saturated stories can become very pervasive. The trouble is their effects are negative and discouraging.' (1997: 94–5). Attempts to demonstrate changes in behaviour can be met with disbelief, minimization and be dismissed as merely manipulative. Indeed, sometimes these attempts may well be less 'genuine' than they could be and it is useful to engage with those who are victims of the violence to recognize their right to feel safe. It is often difficult to see how someone can convince others (and themselves) that they are capable of change, particularly if the focus is solely on the problem behaviour. If the behaviour is not present, how do we know it will not simply reappear? This of course is compounded by the notion that such behaviour is a 'trait' or an integral part of the person, which in effect makes accepting change extremely problematic. People can be asked about how they have resisted the problem in order for the worker and the person to gain clarity about 'what works'. They can also be encouraged to explore other parts of their life away from the problem to identify behaviours that undermine the totalizing nature of the problem. As narrative approaches are underpinned by the notion that identities are heavily influenced through social interactions, a further technique is to allow the person to tell their new story to significant others. This can be a process of testing out their new story initially on those who may be more receptive to hearing it, then learning from this (and gaining in confidence) to 'broadcast' to a wider audience.

Outsider-witnessing is a narrative term used to describe this process, whereby people may be invited to talk about their new or preferred selves in front of an audience consisting of other people with problematic behaviours, group facilitators or visitors. The audience is invited to think about what has been said and to say how it has affected them, so that the person telling the story has the opportunity to hear this. The storyteller will then be invited to talk about how this witnessing has impacted on them, with the intention of producing a more complex, reflective understanding of how they are going to develop and sustain change.

Mark may well feel that he has work to do in order for people to hear the new story he wishes to tell. He may think about who would be useful to discuss this with, how he is going to do this and what benefits this will bring. The onus is on the person to construct their 'case' for change, although we have found that younger people require more encouragement and support in considering how to do this. A range of media can be used, including talk, writing, drawing and other creative and appropriate methods, and it may be to an individual or a group. This can also have the effect of marshalling the resources that others have in supporting the desire to sustain change, and can test the confidence others have in the new story. Where violence has been within the family, it is helpful to gain the views of those who have been subjected to it in order to clarify what the person needs to do to convince actual or potential victims that their safety is being enhanced.

Epston (1998) describes the use of letters or *narrative feedback* as a way of reinforcing the emerging new story and in checking out that the sessions are as free as possible from interpretation. These letters outline the problem, identify the unique outcomes, exceptions and progress the person has made, as well as giving thoughts on where these may be strengthened and developed. This can provide the basis for further work as well as allowing the person to consider whether the worker has represented the session accurately. A written record can be read at the pace of the person, when they have time and space to do this thoughtfully, as well as being a positive document in encouraging progress.

Does narrative therapy work?

Outcome studies in Narrative Therapeutic approaches are limited due to the relatively recent development of such ideas. None the less, in its application across a range of problem areas it has proved to be useful in engaging people, thus reducing drop-out rates which limit the effectiveness of many programmes. Gorey, Thyer and Pawluck (1998: 274) undertook a robust meta-analysis of effective interventions and identified that where there was '*mutual client-worker strategizing*' *to change an external target* (a clear focus of Narrative Therapy), the outcomes were significantly better, particularly when contrasted with cognitive behavioural approaches. Also they identified that when an approach does not locate the problem within the person then outcomes are 'very effective', thus narrative therapeutic approaches fit key elements of research-informed effectiveness. The Dulwich Centre (www.narrativeapproaches.com) has frequent publications, including *The Journal of Community and Narrative Therapy*, which outline research outcomes.

Summary

- Narrative approaches are based explicitly within a postmodernist understanding of people and the world.

- Identity is seen as multiple, contradictory and varied.

- People are viewed as living their lives through 'stories', with some having more influence or power than others.

- People are viewed as primarily 'good', but being invited to be violent or irresponsible by unhelpful social stories.

- The person and the worker co-construct a preferred, problem-free future.

- The focus is on deconstructing the problem behaviour, then creating a local strategy to develop safety and responsibility.

To aid critical reflection we invite you to consider the following two interview forms and then answer the questions below.

FORM A

You will have twenty-five minutes to complete this questionnaire. Please answer questions in order and give as much information as possible in the spaces provided.

Name: Mr, Mrs, Miss, Ms:

Address:

Marital status:

Number of children:

List your academic qualifications in order from highest to lowest:

Past work experience:

Current place of employment:

In the past have you ever suffered from any of the following (please tick):

depression   anxiety

family break up   stress

heart condition   poor physical or mental health

obsessive compulsive disorder   schizophrenia

eating problems   trauma

other (please specify)

Names of two referees:

Address:

Occupation and position

_____

For office use only

FORM B

Reflect on some of the following questions and answer those that interest you. Twenty five minutes has been allowed for this exercise, however you may negotiate more time. The questionnaire belongs to you – all information is confidential and it is up to you who you share it with.

What name do you like to be called? What do you like about that?

Is there a place that holds precious memories for you? What makes this place special for you?

During your life what learnings or knowledges have been positive for you? What contribution have they made to your life?

In your life, what experiences and knowledges do you value?

Think about someone (a person or animal) in your life (alive or no longer living) that is particularly important to you and knows about your special skills. How would this person describe you? What skills, abilities, qualities, values would they talk about? What would they say if they were asked: 'what personal qualities/strengths stand out to you (your name) that will contribute to this course? How would you respond to this? Would you add any to the ones they would talk about?

How have you overcome difficulties in the past? What personal strengths and abilities did you draw upon? What did it take for you to do this? How do your experiences contribute positively to the lives of those who consult you?

Is there anyone you would like to share these reflections with? Why? What contribution would sharing this have on their life and your life?

What do you think about doing these questions and doing this task? What has been interesting to you? What would you like to think more about?

Questions

- What are the differences between Form A and Form B?

- How might the approach in Form B be used in working with people who are violent?

- What do you need to know about someone in order to assist them in changing their behaviour?

CHAPTER 9

Conclusion: Towards Effective Practices with Violence

In the Introduction we identified the move from a more welfare position to one of increasing punitiveness, and we have argued that current criminal justice practices make no attempt to understand violent behaviour, the emphasis being on offending – especially where this is prolific and/or violent – rather than the person. Technocratic and managerial approaches to violence have reinforced this loss of the individual within a welter of protocols and enforced practices that create a climate of despair and inevitability about offending behaviour, leading to the increasing frustration of workers who are directed to engage service users in limited ways of working of dubious effectiveness, particularly in the Probation Service (McIvor, 2004). We enter this arena from a position of respect for service users and for those who are subjected to violence, taking an explicit position that direct work can be effective when it recognizes and responds to the specific person, rather than the narrow construction of 'an offender'.

In our case study, Mark's violent behaviour is likely to be managed through the dominant 'what works' agenda. As we have seen, it has been claimed that re-offending could be reduced through 'high-impact' programmes which were based on a cognitive behavioural perspective, focusing on offending behaviour. The influence of new management practices is reflected in the use of structured programmes with defined aims and objectives, delivered by highly trained professionals, and the management of programmes for high treatment integrity (see, for example, Chapman and Hough, 2001). This includes probation officers to some extent, but psychologists play increasingly significant roles (Worrall, 2002). Garland suggests that treatment is framed in risk rather then welfare and that this has given rise to what he refers to as 'the reinvented prison': 'The prison is used today as a kind of reservation, a quarantine zone in which purportedly dangerous individuals are segregated in the name of public safety' (2001b: 178). Instead of being a last resort on a continuum of treatment, prison practices extend into the community where 'individuals can be identified at any point in their offending cycle – before arrest, whilst in custody, or post sentence' (*Prolific and Other Priority Offender Strategy*, July 2004: 44), and tracked via the national tracking case system. Thus community becomes a supervised space lacking much of the liberty associated with 'normal' life – electronic tagging, partial custody, curfews, drug testing and so on, and the role of the probation service becomes blended with prison and the police. Indeed, the probation service has been reorganized into 42 probation areas to correspond with local police jurisdictions.

Under this system, treatment is a specialist provision, an investment of scarce resources rather than an entitlement, closely monitored and evaluated to make sure it produces returns: 'The Rehabilitate and Resettle strand aims to present PPOs [Prolific and Priority Offenders] with a simple choice: reform or face a very swift return to the courts' (*Prolific and Other Priority Offender Strategy*, July 2004: 12). Should Mark be charged and convicted of a violent offence (which is not unlikely under zero tolerance), he would be expected to attend community-based programmes addressing drug use, anger management, offence reduction and victim empathy, all of which would involve him in a minimum of 18 sessions of two hours. If he received a prison sentence, he would be unlikely to be considered for parole unless he could produce a 'portfolio' of such programmes. Should he show reluctance to undertake 're-education', he would be offered motivational training by way of preparation to maximize his ability to utilize the programmes effectively.

Whatever his judicial disposal, Kelly's safety would be paramount. She would receive 'treatment' in that she would be kept informed, offered support, consulted prior to decision making and requested to make a victim impact statement (for a fuller discussion of restorative justice, see Wright, 1996). Should they separate and Mark remain in the community, he could be subject to restrictions on his movements if she takes out a non-molestation order. It is not impossible that he could be electronically tagged; as Nellis (2004) points out, tagging is increasingly being seen as a desirable ingredient of community supervision. It reduces prison overcrowding and costs; strengthens community punishments; introduces privatization into community punishment; and is a sophisticated way to subject offenders to some of the restrictions of prison without inflicting on them the damage of being removed from their environment; thus more women than men 'qualify' for tagging (Carlen and Worrall, 2004). At the least, his contact with his children would be supervised;

and, as this would most likely take place during the day, he would be restricted to a choice between working and seeing his children. And, despite the emphasis on Kelly's safety, she would have limited choices; the conflation of her safety with her children's interests and zero tolerance means that she would be expected to make a statement whether she wanted to or not. We have found increasingly that where women wish to stay with their violent partners, they are pressured to attend women's groups to raise their victim awareness. Despite his youth, Mark's elder boy could become a target for intervention under a scheme developed to meet the avoidance of crime set out in *Every Child Matters*; as noted earlier, the *Prolific and Other Priority Offender Strategy* specifically targets children in need from a very early age (Section 7). Thus Billy's entitlement to services could depend on him being storied as a potential offender.

The emphasis on offending rather than the person means that offenders' needs are not considered. As Caddick and Lewis (1999) point out, the presumed inability of offenders to exercise self-control must then be addressed by compelled participation in programmes of admonishment, heightened surveillance and additional constraints, management rather than treatment. At one level this involves class; the majority of the prison population are people who lack work, social welfare and family support – as one young prisoner said to us, 'it's like a council estate in here'. These factors all make it more difficult for a prisoner to reintegrate into society but, instead of these being seen as needs, they are re-storied as risk factors. At another level, individual needs arising from such things as drug use and self-harm also become risk factors, particularly with women prisoners who are seen as a potential danger to their children as well as a risk to the community (Malloch, 2004, Mosson, 2003). Thomas and colleagues (2004) found the same to be true of high-risk offenders in secure hospitals: 'Patients had diverse needs that did not fit neatly into clustered subgroups … Future service planning will need to focus on individualized treatment packages that are based on individual assessments of need, risk and responsibility.' This is easier to say than to effect. The young prisoner referred to above opted to work with us on his drug use, unhappy relationship with his father and conflictual relationships with prison staff. Despite making remarkable progress on all these problems, he was refused parole on the grounds that he had not undertaken any programmes provided *within* prison, regardless of the fact that he had been turned down for one course on the grounds that he was assessed as too high a risk and had lost out on the opportunity to attend a specialist drug treatment course (which he took the initiative to apply for) because Group Four would not guarantee his transfer to the specialist prison in under six months.

We would not argue against a focus on offending behaviour and increased victim empathy, but the system of treatment has become inflexible to say the least. This would not matter in terms of public safety if treatment programmes do indeed work.

Effective interventions?

It is difficult to assess treatment outcomes, not only does the evidence from research studies into effectiveness influence the 'facts' selected during the risk-assessment process but this 'evidence' is often distorted. Macdonald (2007) suggests that synthesising the effectiveness literature is fraught with difficulties in that literature reviews often contain biased summaries, much of the research is out of date and rarely updated by the time of publication. And there is also considerable ambiguity about 'what works' and for whom – children, families or society as a whole (Glass, 2001). The goals of these groups of people are not always identical, for example:

- government expressly wishes to be seen to be reducing prolific and violent crime in response to community concerns and media coverage;

- professionals work within a legal mandate, but also have goals that concern the efficient use of scarce resources at management level yet still avoid 'scandals' which would be given a high profile in the media;

- grassroots workers share anxiety about possible 'scandals' so prioritize risk assessment, but also need to have some sort of match with their own ideals and hypotheses if they are to deliver 'treatments' with any sort of conviction;

- service user needs are more complex, being rooted in maintaining relationships at the same time as hoping that safety and welfare needs will be met.

Carlen and Worrall (2004) suggest that the current emphasis on cognitive behavioural treatment works for governance in that it supports a 'get tough' position; for management in that it is seen to be effective and economical; for professionals in that they can be seen to be 'doing something'; and also acts in the interests of restorative justice. As discussed in Chapter 4 on cognitive behavioural approaches, the effectiveness evidence for such programmes is equivocal to say the least, and the adaptation of cognitive behavioural programmes for women is particularly problematic. Kendell (2002) argues that the derogatory nature of it is very worrisome in that offenders are conceptualized as being very different to law-abiding citizens, and that the individualizing of crime as a cognitive deficit has the general effect of holding women responsible for their own oppression. She also argues that it is not cost effective. For example, in April 2001, 68 per cent of adult female prisoners were enrolled in both Reasoning or Rehabilitation or Enhanced Thinking Skills programmes at a cost of £2500.00 and £2000.00 respectively. What, she wonders, might be accomplished if this money was used to assist women with housing and employment? This is particularly pertinent when the reconviction figures are considered (53 per cent for women and 58 per cent for men), the women's reconviction figure being particularly worrying given that one-third of women in prison are first offenders compared with 13 per cent of men. Carlen and Worrall (2004) point out that rather than addressing offending behaviour, prison exacerbates prior offending problems. Equally, cognitive behavioural programmes are not working well for young male offenders on Intensive Supervision and Surveillance Programmes. Half failed to complete, and for those who did, it could hardly be said to be cost effective – each place cost between £50,000 to £165,000, depending on whether it was run by the private sector or local authorities.

Cognitive behavioural programmes focusing on offending behaviour have become the mantra but, as we have seen, it is by no means as successful as its proponents claim (for an overview, see the meta-analysis of Gorey, Thyer and Pawluck, 1998). As long-term evaluations of programmes emerge, they are raising questions about high drop-out rates; recidivism and the inappropriateness for some people. Hollin (2004) suggests that a great deal of work needs to be carried out on the effectiveness of treatment, but rather than trying to prove that existing methods 'work', it may be more effective and efficient to introduce more flexible treatment methods that are based on strengths rather than deficits; partnership rather than coercion and a working relationship rather than the imposition of expert knowledge.

We have explicitly stated our preference for approaches that refuse to pathologize; deal in hope rather than despair and help to provide workers with energy in this often difficult area of work. It is welcome to see that during the writing of this book there have been cautious signs that the current dominance of 'rational-technical' approaches is being questioned through research evidence and through moral positions of seeking ways

of working that respect service users as individuals. 'Mark' (and 'Kelly' and
the children), as any service user, requires thoughtful interventions that
allow him to create meaningful and sustainable change, in order to live
a life free of violence. We are hopeful that this book will aid practitioners
in developing ways of working that are effective, yet retain a sense of constructive values in action.

Summary

■ There is an increased emphasis on the safety of victims, whether
these are individuals or the community in general.

■ Treatment of violent behaviour has developed on the 'what works'
agenda, despite reservations about what actually works in terms of
reducing recidivism.

■ The emphasis in treatment is on offending rather than the offender,
with socio-emotional needs being re-storied as risk factors.

■ Effective practice needs to 'fit' the individual person, rather than the
person 'fit' the practice.

Some final questions

■ Which of the guidance listed in this book do you use most frequently? How do your interventions accord with the theoretical
underpinnings of that guidance?

■ How do you explain the policy and theoretical basis of your interventions to your service users?

■ How do you offer your service users a choice of intervention most
suited to their individual learning styles and personal preferences?

■ How do you generate hope, opportunity and change with service
users and in your everyday work experience?

Bibliography

Abrahams, H. (2001) *Women's Aid Federation of England Domestic Violence Statistical Factsheet.* http://www.womensaid.org.uk/dv/dvfactsh2.htm

Ainsworth, M. D., Blehar, M. C., Waters, E. and Wall, S. (1978) *Patterns of Attachment; Assessed in a Strange Situation and at Home.* Hillsdale, NJ: Lawrence Erlbaum.

Aitkin, L. and Griffin, G. (1996) *Gender Issues in Elder Abuse.* London: Sage.

Alaszewski, A. and Manthorpe, J. (1998) 'Welfare Agencies and Risk: The Missing Link'. *Health and Social Care in the Community,* 6, 1: 4–15.

Alcock, D. (2001) 'Counselling survivors of domestic violence', *Practice,* 13: 45–54.

Appleby, K., Dyson, V., Altman, E. et al. (1996) 'Utility of the chemical use, abuse and dependence scale in screening patients with severe mental illness', *Psychiatric Services,* 47: 647–9.

Auerhahn, K. (1999) 'Selective incapacitation and the problem of prediction'. *Criminology,* 37: 703–34.

BAAF (1996) *Working with Children.* London: BAAF.

Babcock, J. C., Jacobson, N. S., Gottman, J. M. and Yerington, T. P. (2000) 'Attachment, emotional regulation, and the function of marital violence's differences between Secure, Pre-occupied, and Dismissing violent and non-violent husbands', *Journal of Family Violence,* 15: 391–410.

Baldock, J. (1998) 'Do Anger Management Courses Work?', *Prison Research and Development Bulletin,* 7: 2.

Bandura, A. (1975) *Social Learning and Personality Development.* NJ: Holt, Reinhart & Winston.

Bandura, A. (1977) *Social Learning Theory.* Englewood Cliffs, NJ.: Holt, Reinhart & Winston.

Bannister, A. (2000) 'Entering the child's world: Communicating with children to assess their needs', in J. Horwath (ed.), *The Child's World: Assessing Children in Need.* London: Department of Health/NSPCC/ University of Sheffield.

Bannister, A. and Huntington, A. (2002) *Communicating with Children: Action for Change.* London: Jessica Kingsley.

Bartholomew, K. and Horowitz, L. M. (1991) 'Attachment styles among young adults: A test of a four-category model', *Journal of Personal and Social Psychology,* 61: 226–44.

Bateman, A. and Holmes, J. (1995) *Introduction to Psychoanalysis: Contemporary Theory and Practice.* London: Routledge.

Bates, A., Falshaw, L., Corbett, C., Patel and V. Friendship, C. (2004) 'A follow-up study of sex offenders treated by Thames Valley Sex Offender Groupwork Programme. 1995–1999', *Journal of Sexual Aggression*, 10: 29–38.

Baxter, S. and Rogers, L. (2003) 'Stiff upper lip beats stress counselling', *Sunday Times*, 2 March.

Beaumont, B. (1999) 'Assessing risk in work with offenders', in P. Parsloe (ed.), *Risk Assessment in Social Care and Social Work*. London: Jessica Kingsley.

Beck, A. T. (1967) *Depression: Clinical, Experimental and Theoretical Aspects*. London: Hoeber.

Beck, A. T. (1976) *Cognitive Therapy and Emotional Disorders*. New York: International Universities Press.

Beck, U. (1998) 'Politics of risk society', in J. Franklin (ed.), *The Politics of Risk Society*. Cambridge: Polity Press.

Bellack, A. and DiClemente, C. (1999) 'Treating substance abuse among patients with schizophrenia', *Psychiatric Services*, 50: 75–80.

Belsky, J. and Nezworski, T. (eds), (1998) *Clinical Implications of Attachment*. New Jersey: Lawrence Erlbaum.

Berg, I. K. (1994) *Family-Based Services: A Solution-Focused Approach*. New York and London: W. W. Norton.

Berg, I. K. and Miller, S. (1992) *Working with the Problem Drinker: A Solution-Focused Approach*. New York and London: W. W. Norton.

Berlin, S. (1990) 'Dichotomous and complex thinking', *Social Service Review*, March: 46–59.

Berne, E. (1978) *A Layman's Guide to Psychiatry and Psychoanalysis*. London: Penguin.

Bertolino, B. and O'Hanlon, B. (1998) *Invitations to Possibility Land*. Philadelphia, PA: Brunner Mazel.

Besley, A. C. (2002) 'Foucault and the turn to narrative therapy', *British Journal of Guidance and Counselling*, 30, 2: 125–43.

Bird, J. (2000) *The Heart's Narrative: Therapy and Navigating Life's Contradictions*. Auckland: Edge Press.

Blakemore, J. (1999) *Troubling Women: Feminism, Leadership and Educational Change*. Buckingham: Open University Press.

Bograd, M. L. (1990) 'Feminist perspectives on wife abuse: An introduction', in: K. Yllo and M. L. Bograd (eds), *Feminist Perspectives on Wife Abuse*. London: Sage.

Bonta, J. (2002) *An Overview of the What Works Literature and its Relevance to England and Wales*. Home Office and National Probation Service presentation, 12 March, Home Office, London.

Boric, R. and Desnica, M. M. (1996) 'Croatia: three years after', in: C. Corrin (ed.) *Women in a Violent World: Feminist Analyses and Resistance Across 'Europe'*. Edinburgh: Edinburgh University Press.

Bowlby, J. (1953) *Child Care and the Growth of Love*. Harmondsworth: Penguin.

Bowlby, J. (1963) 'Pathological mourning and childhood mourning', *Journal of the American Psychoanalytic Association*, 118: 500–41.

Bowlby, J. (1979) *The Making and Breaking of Affectional Bonds*. London: Tavistock.

Bowlby, J. (1988) *A Secure Base: Clinical Implications of Attachment Theory.* London: Routledge.

Brandon, M. and Lewis, A. (1996) 'Significant harm and children's experiences of domestic violence', *Child and Family Social Work,* 1: 33–42.

Breakwell, G. (1995) 'Theories of violence', in: S. Kidd and C. Stark (eds), *Management of Violence and Aggression in Health Care.* London: Gaskell.

Bretherton, I. (1992) 'The origins of attachment theory: John Bowlby and Mary Ainsworth', *Developmental Psychology,* 28: 759–75.

Bretherton, I. and Waters, E. (eds), (1985) 'Growing points of attachment theory and research', *Monographs of the Society for Research in Child Development,* 50: 209

Briggs, D. (1998) *Assessing Men who Sexually Abuse: A Practice Guide.* London: Jessica Kingsley.

Briggs, S. (2002) *Working with Adolescents: A Contemporary Psychodynamic Approach.* Basingstoke: Palgrave.

Browne, K. and Hamilton, C. E. (1998) 'Physical violence between young adults and their parents: Associations with a history of child maltreatment', *Journal of Family Violence,* 13: 59–80.

Burton, S., Regan, L. and Kelly, L. (1989) *Supporting Women and Challenging Men: Lessons from Domestic Violence Intervention Programmes.* Bristol: Polity Press.

Bush, J. (1995) 'Teaching self-risk management to violent offenders', in J. McGuire (ed.), *What Works: Reducing Reoffending. Guidelines from Research and Practice.* Chichester: Wiley.

Bushman, B. J., Baumeister, R. F. and Stack, A. D. (1999) 'Catharsis, aggression and persuasive influence: Self-fulfilling or self-defeating prophecies?', *Journal of Personality and Social Psychology,* 76: 367–76.

Butcher, N. J., Dahlstrom, W. G., Graham, J. R., Tellegren, A. and Kraemmer, B. (1989) *Minnesota Multiphasic Personality Inventory (MMPI–2): Manual for administration and scoring.* Minneapolis, MN: University of Minnesota Press.

Butler, J. (1992) 'Contingent foundations: Feminism and the question of "postmodernism"', in J. Butler and J. W. Scott (eds), *Feminists Theorize the Political.* London: Routledge.

Butler, M. J. (1995) 'Domestic violence: A nursing imperative', *Journal of Holistic Nursing,* 13: 54–69.

Butt, T. (2003) *Understanding People.* Basingstoke: Palgrave

Byng-Hall, J. (1985) 'The family script: A useful bridge between theory and practice', *Journal of Family Therapy,* 7: 301–5

Byng-Hall, J (1991) 'Understanding and treatment in the family', in C. Murray-Parkes, J. Stevenson-Hinde and P. Marris (eds), *Attachment Across the Life Cycle.* London: Routledge.

Caddick, B. and Lewis, D. (1999) 'Rehabilitation and the distribution of risk', in P. Parsloe (ed.), *Risk Assessment in Social Care and Social Work.* London: Jessica Kingsley Publishing.

Caldwell, M. F. (2002) 'What we do not know about juvenile sexual reoffense risk', *Child Maltreatment,* 7, 4: 291–302.

Campbell, D. (1997) 'Assessment of risk in the family justice system', in Mr Justice Wall (ed.), *Rooted Sorrows: Psychoanalytic Perspectives on Child Protection, Assessment and Treatment*. Bristol: Family Law.

Campbell, J. C. (1986) 'Nursing assessment for risk of homicide with battered women', *Advances in Nursing Science*, 8: 36–51.

Campbell, J. C. (1995) 'Prediction of homicide by battered women', in: J. C. Campbell (ed.), *Assessing Dangerousness*. Newbury Park, CA: Sage.

Campbell, J. C. (2002) 'Health consequences of intimate partner violence', *The Lancet*, 359: 1331–6.

Cann, J. (2006) 'Cognitive skills programmes: Impact on reducing reconviction among a sample of female prisoners', *Home Office Findings 276*. London: Home Office.

Cann, J., Falshaw, L. Nugent, F. and Friendship, C. (2003) 'Understanding what works: Accredited cognitive skills programmes for adult men and young offenders', *Home Office Findings 226*. London: Home Office.

Caplan, G. (1961) *An Approach to Community Mental Health*. London: Tavistock.

Carey, K. (1995) 'Treatment of substance abuse disorders and schizophrenia', in A. Lehman and L. Dixon (eds), *Double Jeopardy: Chronic Mental Illness and Substance Use Disorders*. Chur, Switzerland: Harwood Academic.

Carlen, P. (2002) 'Introduction: Women and punishment', in P. Carlen (ed.), *Women and Punishment: The Struggle for Justice*. Cullompton, Devon: Willan Publishing.

Carlen, P. and Worrall, A. (2004) *Analysing Women's Imprisonment*. Cullompton, Devon: Willan Publishing.

Castel, R. (1991) 'From dangerousness to risk', in G. Burchell, C. Gordon and P. Miller (eds), *The Foucault Effect: Studies in Governmentality*. Chicago: University of Chicago Press.

Cavanagh, K. and Lewis, R. (1996) 'Interviewing violent men: Challenge or compromise?', in K. Cavanagh and V. Cree (eds), *Working with Men: Feminism and Social Work*. London: Routledge.

Cavender, G. (2004) 'Media and crime policy', *Punishment and Society*, 6: 318–45.

Cayouette, S. (1999) 'Running batterers' groups for lesbians', in B. Levanthal and S. E. Lundy (eds), *Same-Sex Domestic Violence: Strategies for Change*. London: Sage.

Chapman, T. and Hough, M. (2001) *Evidence-Based Practice: A Guide to Effective Practice*. London: H.O.I.P.

Chandler, T. and Taylor, J. (1995) *Lesbians Talk: Violent Relationships*. London: Scarlet Books.

Cicirelli, V. G. (1991) 'Attachment theory in old age: Protection of the attachment figure', in K. Pillemer and K. McCartney (eds), *Parent-Child Relations Across the Life Course*. Hillsdale, NJ: Lawrence Erlbaum.

Cigno, K. (1998) 'Cognitive behaviour practice', in R. Adams, L. Dominelli and M. Payne (eds), *Social Work: Themes, Issues and Critical Debates*. Basingstoke: Palgrave Macmillan.

Colledge, R. (2002) *Mastering Counselling Theory*. Basingstoke: Palgrave.

College Research Unit (1998) *Management of Imminent Violence: Clinical Guidelines to Support Mental Health Services. Occasional Paper OP41: Assessing the Risk of Violence on Wards*. London: Royal College of Psychiatrists' Research Unit.

Cordery, J. and Whitehead, A. (1992) 'Boys don't cry: Empathy, collusion and crime', in P. Senior and B. Woodhill (eds), *Gender, Crime and Probation Practice*. Sheffield: Pavic Publications, Sheffield City Polytechnic.

Corrin, C. (1996) 'Introduction: Feminist campaigning and networking', in C. Corrin (ed.), *Women in a Violent World: Feminist Analyses and Resistance Across 'Europe'*. Edinburgh: Edinburgh University Press.

Cosgrove, K. (1996) 'No man has the right', in C. Corrin (ed.), *Women in a Violent World: Feminist Analyses and Resistance Across 'Europe'*. Edinburgh: Edinburgh University Press.

Counts, D. A., Brown, J. K. and Campbell, J. (1992) *Sanctions And Sanctuary: Cultural Perspectives on the Beating of Wives*. Thousand Oaks, CA: Sage.

Craig, L. A. (2004) 'Limitations in actuarial risk assessment of sexual offenders: A methodological note', *British Journal of Forensic Practice*, 6, 1: 16–32.

Crittenden, P. M. (1988) 'Family and dyadic patterns of functioning in maltreating families', in: K. Browne, K. D. Davis and P. Stratton (eds), *Early Prediction and Prevention of Child Abuse*. Chichester: Wiley.

Crittenden, P. M. (1999) 'Child neglect: Causes and contributors', in: H. Dubowitz (ed.), *Neglected Children: Research, Practice and Policy*. Thousand Oaks, CA: Sage.

Crome, I. B. (1999) 'Substance misuse and psychiatric comorbidity: Towards improved service provision', *Drugs, Education, Prevention and Policy*, 68: 151–74.

Cullen, M. and Freeman-Longo, R. E. (1995) *Men and Anger: Understanding and Managing Your Anger*. Holyoke, MA: NEARI Press.

Currie, D. H. (1990) 'Battered women and the state: From failure of theory to a theory of failure', *Journal of Human Justice*, 1: 77–96.

Daly, M. and Wilson, M. (1988) *Homicide*. New York: Aldine.

Davies, K. and Edwards, G. (1999) 'Domestic violence: A challenge to accident and emergency nurses', *Accident and Emergency Nursing*, 7: 26–30.

De Jong, P. and Berg, I. K. (2002) *Interviewing for Solutions*. 2nd edn, Pacific Grove, CA: Brooks/Cole.

De Shazer, S. (1985) *Keys to Solutions in Brief Therapy*. New York and London: W. W. Norton.

De Shazer, S. (1988) *Clues: Investigating Solutions in Brief Therapy*. New York and London: W. W. Norton.

De Shazer, S. (1991) *Putting Difference to Work*. New York and London: W. W. Norton.

De Shazer, S. (1994) *Words Were Originally Magic*. New York and London: W. W. Norton.

Debbonaire, T. (1994) 'Work with children in women's aid refuges and after', in A. Mullender and R. Morley (eds), *Children Living with Domestic Violence: Putting Men's Abuse of Children on the Child Care Agenda*. London: Whiting and Birch.

Department of Health (1988) *Protecting Children: A Guide for Social Workers Undertaking a Comprehensive Assessment*. London: HMSO.

Department of Health/Department for Education and Employment/Home Office (2000) *Framework for the Assessment of Children in Need and their Families*. London: HMSO.

Department of Health (2002a) *Publication of Draft Mental Health Bill: Press Release 26 June 2002*, 2002/0284: www.doh.gov.uk/PublicationsandStatistics/PressReleases.

Department of Health. (2002b) *Mental Health Policy Implementation Guide: Dual Diagnosis Good Practice Guide*. www.doh.gov.uk/mentalhealth.

Department of Health (2003) *Mainsteaming Gender and Women's Mental Health*. www.doh.uk/mentalhealth.

Department of Health (2004a) *Domestic Violence: A Resource Manual for Healthcare Professionals*. www.doh.uk.gov/domestic.htm.

Department of Health (2004b) *National Task Force on Violence Against Social Care Staff*. www.doh.gov.uk/violencetaskforce/overview.htm.

Derlet, R. W. and Richards, J. R. (2000) 'Overcrowding – the nation's emergency departments: Complex causes and disturbing effects', *Annals of Emergency Medicine*, 35: 63–8.

Dermer, S. B., Hemesath, C. W. and Russell, C. S. (1998) 'A feminist critique of solution focused therapy', *American Journal of Family Therapy*, 26: 239–50.

Derrida, J. (1973) *Writing and Difference*. Chicago: Chicago University Press.

Dexheimer, M. (2002) 'Coming to know ourselves as a community through a nursing partnership with adolescents convicted of murder', *Advances in Nursing Science*, 24: 21–42.

Dobash, R. E. and Dobash, R. P. (1992) *Women, Violence and Social Change*. London: Routledge.

Dobash, R. E., Dobash, R. P., Cavanagh, K. and Lewis, R. (1995) 'Evaluating programmes for violent men: Can violent men change?', in R. E. Dobash, R. P. Dobash and L. Noaks (eds), *Gender and Crime*. Cardiff: University of Wales Press; Concord, MA: Paul.

Dobash, R. E., Dobash, R. P., Cavanagh, K. and Lewis, R. (1996) *Research Evaluation of Programmes for Violent Men*. Edinburgh: HMSO.

Dobash, R. E., Dobash, R. P., Cavanagh, K. and Lewis, R. (1998) 'Separate and intersecting realities: A comparison of men's and women's accounts of violence against women', *Violence Against Women*, 4: 382–414.

Dobash, R. E., Dobash, R. P., Cavanagh, K. and Lewis, R. (2000) *Changing Violent Men*. London: Sage.

Dogra, N., Parkin, A., Gale, F. and Frake, C. (2002) *A Multidisciplinary Handbook of Child and Adolescent Mental Health for Front Line Professionals*. London: Jessica Kingsley.

Dolan, Y. (1998) *One Small Step: Moving beyond Trauma and Therapy to a Life of Joy*. Watsonville, CA, Papier Mache Press.

Dominelli, L. and Cowburn, M. (2001) Masking hegemonic masculinity: Reconstructing the paedophile as the dangerous stranger. *British Journal of Social Work*, 31, 3: 399–415.

Donaghy, M. (2003) 'Models of mental health disorder', in T. Everett., M. Donaghy and S. Feaver (eds), *Interventions for Mental Health: An Evidence-Based Approach for Physiotherapists and Occupational Therapists*. London: Butterworth Heineman.

Douglas, M. (1992) *Risk and Blame: Essays in Cultural Theory*. London, Routledge.

Downes, D. (2001) 'The macho penal policy: Mass incarceration in the United States – a European perspective', in D. Garland (ed.), *Mass Imprisonment: Social Causes and Consequences*. London: Sage.

Durrant, M. (1993) *Creative Strategies for School Problems*. Epping, NSW: Eastwood Family Therapy Centre.

Dutton, D. G., Saunders, K., Starzowski, A. and Bartholomew, K. (1994) 'Intimacy – anger and insecure attachment as precursors of abuse in intimate relationships', *Journal of Applied Social Psychology*, 24: 1367–86.

Elliott, A. (2001) *Concepts of the Self*. Cambridge: Polity.

Elliott, A. (2002) *Psychoanalysis: An Introduction*. 2nd edn, Basingstoke: Palgrave.

Ellis, A. (1962) *Reason and Emotion in Psychotherapy*. New York: Lyle Stuart.

Epston, D. (1998) *Catching Up with David Epston: A Collection of Narrative Practice-Based Papers, 1991–1996*. Adelaide: Dulwich Centre Publications.

Erickson, E. H. (1948) *Childhood and Society*. Harmondsworth: Penguin.

Erickson, M. H. (1959) *Hypnotherapy: An Exploratory Casebook*. New York: Irvington.

Essex, S., Gumbelton, J. and Luger, C. (1996) 'Resolutions: Working with families where responsibility for abuse is denied', *Child Abuse Review*, 5: 191–201.

Everett, T., Donaghy, M. and Feaver, S. (2003) *Interventions for Mental Health: An Evidence-Based Approach for Physiotherapists and Occupational Therapists*. London: Heinemann.

Fahlberg, V. (1981a) *Attachment and Separation*. London: BAAF.

Fahlberg, V. (1981b) *Helping Children When They Must Move*. London: BAAF.

Fahlberg, V. (1982) *Child Development*. London: BAAF.

Fahlberg, V. (1984) 'The child who is "stuck"', in: M. Adcock and R. White (eds), *In Touch with Parents*. London: BAAF.

Fahlberg, V. (1988a) *Putting the Pieces Together*. London: BAAF.

Fahlberg, V. (1988b) *The Child in Placement*. London: BAAF.

Falshaw, L., Friendship, C., Travers, R. and Nugent, F. (2003) 'Searching for "What Works": An evaluation of the cognitive skills programmes', *Home Office Findings 206*. London: Home Office.

Falshaw, L., Friendship, C. Travers, R. and Nugent, F. (2004) 'Searching for "What Works": HM Prison Service accredited cognitive skills programmes', *The British Journal of Forensic Practice*, 6, 2: 3–11.

Farmer, E. and Owen, M. (1995) *Child Protection: Private Risks and Public Remedies*. London: HMSO.

Farringdon, D. P., Hancock, G., Livingston, M. Painter, K. and Towl, G. (2000) 'Evaluation of Intensive Regimes for Young Offenders'. *Home Office Research Findings 163*. London: Home Office.

Featherstone, B. (1999) 'Mothering and the child protection system', in The Violence Against Children Study Group (editorial collective), *Children, Child Abuse and Child Protection: Placing Children Centrally*. Chichester: Wiley.

Feeley, M. M. and Simon, J. (1992) 'The new penology: Notes on the emerging strategy of corrections and its implications', *Criminology*, 30: 449–74.

Finkelhor, D. (1983) 'Common features of family abuse', in D. Finkelhor, R. Gelles, G. Hotaling and M. Straus (eds), *The Dark Side of Families: Current Family Violence Research*. Beverley Hills: Sage.

Fitzroy, L. (2002) 'Violent women: Questions for feminist theory, practice and policy', *Critical Social Policy*, 21: 7–34.

Fonagy, P. (1999) 'Psychoanalytic theory from the standpoint of attachment theory and research', in J. Cassidy and P. R. Shaver (eds), *Handbook of Attachment: Theory, Research and Clinical Applications*. New York: Guilford Press.

Fonagy, P. (2003) 'Towards a developmental understanding of violence', *British Journal of Psychiatry*: 190–2.

Fook, J. (2002) *Social Work: Critical Theory and Practice*. London, Sage.

Foucault, M. (1965) *Madness and Civilisation: A History of Insanity in the Age of Reason*, trans. R. Howard. London, Routledge.

Foucault, M. (1973) *The Birth of the Clinic: an Archaeology of Medical Perception*, trans. A. M. Sheridan. London, Tavistock.

Fraiberg, S. (1980) *Clinical Studies in Infant Mental Health*. London: Tavistock.

Fraiberg, S., Adelson, E. and Shapiro, V. (1975) 'Ghosts in the nursery: A psycho-analytic approach to the problems of impaired infant-mother relationships', *Journal of the American Academy of Child Psychiatry*, 14: 387–421.

Freeman, J., Epston, D. and Lebovits, D. (1997) *Playful Approaches to Serious Problems*. New York: W. W. Norton.

Freud, S. (1962) 'The ego and the id', in J. Strachey (ed), *Standard Edition of the Complete Works of Sigmund Freud 19*. London: Hogarth.

Fromm, E. (1985) 'The mode and function of an analytic social psychology: Notes on psychoanalytic and historical materialism', in A. Arato and E. Gebhurdt (eds), *The Essential Frankfurt School Reader*. New York: Continuum.

Frost, M. (1997) 'Health visitors' perceptions of domestic violence', *Health Visitor*, 70: 258–9.

Fuller, C. and Taylor, P. (undated) *Toolkit of Motivational Skills: A Practice Handbook for Using Motivational Skills in the Work of the Probation Service*. London: National Probation Service.

Furman, B. and Ahola, T. (1992) *Solution Talk: Hosting Therapeutic Conversations*. New York and London: W. W. Norton.

Gallwey, P. (1997) 'Bad parenting and pseudo-parenting', in Mr Justice Wall (ed.), *Rooted Sorrows: Psychoanalytic Perspectives on Child Protection, Assessment and Treatment*. Bristol: Family Law.

Garland, D. (2001a) 'The meaning of mass imprisonment', in D. Garland (ed.), *Mass Imprisonment: Social Causes and Consequences*. London: Sage.

Garland, D. (2001b) *The Culture of Control: Crime and Social Order in Contemporary Society*. Oxford: Oxford University Press.

Genders, E. and Morrison, S. (1996) 'When violence is the norm', in N. Walker (ed.), *Dangerous People*. London: Blackstone Press.

Gibb, R. C. and Macpherson, G. J. D. (2000) 'A common language of classification and understanding', in T. Thompson and P. Matthias (eds), *Lyttle's Mental Health and Disorder*. 3rd edn, London: Balliere Tyndall/Royal College of Nursing.

Gilchrist, E., Johnson, R., Takriti, R., Weston, S., Beech, A. and Kebbell, M. (2003) 'Domestic violence offenders: Characteristics and offending related needs', *Home Office Findings 217*. London: Home Office.

Glass, N. (2001) 'What works for children – the political issues', *Children and Society*, 15: 14–20.

Goldstein, J., Freud, A. and Solnit, A. (1973) *Beyond the Best Interests of the Child*. London, Collier-Macmillan.

Goldstein, J., Freud, A. and Solnit, A. (1979) *Before the Best Interests of the Child*. New York, Free Press.

Goldstein, J., Freud, A. and Solnit, A. (1985) *In the Best Interests of the Child*. New York, Free Press.

Gondolf, E. (1998) 'Do batterer programs work? A 15-month follow-up of a multi-site evaluation', *Domestic Violence Report*, 3: 64–5 and 87–9.

Gondolf, E. W. and White, R. J. (2001) 'Batterer program participants who repeatedly reassault: Psychopathic tendencies and other disorders', *Journal of Interpersonal Violence*, 16: 361–80.

Gorer, G. (1966) 'Psychoanalysis in the world', in C. Rycroft, G. Gorer, A. Storr, J. Wren-Lewis and P. Lomas (eds), *Psychoanalysis Observed*. Harmondsworth: Penguin.

Gorey, K. M., Thyer, B. A. and Pawluck, D. E. (1998) 'Differential effectiveness of prevalent social work practice models: A meta-analysis', *Social Work*, 43, 3: 269–78.

Graddol, D. and Swann, J. (1989) *Gender Voices*. New York: W. W. Norton.

Grady, A. (2002) 'Female-on-male domestic abuse: Uncommon or ignored?', in R. Young and C. Hoyle (eds), *New Visions of Crime Victims*. Oxford: Hart.

Greenwood, P. W. and Abrahamse, A. (1982) *Selective Incapacitation*. Santa Monica, CA: RAND.

Grevatt, M., Thomas-Peter, B. and Hughes, G. (2004) 'Violence, mental disorder and risk assessment: Can structural clinical assessments predict the short-term risk of inpatient violence?', *Journal of Forensic Psychiatry and Psychology*, 15: 278–92.

Grossman, K., Grossman, K. E. and Spangler, G. (1985) 'Maternal sensitivity and newborns' orientation responses as related to quality of attachment in Northern Germany', in I. Bretherton and E. Waters (eds), *Growing Points of Attachment Theory and Research*, Monographs of the Society for Research in Child Development 50. Chicago: University of Chicago Press, p. 209.

Grubin, D. (1998). *Sex Offending Against Children: Understanding the Risk*. Police Research Series Paper 99. London: Home Office.

Gupta, R. (2003) *From Homebreakers to Jailbreakers*. Zed Books. zed@zedbooks.demon.co.uk

Hackett, S. (2000). 'Sexual aggression, diversity and the challenge of anti-oppressive practice', *The Journal of Sexual Aggression*, 5, 1: 4–20.

Halliday, M. A. K. (ed.), (1978) *Language as Social Semiotic: The Social Interpretation of Language and Meaning*. London, Arnold.

Hanmer, J. (1990) 'Men, power and the exploitation of women', in J. Hearn and D. Morgan (eds), *Men, Masculinities and Social Theory*. London: Unwin Hyman.

Hanmer, J. (1995) 'Patterns of agency contacts with Women who have experienced violence from known men', *Research Unit on Violence, Abuse and Gender Relations*, University of Bradford, Research Paper No. 12.

Hanmer, J. and Saunders, S. (1984) *Well-Founded Fear: A Community Study of Violence to Women*. London: Hutchinson.

Hanson, B. and Maroney, T. (1999) 'HIV and same-sex domestic violence', in B. Leventhal and S. E. Lundy (eds), *Same Sex Domestic Violence: Strategies for Change*. London: Sage.

Hanson, R. K. (2004) 'Sex offender risk assessment', in C. R. Hollin (ed), *The Essential Handbook of Offender Assessment and Treatment*. Chichester: Wiley.

Hanson, R. K. and Thornton, D. (1999) *Static-99: Improving Actuarial Risk Assessments for Sex Offenders*. Ottawa: Department of the Solicitor General of Canada.

Hardy, M. S. (2001) 'Physical aggression and sexual behaviour among siblings: A retrospective study', *Journal of Family Violence*, 16: 255–268.

Hart, B. J. and Gondolf, E. W. (1994) 'Lethality and dangerousness in assessment', *Violence Update*, 4: 7–10.

Hart, D. A. and Kirby, S. D. (2004) 'Risk prevention', in S. D. Kirby., D. A. Hart., D. Cross and G. Mitchell. *Mental Health Nursing. Competence for Practice*. Basingstoke: Macmillan.

Harty, M.-A., Shaw, J., Thomas, S., Dolan, M., Davies, L., Thornicroft, G., Carlisle, J., Morend, M., Leese, M., Appleby, L. and Jones, P. (2004) 'The security, clinical and social needs of patients in high security psychiatric hospitals in England', *Journal of Forensic Psychiatry and Psychology*, 15: 209–21.

Hasin, D., Trautman, K., Miele, G. et al. (1996) 'Psychiatric research interview for substance and mental disorders (PRISM): Reliability for substance abusers', *American Journal of Psychiatry*, 153: 1195–201.

Hazan, C. and Shaver, P. (1987) 'Romantic love conceptualized as an attachment process', *Journal of Personal and Social Psychology*, 52: 511–24.

Healey, A., Knapp, M., Astin, J., Glossop, M., Marsden, J., Stewart, D., Lehman, P. and Godfrey, C. (1998) 'Economic burden of drug dependency', *British Journal of Psychiatry*, 173: 160–5.

Healy, K. (2000) *Social Work Practices*. London: Sage.

Hearn, J. (1990) '"Child abuse" and men's violence', in Violence Against Children Study Group (editorial collective), *Taking Child Abuse Seriously: Contemporary Issues in Child Protection Theory and Practice*. London: Unwin Hyman.

Hearn, J. (1998) *The Violences of Men: How Men Talk About and How Agencies Respond to Men's Violence to Women*. London: Sage.

Hearn, J. (1999) 'Ageism, violence and abuse – theoretical and practical perspectives on the links between "child abuse" and "elder abuse"', in The Violence

Against Children Study Group (editorial collective), *Children, Child Abuse and Child Protection. Placing Children Centrally*. Chichester: Wiley.

Hearn, J. and Morgan, D. (eds), (1990) *Men, Masculinities and Social Theory*. London: Unwin Hyman.

Hearn, J. and Parkin, W. (1987) '"Sex" at "Work"', *The Power and Paradox of Organisational Sexuality*. Brighton: Wheatsheaf Books.

Henning, K., Jones, A. R. and Holdford, R. (2005) 'I didn't do it, but if I did I had good reason: Minimization, denial and attributions of blame among male and female domestic violence offenders', *Journal of Family Therapy*, 20 (June): 131–6.

Hesse, E. (1999) 'The adult attachment interview: Historical and current perspectives', in J. Cassidy and P. R. Shaver (eds), *Handbook of Attachment: Theory, Research and Clinical Implications*. New York: Guilford Press.

Hester, M., Kelly, L. and Radford, J. (eds), (1996) *Women, Violence and Male Power*. Buckingham: Open University Press.

Hester, M., Pearson, C. and Harwin, N. (1999) *Making an Impact: Children and Domestic Violence – a Reader*. London: Jessica Kingsley.

Hester, M., Pearson, C. and Radford, L. (1997) *Domestic Violence: A National Survey of Court Welfare and Voluntary Sector Mediation Practice*. Bristol: Polity Press.

Hester, M., Humphries, J., Pearson, C., Qaiser, K., Radford, L. and Woodfield, K.-S. (1994) 'Domestic violence and child contact', in A. Mullender and R. Morley (eds), *Children Living with Domestic Violence: Putting Men's Abuse of Women on the Child Care Agenda*. London: Whiting and Birch.

Hodge, J., Williams, B., Andreou, C., Lanyardo, M., Bentovim, A. and Skuse, D. (1997) 'Children who sexually abuse other children', in Mr Justice Wall (ed.), *Rooted Sorrows. Psychoanalytic Perspectives on Child Protection, Assessment and Treatment*. Bristol: Family Law.

Hollin, C. R. (1990) 'Social skills training and delinquents: A look at the evidence and some recommendations for practice', *British Journal of Social Work*, 20, 5: 483–93.

Hollin, C. R. (1999) 'Treatment programmes for offenders: New findings on criminal rehabilitation', *International Journal of Law and Psychiatry*, 22, 3: 361–72.

Hollin, C. R. (2004) 'To treat or not to treat? An historical perspective', in C. R. Holliin (ed.), *The Essential Handbook of Offender Assessment and Treatment*. Chichester: Wiley.

Home Office/Department of Health/Welsh Office (1995) *National Standards for the Supervision of Offenders in the Community*. London: Home Office Probation Services Division.

Home Office (2002) *Justice for All*. London: Stationery Office.

Home Office (2003a) *Living Without Fear: An Integrated Approach to Tackling Violence Against Women*. London: Home Office.

Home Office (2003b) *Safety and Justice: The Government's Proposals on Domestic Violence*. London: Home Office.

Home Office (2004) *The Prolific and Other Priority Offenders Strategy*. London: Home Office.

Horsefield, A. (2003) 'Risk assessment: Who needs it?' *Probation Journal*, 50, 4: 374–9.

Horwath, J. (ed.), (2000) *The Child's World. Assessing Children In Need*. London: Department of Health/NSPCC/University of Sheffield.

Howe, D. (1995) *Attachment Theory for Social Work Practice*. Basingstoke: Macmillan.

Howe, D. (2000) 'Attachment', in: J. Horwath (ed.), *The Child's World: Assessing Children In Need*. London: Department of Health/NSPCC/University of Sheffield.

Howell, M. J. and Pugliesi, K. L. (1998) 'Husbands who harm: Predicting spousal violence by men', *Journal of Family Violence*, 3: 15–28.

Hoyle, C. (1998) *Negotiating Domestic Violence: Police, Criminal Justice and Victims*. Oxford: Oxford University Press.

Humphreys, C. (1999) 'Avoidances and confrontations: Social work practice in relation to domestic violence and child abuse', *Child and Family Social Work*, 4: 77–87.

Humphreys. C. (2000) *Social Work, Domestic Violence and Child Protection: Challenging Practice*. Bristol: The Policy Press.

Humphreys, C., Hester, M., Hague, G., Mullender, A., Abrahams, H. and Lowe, P. (2000) *From Good Intentions to Good Practice: Mapping Services Working with Families where there is Domestic Violence*. Bristol: The Policy Press.

Humphreys, C., Mullender, A., Lowe, P., Hague, G., Abrahams, H. and Hester, M. (2001) 'Domestic violence and child abuse: Developing sensitive policies and guidance', *Child Abuse Review*, 10: 183–97.

Hunt, S. C. and Martin, A. M. (2001) *Pregnant Women, Violent Men: What Midwives Need to Know*. Oxford: BFM/Books for Midwives.

Ingram, R. (1994) 'Taking a proactive approach: Communicating with women experiencing violence from a known man in the Emergency department', *Accident and Emergency Nursing*, 2: 143–8.

Island, D. and Lettelier, P. (1991) *Men Who Beat the Men Who Love Them: Battered Men and Domestic Violence*. New York: Haworth.

Jacobs, M. (1988) *Psychodynamic Counselling in Action*. London: Sage.

Jenkins, A. (1990) *Invitations to Responsibility*. Adelaide: Dulwich Centre Publications.

Jenkins, A. (1996) 'Moving towards respect: a quest for balance', in C. McClean, M. Carey and C. White (eds), *Men's Ways of Being*. Colorado, Oxford: Westview Press.

Johnson, H. and Sacco, V. (1995) 'Researching violence against women: Statistics of Canada's National Survey', *Canadian Journal of Criminology*, July: 281–304.

Johnstone, M. (2000) 'Men, masculinity and offending', *Probation Journal*, 48: 10–16.

Jones, D. (2000) 'The assessment of parental capacity', in J. Horwath (ed.), *The Child's World: Assessing Children In Need*. London: Department of Health/NSPCC/University of Sheffield.

Jordan, J. V. (1997) 'A relational perspective for understanding women's development', in J. V. Jordan (ed.), *Women's Growth and Diversity: More Writings from the Stone Centre*. New York: Guilford Press.

Joseph, G. (1981) 'Black mothers and daughters: Their role and functions in American society', in G. Joseph and J. Lewis (eds), *Common Differences*. Garden City, NY: Anchor.

Jukes, A. (1996) 'Working with men who are violent to women', in S. Palmer, S. Dainow and P. Milner (eds), *Counselling: The BAC Counselling Reader*. London: Sage.

Kearney, R. (2002) *On Stories*. London and New York: Routledge.

Kemshall, H. (ed.), (2000) *Good Practice in Working with Victims of Violence*. London: Jessica Kingsley.

Kemshall, H. (2001) *Risk Assessment and Management of Known Sexual and Dangerous Offenders*. London: Home Office Policy and Reducing Crime Unit Paper 140.

Kendell, R. E. (2002) 'The distinction between personality disorder and mental illness', *British Journal of Psychiatry*: 101–15.

Kennedy, R. (1997) 'Assessment of parenting', in Mr Justice Wall (ed.), *Rooted Sorrows: Psychoanalytic Perspectives on Child Protection, Assessment and Treatment*. Bristol: Family Law.

Kesner, D. E. and McKenry, P. C. (1998) 'The role of childhood attachment factors in predicting male violence toward female intimates', *Journal of Family Violence*, 13: 417–32.

Kingston, P. and Penhale, B. (1995) 'Elder abuse and neglect: Issues in the Accident and Emergency department', *Accident and Emergency Nursing*, 3: 122–8.

Kirby, S. D. and Hart, D. A. (2004) 'Risk prevention', in: S. D. Kirby, D. A. Hart, D. Cross and G. Mitchell (eds), *Mental Health Nursing: Competence for Practice*. Basingstoke: Palgrave.

Kirkwood, C. (1993) *Leaving Abusive Partners: From the Scars of Survival to the Wisdom for Change*. London: Sage.

Klassen, D. and O'Connor, W. A. (1988) 'Crime, inpatient admissions and violence amongst male mental patients', *International Journal of Law and Psychiatry*, 11: 305–12.

Klein, M. (1988) *Love, Guilt and Reparation and Other Works: 1921–1945*. London: Virago.

Kreisman, J. J. and Straus, H. (1989) *'I hate you, don't leave me': Understanding the Borderline Personality*. New York: Avon Books.

Langan, M. and Day, L. (1992) *Women, Oppression and Social Work: Issues in Anti-Discriminatory Practice*. London, Routledge.

Lee, M. Y., Sebold, J. and Uken, A. (2003) *Solution Focused Treatment of Domestic Violence Offenders: Accountability for Change*. Oxford: Oxford University Press.

Leventhal, B. and Lundy, S. E. (1999) *Same-Sex Domestic Violence: Strategies for Change*. London: Sage.

Lipchik, E. (1994) 'The rush to be brief', *Networker*, March/April: 35–9.

Lipchik, E. and Kubicki, A. D. (1996) 'Solution-focused domestic violence: Bridges towards a new reality in couples therapy', in S. D. Miller and B. L. Duncan (eds), *Handbook of Solution-Focused Brief Therapy*. San Francisco: Jossey Bass.

Lipchik, E. and Turnell, A (1999) 'The role of empathy in brief therapy: The overlooked but vital context', *The Australian and New Zealand Journal of Family Therapy*, 20: 29–36.

Loizidou, E. (2004) 'Criminal law and punishment', *Punishment and Society*, 6: 303–18.

Longo, R. E. (2002) 'A holistic approach to treating young people who sexually abuse', in M. C. Calder (ed.), *Young People who Sexually Abuse: Building the Evidence Base for your Practice*. Lyme Regis: Russell House Press.

Luhman, N. (1993) *Risk: A Sociological Theory*. Berlin, Walter De Gruyter.

M.A.P. (2003) 'The "understanding sexual abuse" programme: A group for men who deny their offending behaviour. The M.A.P. Initiative', *Nota News*, 45: 16–18.

Macdonald, A. J. (2007) *Solution Focused Therapy: Theory, Research and Practice*. London: Sage.

Macdonald, G. (1998) 'Promoting evidence-based practice in child protection', *Clinical Child Psychology and Psychiatry*, 3: 71–85.

Macleod, J. (2000) 'The development of narrative-informed theory, research and practice in counselling and psychotherapy: European perspectives', *European Journal of Psychotherapy, Counselling and Health*, 3: 331–3.

Maden, T. (1993) 'Women as violent offenders and violent patients', in P. J. Taylor (ed.), *Violence in Society*. London: Royal College of Physicians of London.

Main, M. and Weston, D. (1981) 'Quality of attachment to mother and to father: Related to conflict behaviour and the readiness for establishing new relationships', *Child Development*, 52: 932–40.

Main, M., Kaplan, N. and Cassidy, J. (1985) 'Security in infancy, childhood and adulthood: A move to the level of representation', in I. Bretherton and E. Waters (eds), *Growing Points in Attachment: Theory and Research*. Monographs of the Society for Research In Child Development Serial 209. Chicago: University of Chicago Press, pp. 66–104.

Maisto, S., Carey, M., Carey, K. et al. (2000) 'Use of the AUDIT and the DAST-10 to identify alcohol and drug user disorders among adults with severe and persistent mental illness', *Psychological Assessment*, 12: 186–92.

Malloch, M. S. (2004) 'Not "fragrant" at all: Criminal justice responses to "risky" women', *Critical Social Policy*, 24: 385–405.

Mama, A. (1989) *The Hidden Struggle: Statutory and Voluntary Sector Responses to Violence and the Caring Profession*. London: Runnymede Trust.

Mangan, M. (2003) *Staging Masculinities: History, Gender, Performance*. Basingstoke: Palgrave.

Margolin, G., John, R. S. and Foo, L. (1998) 'Interactive and unique risk factors for husbands' emotional and physical abuse of their wives', *Journal of Family Violence*, 13: 315–44.

Marsden, J., Gossop, M., Stewart, D. et al. (1997) 'The Maudsley Addiction Profile (MAP): A brief instrument for assessing treatment outcome', *Addiction*, 93: 1857–68.

Marshall, W. L., Serran, G. A., Fernandez, Y. M., Mulloy, R., Mann, R. E. and Thornton, D. (2003) 'Therapist characteristics in the treatment of sexual offenders: Tentative data on their relationship with indices on behaviour change', *Journal of Sexual Aggression*, 9: 25–30.

Marvin, R. S. and Stewart, R. B. (1990) 'A family system framework for the study of attachment', in M. Greenberg; D. Cichetti. and M. Cummings (eds), *Attachment Beyond the Pre-School Years*. Chicago: University of Chicago Press.

Matthews, R. (2004) 'Researchers ignore "inconvenient" drug trial results', *Sunday Telegraph*, 30 May: 6.

Mayer, J. E. and Timms, N. (1970) *The Client Speaks*. London: Routledge & Kegan Paul.

McGibbon, A., Cooper, L. and Kelly, L. (1989) 'What Support?' An Exploratory Study of Council Policy and Practice and Local Support Services in the Area of Domestic Violence within Hammersmith and Fulham. London: Hammersmith and Fulham Council.

McIvor, G. (2004) 'Getting personal: Developments in policy and practice in Scotland', in G. Mair (ed.), *What Matters in Probation*. Cullompton: Willan Publishing.

McKeowan, K., Haase, T. and Pratschke, J. (2001) *Distressed Relationships: Does Counselling Help?*. Dublin: Marital and Relationship Counselling Services.

McLeod, J. (2003) *An Introduction to Counselling*. 3rd edn, Maidenhead: Open University Press.

McMurran, M. and Hollin, C. R. (1993) *Young Offenders and Alcohol-Related Crime*. Chichester: Wiley.

McMurran, M. (1999/2000) 'COV-AID: Control of violence – anger, impulsivity, and drinking', *Dialogue*, 3: 4.

McNiel, D. E. and Binder, R. L. (1991) 'Clinical assessment of the risk of violence among psychiatric inpatients', *American Journal of Psychiatry*, 148: 1317–21.

Menzies, R. J., Webster, C. D. and Sepejak, D. S. (1985) 'Hitting the forensic sound barrier: Predictions of dangerousness in a pre-trial psychiatric clinic', in C. D. Webster, M. H. Ben-Aron and S. J. Hucker (eds), *Dangerousness: Probability and Prediction, Psychiatry and Public Policy*. New York: Cambridge University Press.

Messerschmidt, J. W. (1993) *Masculinities and Crime: Critique and Reconceptualisation of Theory*. Lanham, MD: Rowman & Littlefield.

Miller, W. R. and Rollnick, S. (1991) *Motivational Interviewing – Preparing People to Change Addictive Behaviour*. New York: Guilford Press.

Miller, W. R. and Rollnick, S (2002). *Motivational Interviewing – Preparing People to Change*. 2nd edn, New York: Guilford Press.

Milner, J. (2001) *Women and Social Work: Narrative Approaches*. Basingstoke: Palgrave.

Milner, J. (2004) 'From "disappearing" to "demonized": The effects on men and women of professional interventions based on challenging men who are violent', *Critical Social Policy*, 24: 79–101.

Milner, J. and Jessop, D. (2003) 'Domestic violence: Narratives and solutions', *Probation Journal*, 50: 127–41.

Milner, J. and O'Byrne, P. (2002) *Brief Counselling: Narratives and Solutions*. Basingstoke: Palgrave.

Mirlees-Black, C. (1995) 'Estimating the extent of domestic violence: Findings from the British Crime Survey, *Home Office Research Bulletin*, 37: 1–18.

Mirlees-Black, C. (1999) *Domestic Violence: Findings from a New British Crime Survey Self-completion Questionnaire*, Home Office Research Study 191. London: Home Office.

Mladjenovic, L. and Matijasevic (1996) 'SOS Belgrade July 1993–1995: Dirty streets', in: C. Corrin (ed.), *Women in a Violent World: Feminist Analyses and Resistance Across 'Europe'*. Edinburgh: Edinburgh University Press.

Monahan, J. (2004) 'The future of violence risk management', in M. Tonry (ed.), *The Future of Imprisonment*. New York: Oxford University Press.

Morgan, A. (2000) *What is Narrative Therapy? An Easy to Read Introduction*. Adelaide: Dulwich Centre Publications.

Morgan, D. (1981) 'Men, masculinity and the process of sociological enquiry', in H. Roberts (ed.) *Doing Feminist Research*. London: Routledge & Kegan Paul.

Mortlock, T. (1996) 'The battered woman in the Accident and Emergency department', *Accident and Emergency Nursing*, 4: 187–9.

Mosson, L. (2003) 'Working with women prisoners', in: G. Towl (ed.), *Psychology in Prisons*. Oxford: BPS/Basil Blackwell.

Mullender, A. (1996) *Rethinking Domestic Violence: The Social Work and Probation Response*. London: Routledge.

Mullender, A. (2002) 'Persistent oppressions: The example of domestic violence', in: R. Adams, L. Dominelli and M. Payne (eds), *Critical Practice in Social Work*. Basingstoke: Palgrave.

Mullender, A. and Burton, S. (2001) 'Good practice with perpetrators of domestic violence', *Probation Journal*, 48: 260–9.

Mullender, A. and Morley, R. (eds), (1994a) *Children Living with Domestic Violence: Putting Men's Abuse of Women on the Child Care Agenda*. London: Whiting & Birch.

Mullender, A. and Morley, R. (1994b) 'Context and content of a new agenda' in A. Mullender and R. Morley (eds), *Children Living with Domestic Violence: Putting Men's Abuse of Women on the Child Care Agenda*. London: Whiting & Birch.

Mullender, A., Hague, G., Imam, U., Kelly, L., Malos, E. and Regan, L. (2002) *Children's Perspectives on Domestic Violence*. London: Sage.

Musker, M. (2000) 'Anger management', in T. Thompson and P. Matthias (eds), *Lyttle's Mental Health and Disorder*. 3rd edn, London: Balliere Tyndall/Royal College of Nursing.

Myake, K., Chen, S., Campos, J. and Waters, E. (1985) 'Infants' temperament, mothers' mode of interaction and attachment in Japan: an interim report', in I. Bretherton and E. Waters (eds), *Growing Points of Attachment Theory and Research*. Monographs of the Society for Research in Child Development 50. Chicago: University of Chicago Press, p. 209.

Myers, S. (2005) 'A signs of safety approach to assessing children with sexually concerning or harmful behaviour', *Child Abuse Review*, 14: 97–112.

Myers, S. with McLaughlin, M. and Warwick, K. (2003) '"The day the Touching Monster came": Solution-focused and narrative approaches to working with children and young people with sexually inappropriate behaviour', *Educational and Child Psychology*, 20,1: 76–89.

National Institute for Mental Health (NIMH) (2003) *Personality Disorder: No Longer a Diagnosis of Exclusion*. London: NIMH.

Nellis, M. (2004) '"I know where you live": Electronic monitoring and penal policy in England and Wales', *British Journal of Community Justice*, 2: 33–59.

Newton, J. (1988) 'History as usual? Feminism and the New Historicism'. *Cultural Critique*, 9: 87–121.

Norton, K. (1999) 'Management of patients with personality disorders', in A. Lee (ed.), *Affective and Non-psychotic Disorders: Recent Advances in Psychiatric Treatment. Vol. 2*. London: Gaskell.

O'Connell, B. (2001) *Solution-Focused Stress Counselling*. London and New York: Continuum.

O'Hanlon, B. (1995) *Breaking the Bad Trance*. London Conference, B. T. Practice.

O'Malley, P. (1992) 'Risk, power and crime prevention', *Economy and Society*, 21: 252–75.

Onega, S. and Landa, J. A. G. (eds), (1996) *Narratology: An Introduction*. London and New York: Longman.

Pagelow, M. (1985) 'The "battered husband syndrome": Social problem or much ado about nothing?', in N. Johnson (ed.), *Marital Violence*. London: Sage.

Parton, C. (1990) 'Women, gender and child abuse', in Violence Against Children Study Group (editorial collective), *Taking Child Abuse Seriously: Contemporary Issues in Child Protection Theory and Practice*. London: Unwin Hyman.

Parton, N. and O'Byrne, P. (2000) *Constructive Social Work*. Basingstoke: Palgrave Macmillan.

Parton, N., Thorpe, D. and Wattam, C. (1997) *Child Protection: Risk and the Moral Order*. Basingstoke: Macmillan.

Pavlov, I. P. (1960) *Conditional Reflexes: An Investigation of the Psychological Activity of the Cerebral Cortex* (translation). New York: Dover Publications.

Payne, M. (1997) *Modern Social Work Theory*. 3rd edn, Basingstoke: Palgrave Macmillan.

Payne, M. (2000) *Narrative Therapy: An Introduction for Counsellors*. London, Sage.

Pence, E. (1983) 'The Duluth domestic abuse intervention project', *Hamline Law Review*, 6: 247–75.

Pence, E. and Paymar, M. (1985, 1990, rev. edn) *Power and Control: The Tactics of Men Who Batter: An Educational Curriculum*. Duluth, MN: Minnesota Program Development.

Pence, E. and Paymar, M. (1993) *Education Groups for Men Who Batter*. New York: Springer Publishing.

Penfield, W. (1952) 'Memory mechanisms', *AMA Archives of Neurology and Psychiatry*, 67: 178–98.

Peters, M. A. (1999) *Poststructuralism, Politics and Education*. Westport, CT, Bergin and Garvey.

Poon, N. (1995) 'Conceptual issues in defining male domestic violence', in T. Haddad (ed.), *Men and Masculinities: A Critical Anthology*. Toronto: Canadian Scholars Press.

Powis, B. (2002) *Offenders' Risk of Serious Harm: A Literature Review*. Home Office Research, Development and Statistics Directorate, Occasional Paper 81. London: Home Office.

Prins, H. (1995) *Offenders, Deviants or Patients?* 2nd edn, London: Routledge.

Pritchard, J. (ed.), (1999) *Elder Abuse: Best Practice in Britain and Canada*. London: Jessica Kingsley.

Quinsey, V. L., Rice, M. E. and Harris, G. T. (1995) 'Actuarial prediction of sexual recidivism', *Journal of Interpersonal Violence*, 10, 1: 85–105.

Quinsey, V. L., Harris, G. T., Rice, M. E. and Cormier, C. A. (1998) *Violent Offenders: Appraising and Managing Risk*. Washington DC: American Psychological Association.

Ramon, S. (1986) 'The category of psychopathy: The professional and social context in Britain', in P. Miller and N. Rose (eds), *The Power of Psychiatry*. Cambridge: Polity Press.

Ramsey, J., Richardson, J., Carter, H., Davidson, L. and Feder, G. (2002) 'Should health service professionals screen women for domestic violence? A systematic review', *British Medical Journal*, 325: 314.

Randall, P. (1997) *Adult Bullying: Perpetrators and Victims*. London: Routledge.

Rasool, G. H. (2002) *Dual Diagnosis: Substance Misuse and Psychiatric Disorder*. Oxford: Basil Blackwell.

Raynor, P., Smith, D. and Vanstone, M. (1994) *Effective Probation Practice*. Basingstoke: Macmillan.

Reichman, N. (1986) 'Managing crime risks: Towards an insurance-based model of social control', *Research in Law, Deviance and Social Control*, 8: 151–72.

Renwick, S. J., Dunbar, G. and Davidson, R. (1983) 'Development of a questionnaire to measure alcohol dependence', *British Journal of Addiction*, 76: 89–95.

Renzetti. C. M. (1992) *Violent Betrayal: Partner Abuse in Lesbian Relationships*. London: Sage.

Respect (2000) *Statement of Principles and Minimum Standards of Practice*. DVIP, P.O. Box 2838, London, W6 9ZE.

Rey, J. M. and Tennant, C. T. (2002) 'Cannabis and Mental Health', *British Medical Journal*, 2002: 1183–4.

Richardson, J. and Feder, G. (1996) 'Domestic violence: A hidden problem for general practice', *British Journal of General Practice*, 46: 239–42.

Robinson, D. and Poporino, F. J. (2001) 'Programming in cognitive skills: The reasoning and rehabilitation programme', in C. R. Hollin (ed.), *Handbook of Offender Assessment and Treatment*. Chichester: Wiley.

Robinson, L. (1995) *Psychology for Social Workers: Black Perspectives*. London; Routledge.

Rorty, R. (ed.), (1967) *The Linguistic Turn: Recent Essays in Philosophical Method*. Chicago: University of Chicago Press.

Rose, N. (1985) *The Psychological Complex: Psychology, Politics and Society in England, 1896–1939*. London: Routledge & Kegan Paul.

Rosenberg, S., Drake, R., Wolford, G. et al (1998) 'Dartmouth Assessment of Lifestyle Instrument (DALI): A substance-use disorder screen for people with severe mental illness', *American Journal of Psychiatry*, 155: 232–8.

Royal College of Psychiatrists (1996) *Assessment and Clinical Management of Risk of Harm to Other People*. London: Royal College of Psychiatrists.

Russo, A. (1999) 'Lesbians organising lesbians against battering' in B. Leventhal and S. E. Lundy (eds), *Same Sex Domestic Violence: Strategies for Change*. London: Sage.

Rutter, S., Gudjonsson, G. and Rabe-Hesketh, S. (2004) 'Violent incidents in a medium secure unit: The characteristics of persistent perpetrators of violence', *Journal of Forensic Psychiatry and Psychology*, 15: 293–302.

Ryan, M. (2002) *Penal Policy and Political Culture in England and Wales*. Winchester: Waterside Press.

Ryan, T. (1996) 'Risk management and people with mental health problems', in H. Kemshall and J. Pritchard (eds), *Good Practice in Risk Assessment and Risk Management*. London: Jessica Kingsley.

Rycroft, C. (1966) 'Introduction: Causes and meaning', in C. Rycroft, G. Gorer, A. Storr, J. Wren-Lewis and P. Lomas (eds), *Psychoanalysis Observed*. Harmondsworth: Penguin.

Sagi, A., Lamb, M. E. and Lewkowicz, K. S. (1985) 'Security of infant-mother – father and – metaplet among Kibbutz reared Israeli children', in I. Bretherton. and E. Waters (eds), *Growing Points of Attachment Theory and Research*, Monographs of the Society for Research in Child Development, 50. Chicago: University of Chicago Press, p. 209.

Salter, A. C. (1988) *Treating Child Sex Offenders and Victims: A Practical Guide*. London and Newbury Park, CA: Sage.

Sands, R. (1996) 'The elusiveness of identity in social work with women', *Clinical Social Work Journal*, 24, 2:167–86.

Schechter, S. (1982) *Women and Male Violence: The Visions and the Struggles of the Battered Women's Movement*. Boston, MA: South End Press.

Schneider, V. and Marren, U. (1995) 'Violence in the Accident and Emergency department', *Annals of Emergency Medicine*, 3: 74–8.

Schornstein, S. L. (1997) *Domestic Violence and Health Care: What Every Professional Needs to Know*. London: Sage.

Schwartz, A. and Goldiamond, I. (1975) *Social Casework: A Behavioural Approach*. New York: Columbia University Press.

Scourfield, J. (2003) *Gender and Child Protection*. Basingstoke: Palgrave.

Scourfield, J. and Dobash, R. P. (1999) 'Programmes for violent men: Recent developments in the UK', *Howard Journal of Criminal Justice*, 38: 128–43.

Scourfield, J. and Drakeford, M. (2002) 'New Labour and the "problem of men"', *Critical Social Policy*, 22: 619–40.

Sharry, J., Madden, B. and Darmody, M. (2001) *Becoming a Solution Detective: A Strengths Guide to Brief therapy*. London: B. T. Press.

Sheldon, B. (1982) *Behaviour Modification: Theory, Practice and Philosophy*. London: Tavistock.

Sheldon, B. (1995) *Cognitive-Behavioural Therapy: Research, Practice and Philosophy*. London and New York: Routledge.

Shepherd, J. (1998) 'Victims of violent crime', *Accident and Emergency Nursing*, 6: 15–17.

Shorter, E. and Tyrer, P. (2003) 'Separation of anxiety and depression disorders: Blind alley in psychopharmocology and classification of disease', *British Medical Journal*, 2003: 158–60.

Silver, E. and Miller, L. L. (2002) 'A cautionary note on the use of actuarial risk assessment tools for social control', *Crime and Delinquency*, 48, 1, 138–61.

Sims, A. (2003) *Symptoms in the Mind: An Introduction to Descriptive Psychopathology*. 3rd edn, Edinburgh: Saunders.

Simmons, J. et al. (2002) *Crime in England and Wales, 2001–2002*. London: Home Office.

Skinner, B. F. (1958) 'Reinforcement theory', *American Psychologist*, 13: 94–9.

Slattery, G. (2003) 'Working with young men: Taking a stand against sexual abuse and sexual harassment', in *Responding to Violence: A Collection of Papers Relating to Child Sexual Abuse and Violence in Intimate Relationships*. Adelaide: Dulwich Centre Publications.

Smale, G. and Tuson, G., with Brehal, N. and Marsh, P. (1993) *Empowerment, Assessment, Care Management and the Skilled Worker*. London: National Institute for Social Work.

Speedy, J. (2000) 'The "storied" helper', *European Journal of Psychotherapy, Counselling and Health*, 3: 361–74.

Spender, D. (1995) *Man Made Language*. 2nd edn, London: Routledge.

Stanko, E. (1985) *Intimate Intrusions*. London: Unwin Hyman.

Stanko, E. A., Crisp, D., Hale, C. and Lucraft, H. (1998) *Counting the Costs: Estimating the Impact of Domestic Violence in the London Borough of Hackney*. Swindon: Crime Concern.

Stanley, N. (1997) 'Domestic violence and child abuse: Developing social work practice', *Child and Family Social Work*, 2: 135–45.

Stirling, G., Higgins, J. E. and Cooke, M. W. (2001) 'Violence in A and E departments: A systematic review of the literature', *Accident and Emergency Nursing*, 9: 77–85.

Stiver, I. P. (1991) 'The meanings of "dependency" in female-male relationships', in J. V. Jordan, A. G. Kaplan, J. B. Miller, I. P. Stiver and J. L. Surrey (eds), *Women's Growth in Connection: Writings from the Stone Centre*. New York: Guilford Press.

Storr, A. (1966) 'The Concept of Cure', in C. Rycroft, G. Gorer, A. Storr, J. Wren-Lewis and P. Lomas (eds), *Psychoanalysis Observed*. Harmondsworth: Penguin.

Stuart, R. B. (1974) 'Behaviour modification: A technology for social change', in F. J. Turner (ed.), *Social Work Treatment*. New York: Free Press.

Sullivan, M. (2005) 'Understanding male sexual assault', in *Improving Outcomes for Victims of Sexual Violence: A Strategic Partnership Approach* (Conference Report). London: Home Office.

Suserud, B.-O., Blomquist, M. and Johansson, I. (2002) 'Experiences of threats and violence in the Swedish ambulance service', *Accident and Emergency Nursing,* 10: 127–35.

Swanson, J., Holzer, C., Ganju, V. and Jono, R. (1990) 'Violence and psychiatric disorder in the community: Evidence from the Epidemiological Catchment Area Surveys', *Hospital and Community Psychiatry,* 41: 761–70.

Szmukler, G. (2001) 'Violence risk prediction in practice', *British Journal of Psychiatry,* 178: 84–5.

Taft, C. T., Murphy, C. M., Elliott, J. D. and Keaser, M. C. (2001) 'Race and demographic factors in treatment attendance for domestically abusive men', *Journal of Family Violence,* 16: 385–400.

Tardiff, K. (1989) *Assessment and Management of Violent Patients.* Washington DC and London: American Psychiatric Press.

Taylor, P. J. (1993) 'Mental illness and violence', in P. J. Taylor (ed.), *Violence in Society.* London: Royal College of Physicians of London.

Teft, P. (1999) 'Work with men who are violent to their partners: Time to re-assert a pro-feminist analysis', *Probation Journal,* 46: 11–18.

Thomas, S., Lese, M., Dolan, M., Harty, M.-A., Shaw, J., Middleton, H., Carlisle, J., Davies, L., Thornicroft, G. and Appleby, L. (2004) 'The individual needs of patients in high security psychiatric hospitals in England', *Journal of Forensic Psychiatry and Psychology,* 15: 222–43.

Thompson, N. (2003) *Language and Communication.* Basingstoke: Palgrave.

Thorpe, M. (1997) 'The impact of psychoanalytic practice on the Family Justice System', in Mr Justice Wall (ed.), *Rooted Sorrows: Psychoanalytic Perspectives on Child Protection, Assessment and Treatment.* Bristol: Family Law.

Tilley, N. (2001) 'Evaluation and evidence-led crime reduction policy and practice', in R. Matthews and J. Pitts (eds), *Crime, Disorder and Community Safety.* London: Routledge.

Tonry, M. (2004) *Punishment and Politics: Evidence and Evaluation in the Making of English Crime Control Policy.* Cullompton, Devon: Willan.

Towl, G. (ed.), (2003) *Psychology in Prisons.* Oxford: BPS/Basil Blackwell.

Turell, S. C. (2000) 'A descriptive analysis of same sex relationship violence for a diverse sample', *Journal of Family Violence,* 15: 281–93.

Turnell, A. and Edwards, S. (1999) *Signs of Safety. A Solution and Safety Oriented Approach to Child Protection Casework.* London: W. W. Norton.

Tutty, L. M., Bigood, B. A. and Rothery, M. A. (1993) 'Support groups for battered women: Research on their efficacy'. *Journal of Family Violence,* 8, 4: 325–43.

Ungar, M. (2004) 'A constructionist discourse on resilience: Multiple contexts, multiple realities among at-risk children and youth', *Youth and Society,* 35, 3 (March): 341–65.

Valios, N. (2003) 'Up in the air', *Community Care,* 1488: 4–10.

Vizard, E. (2002). 'The assessment of young sexual abusers', in M. Calder (ed.), *Young People who Sexually Abuse: Building the Evidence Base for your Practice.* Lyme Regis: Russell House Press.

Wake, D. (2004) 'The influence of dual diagnosis', in S. D. Kirby, D. A. Hart, D. Cross and G. Mitchell (eds), *Mental Health Nursing: Competence for Practice*. Basingstoke: Palgrave.

Walsh, E., Buchanan, A. and Fahy, T. (2002) 'Violence and schizophrenia: Examining the evidence', *British Journal of Psychiatry*, 2002: 490–5.

Wampold, B. E. (2001) *The Great Psychotherapy Debate: Models, Methods and Findings*. Mahwah, NJ: Lawrence Erlbaum Associates.

Waugh, F. and Bonner, M. (2002) 'Domestic violence and child protection: Issues in safety planning', *Child Abuse Review*, 11: 282–95.

Webster, C. D. and Bailes, G. (2004) 'Assessing violence in mentally disordered and personality disordered individuals', in C. R. Hollin (ed.), *The Essential Handbook of Offender Assessment and Treatment*. Chichester: Wiley.

Webster, C. D., Douglas, K., Eaves, D. and Hart, S. D. (1997) *HCR-20: Assessing Risk for Violence*. 2nd edn, Vancouver: Simon Fraser University.

Webster, C. D., Harris, G. T., Rice, M. E. Cormier, C. and Quinsey, V. L. (1994) *The Violence Prediction Scheme*. Toronto: Centre of Criminology, University of Toronto.

Weiss, J. S. (1991) 'The attachment bond in childhood and adulthood', in C. Murray-Parkes, J. Stevenson-Hinde and P. Marris (eds), *Attachment Across the Life Cycle*. London: Routledge.

Weiss, R. S. (1982) 'Attachment in adult life', in C. Murray-Parkes and J. Stevenson-Hinde (eds), *The Place of Attachment in Human Behaviour*. New York: Wiley.

Werner, H. D. (1970) *New Understandings of Human Behaviour*. New York: Association Press.

Whiston, S. C. (2000) *Principles and Applications of Assessment in Counselling*. Belmont, CA: Wadsworth.

White, M. (1995) *Re-Authoring Lives: Interviews and Essays*. Adelaide: Dulwich Centre.

White, M. and Epston, D. (1989) *Literate Means to Therapeutic Ends*. Adelaide: Dulwich Centre.

White, M. and Epston, D. (1990) *Narrative Means to Therapeutic Ends*. New York: W. W. Norton.

Whitfield, C., Anda, R. F., Dube, S. R. and Felitti, V. J. (2003) 'Violent childhood experience and the risk of intimate partner violence in adults: Assessment in a large health maintenance organization', *Journal of Interpersonal Violence*, 18: 166–85.

Whittington, R. and Patterson, P. (1996) 'Verbal and non-verbal behaviour immediately prior to aggression by mentally disorded people: Enhancing risk assessment', *Journal of Psychiatric and Mental Health Nursing*, 3: 47–54.

Williams, E. (2003) 'Aggression and mental disorder', in T. Everett, M. Donaghy and S. Feaver (eds), *Interventions for Mental Health: An Evidence-Based Approach for Physiotherapists and Occupational Therapists*. London: Butterworth Heineman.

Winnicott, C. (1986) 'Face to face with children', in *Working with Children*. London: BAAF.

Winnicott, D. W. (1971) *Playing and Reality*. London: Tavistock.

Wirtz, H. and Schweitzer, R. (2003) 'Groupwork with men who engage in violent and abusive actions', in *Responding to Violence: A Collection of Papers Relating to Child Sexual Abuse and Violence in Intimate Relationships*. Adelaide: Dulwich Centre Publications.

Wittgenstein, l. (1980) *Remarks on the Philosophy of Psychology*. Oxford: Blackwell.

Waldron-Haugurd, L., Gratch, L. and Magruder, B. (1997) 'Victimization and perpetration rates of violence in gay and lesbian relationships: Gender issues explored', *Violence Victims*, 12: 173–84.

Wolf, S. (1984) 'A multi-factor model of deviant sexuality'. *Paper presented at the Third International Conference on Victimology*. Lisbon, Portugal.

Wood, J. and Phillip, I. (1999/2000) '"Dangerous people": A dangerous rhetoric?', *Dialogue*, 3: 1–2.

World Health Organisation (2002) *World Report on Violence and Health*. Geneva: WHO. http://www.who.int/violence_injury_prevention/htm

World Health Organization (2004) *Injuries and Violence Prevention: Links Across Types of Violence*. Geneva: WHO. www.who.int/violence_injury_prevention/violence/arms.htm

Worrall, A. (2002) 'Rendering women punishable: The making of a penal crisis', in P. Carlen (ed.), *Women and Punishment: The Struggle for Justice*. Cullompton, Devon: Willan Publishing.

Wright, M. (1996) *Justice for Victims and Offenders: A Restorative Response to Crime*. Winchester: Waterside Press.

Yan, E. and So-Kum Tang, C (2003) 'Proclivity to elder abuse', *Journal of Interpersonal Violence*, 18: 999–1017.

Yick, A. G. (2000) 'Predictors of physical spousal/intimate violence in Chinese American families', *Journal of Family Violence*, 5: 249–68.

Index of Authors

Index of Subjects